REIMAGINING MASCULINITY AND VIOLENCE IN *GAME OF THRONES* AND *A SONG OF ICE AND FIRE*

Liverpool Science Fiction Texts and Studies, 76

Liverpool Science Fiction Texts and Studies

Editors
David Seed, *University of Liverpool*
Sherryl Vint, *University of California Riverside*

Editorial Board
Stacey Abbott, *University of Roehampton*
Mark Bould, *University of the West of England*
Veronica Hollinger, *Trent University*
Roger Luckhurst, *Birkbeck College, University of London*
Andrew Milner, *Monash University*
Andy Sawyer, *University of Liverpool*

Recent titles in the series

60. Curtis D. Carbonell, *Dread Trident: Tabletop Role-Playing Games and the Modern Fantastic*

61. Upamanyu Pablo Mukherjee, *Final Frontiers: Science Fiction and Techno-Science in Non-Aligned India*

62. Gavin Miller, *Science Fiction and Psychology*

63. Andrew Milner and J.R. Burgmann, *Science Fiction and Climate Change: A Sociological Approach*

64. Regina Yung Lee and Una McCormack (eds), *Biology and Manners: Essays on the Worlds and Works of Lois McMaster Bujold*

65. Joseph Norman, *The Culture of "The Culture": Utopian Processes in Iain M. Banks's Space Opera Series*

66. Jeremy Withers, *Futuristic Cars and Space Bicycles: Contesting the Road in American Science Fiction*

67. Sabrina Mittermeier and Mareike Spychala, *Fighting for the Future: Essays on Star Trek: Discovery*

68. Richard Howard, *Space for Peace: Fragments of the Irish Troubles in the Science Fiction of Bob Shaw and James White*

69. Thomas Connolly, *After Human: A Critical History of the Human in Science Fiction from Shelley to Le Guin*

70. John Rieder, *Speculative Epistemologies: An Eccentric Account of SF from the 1960s to the Present*

71. Sarah Annes Brown, *Shakespeare and Science Fiction*

72. Christopher Palmer, *Apocalypse in Crisis: Fiction from 'The War of the Worlds' to 'Dead Astronauts'*

73. Mike Ashley, *The Rise of the Cyberzines: The Story of the Science-Fiction Magazines from 1991 to 2020: The History of the Science-Fiction Magazine Volume V*

74. J. Jesse Ramírez, *Un-American Dreams: Apocalyptic Science Fiction, Disimagined Community, and Bad Hope in the American Century*

75. Istvan Csicsery-Ronay, Jr., *Mutopia: Science Fiction and Fantastic Knowledge*

REIMAGINING MASCULINITY AND VIOLENCE IN *GAME OF THRONES* AND *A SONG OF ICE AND FIRE*

TOBI EVANS

LIVERPOOL UNIVERSITY PRESS

First published 2022 by
Liverpool University Press
4 Cambridge Street
Liverpool
L69 7ZU

Copyright © 2022 Tobi Evans

Tobi Evans has asserted the right to be identified as
the author of this book in accordance with the Copyright, Designs and
Patents Act 1988.

All rights reserved. No part of this book may be reproduced, stored in a
retrieval system, or transmitted, in any form or by any means, electronic,
mechanical, photocopying, recording, or otherwise, without the prior
written permission of the publisher.

British Library Cataloguing-in-Publication data
A British Library CIP record is available

ISBN 978-1-80085-536-6 cased

Typeset by Carnegie Book Production, Lancaster
Printed and bound by CPI Group (UK) Ltd, Croydon CR0 4YY

This one's for you, Dad

Contents

List of Abbreviations	viii
Acknowledgements	ix
Introduction	1
1 Some Knights Are Dark and Full of Terror	27
2 Undoing Sovereign Violence	49
3 Vile, Scheming, Evil Bitches?	87
4 Disabled Masculinities and the Potential and Limits of Queered Masculine Violence	127
5 Queer Magical Violence and Gender Fluidity	173
Bibliography	209
Index	223

Abbreviations

AFAB   assigned female at birth
AMAB   assigned male at birth
GoT   *A Game of Thrones*. 4th ed. London: Harper Voyager
CoK   *A Clash of Kings*. 4th ed. London: Harper Voyager
SoS1   *A Storm of Swords 1: Steel and Snow*. 4th ed. London: Harper Voyager
SoS2   *A Storm of Swords 2: Blood and Gold*. 4th ed. London: Harper Voyager
FfC   *A Feast for Crows*. 3rd ed. London: Harper Voyager
DwD   *A Dance with Dragons*. 2nd ed. London: Harper Voyager

Acknowledgements

This book was written on the unceded lands of the Ngunnawal people in Canberra and the Wurundjeri Willam people in Naarm (Melbourne). I would like to acknowledge and celebrate elders past and present for the work they have undertaken for country and community, especially the care they have taken for the lands that I call home.

The bulk of the research for this book was generously funded by an Australian Government Research Training Program Stipend Scholarship. Additional funding for presenting earlier chapters at international conferences was provided by an Australian National University (ANU) Vice Chancellor's Higher Degree Research Travel Grant and a Madonna and Michael Marsden International Travel Grant from the Popular Culture Association/American Culture Association. The opportunity to complete a large research project (and to take it on the road no less) would have been financially inaccessible to me if not for this funding.

I am incredibly grateful to Liverpool University Press for taking a chance on this book, especially my editor, Christabel Scaife, the series editors David Seed and Sherryl Vint, and the anonymous reviewers who gave valuable feedback on the manuscript.

Warm thanks to my supervisory panel at the ANU, Katherine Bode, Katie Sutton, and Kate Mitchell, whose academic rigour and generous advice made this book not only possible, but infinitely better than I could have imagined. I am especially grateful to Kath, who saw this project through from my application to thesis submission to book contract and revisions. We did it!

Special thanks to my friends and colleagues in fantasy studies, especially Chuckie Palmer-Patel, for the tireless and often unpaid work she does for the field of fantasy studies: running *Fantastika* journal, conferences, and other media; supporting emerging researchers like myself with long email conversations about fantasy; volunteering to read several chapters of this book; giving sound and encouraging editorial advice; *and* her own incredible scholarship. Chuckie, I don't know how you do it—but I'm grateful that you do.

I owe a very important debt to Penny Holliday and Vivienne Muller at the Queensland University of Technology (QUT), as well as Jason Sternberg, who was the first person to imagine that this research could become a book.

Thank you to the PhD Coffee Coven at the ANU, especially Dr Lauren Sadow and Dr Katie Cox. Y'all are legends in human skin and your love and support made this research not only possible, but fun. Down the road at the ANU, I'd like to thank Dr Blair Williams for being a wonderful friend, colleague, and activist. Your work keeps me believing in the real-world value of gender studies. Also in Canberra (for the moment), an endless debt of gratitude to Allison Kephart for her support with this book and a million other things. LOVE YOU!

To my chosen family in Melbourne who have seen the tail end of this book come to life, thank you for your excitement and encouragement. I am especially grateful to my furry daughter/tiny demon Callie and my partner Ezra, who have not only supported me but expanded and enriched my understanding of masculinity and care.

Big thanks to my family for their patience and enthusiasm for this research, which is all the more lovely for their not understanding it but cheering me on anyway. Special thanks to my Grandma, Jackie Watkins, whose support, belief, and enthusiasm for this book has not wavered. Your regular and gentle inquiries about how my book is going, and your own love for words, are a gift I treasure. Finally, thank you to my Dad, Les Evans, for cheering me on every step of the way and being endlessly proud and supportive.

Author's Note

One of the joys and challenges of writing on current popular cultural texts and their intersection with the rapidly changing landscape of gender, sex, and sexuality is that as soon as anything is committed to print, it is liable to become outdated. As our thinking and language around the texts and ideas in this book continue to evolve, please know that I will be travelling with you, excited for new and more nuanced language with which to think about our worlds.

Introduction

At the end of *A Game of Thrones* by George R.R. Martin, one of many fantasy novels owing heritage to J.R.R. Tolkien's *The Lord of the Rings* trilogy and the progenitor of the now infamous *Game of Thrones* television show, a fourteen-year-old orphan called Daenerys Targaryen is betrayed by a medicine woman whom she saved from rape and murder at the hands of her warlord husband Drogo's warriors. Daenerys allies with the woman and trusts her when she offers to save Drogo's life in exchange for that of her unborn child. The "life" that the medicine woman grants is "monstrous" and is intended as vengeance against the Dothraki tribe who destroyed her village. In response, Daenerys burns the woman in Drogo's funeral pyre before walking into the flames herself. She arises unburnt with three newly hatched dragons. Two of the creatures suckle milk from her breasts, and around her the Dothraki tribe bows in awe as they accept her as their new leader. Standing naked with dragons wrapped around her magical flesh, Daenerys's violence causes her to face two corpses and the possibility of her own death. Her skin, the border that marks the difference between her body and the outside world, is magically unbroken by the experience. At the same time, she opens her body and its fluids to three dragons, becoming a mother to the non-human Other and entering a relation of queer kinship that brings her political and social power.

My subject is violent bodies, and I begin at Daenerys's transformation on the Dothraki Sea because it dramatises precisely the cycle of repeated violence, bodily instability and failure, and relation between self and Other with which audiences of both *A Song of Ice and Fire* and *Game of Thrones* are invited to engage. Where violence is used to dominate the Other, as in the medicine woman's case, it is reversed and is shown to be part of a destructive cycle. While Daenerys too seeks to dominate the Other, she does so because she recognises that the woman will continue to punish her and her people if left alive. Daenerys acknowledges their relationality and uses violence on behalf of her tribe as well as herself, and this ambiguity leads her to maintain the boundaries that make her who she is, even as these boundaries are troubled by the way she embraces her dragons.

The image of a woman avenging her husband and child and then breastfeeding newborn dragons draws attention to the complex and sometimes radical ways in which masculinity is imagined in this fictional universe. I read Daenerys as one of several characters in *A Song of Ice and Fire* and *Game of Thrones* whom audiences are invited to view as moving between masculinity and femininity. What I suggest is that *A Song of Ice and Fire* and *Game of Thrones* both privilege masculinities that reject individualistic models which reify existing matrices of power and instead open themselves to radical connections with other subjects. The others I examine are variously figured—as squires, enemies, trees, dragons, wolves, or birds. But in the real world they could just as easily be co-workers, mentors, or friends. These types of connections are the only way in which humankind can face the threats of the future, whether they be societal challenges, such as mental health and sexual violence, or existential threats including war or environmental change.

Westerosi Dreams

Game of Thrones had millions of viewers in the 2010s and brought a large audience to the book series on which it was based. However, both texts' popularity suffered from the eighth and final season of *Game of Thrones*. The franchise vanished from the cultural landscape as if by magic, casting a shadow over the entire series. When viewed as complete (or partial, in the case of the novels) texts, *Game of Thrones* and *A Song of Ice and Fire* imagine masculinity and violence in ways that can help us think about the possibilities for masculinity in our own lives and our own world. Fantasy and science fiction texts have a long history of imagining sex, gender, and sexuality in radically different ways, and Martin's novels and their television adaptation continue this generic legacy in a way that reached an immense audience.

A Song of Ice and Fire and *Game of Thrones* contain multiple narrators and hundreds of named characters, but they privilege three families: the Starks, the Lannisters, and the Targaryens. Each family is involved in one of three central plotlines, although there is considerable overlap. The first concerns Daenerys Targaryen, the dispossessed leader of Westeros and Mother of Dragons, and her quest to reclaim the Iron Throne; the second focuses on the events in Westeros's political capital, King's

INTRODUCTION 3

Landing, and the intrigues of court; and the third is an army of the living dead, known as "wights," "Others," and "white walkers," who are gaining numbers in the icy north of Westeros with the intent of bringing about an apocalyptic everlasting winter. These plotlines are loosely based on real history, especially the War of the Roses (Larrington 2016). The narrative is set in pseudo-medieval Westeros (the fictionalised West) and Essos (the fictionalised East).

A Song of Ice and Fire is at the time of writing comprised of five novels: *A Game of Thrones* (1996), *A Clash of Kings* (1998), *A Storm of Swords* (2000), *A Feast for Crows* (2005), and *A Dance with Dragons* (2011), two of which are physically so large that they are sold in two volumes in some countries. Two more books are planned, *The Winds of Winter* and *A Dream of Spring*, though no publication dates have been announced. The books are chronological, although each chapter is told from the point of view of a specific character. Perspective chapters are almost always given to the series' most important characters, with occasional chapters from minor characters. This format allows Martin to show different ways of looking at the world, as well as different physical locations, while using omniscient third-person narration.

Conversations between Martin and *Game of Thrones* creators David Benioff and D.B. Weiss began in 2006, and the television series premiered on Home Box Office (HBO) in 2011 to widespread popular and critical acclaim prior to its final season. The decision to approach HBO was presented as destiny; while Martin claimed that the series was "unfilmable" and rejected numerous offers to make it into a feature film, Benioff immediately had HBO in mind because "a fantasy movie of this scope, financed by a major studio, would almost certainly need a PG-13 rating. That means no sex, no blood, no profanity. Fuck that." Martin appears to have been of a similar mind and is credited as saying that he "never imagined it anywhere else" but HBO (Cogman 2012).

Game of Thrones is complete, having overtaken the narrative in the novels in its fourth season. The show spans eight seasons of roughly ten hour-length episodes and is understood as a television series by most fans and critics because of its serial narrative and global broadcast, although it blurs the line between television and film in multiple ways. The series was one of the first television series to have individual episodes screened in cinemas in the United States, and towards the end of the series single episodes frequently ran to feature length. *Game of Thrones* was a massive undertaking, both in terms of authorial voices, finance, and branding. The HBO brand—with the tagline "It's not television, it's HBO"—connotes quality entertainment for an intelligent and affluent audience, and it lends this connotation to the programmes it commissions. Alongside this brand identity, each episode involved a team of script writers and at least two directors, not to mention sound teams, cinematographers, costume designers, and actors. Many of these individuals worked from Martin's novels and, later, from book outlines for *The Winds of Winter* and *A Dream of Spring*. Martin also wrote one episode per season for the first four seasons and continued to provide notes on each episode during production. Martin, Benioff, and Weiss remained central figures, although the sheer size of the series' production necessitated an acknowledgement of multiple authors.

Both the novels and television series were immensely popular and had an audience of millions between 2011 and 2019, although *Game of Thrones* has a far larger audience base and brought the books much of their mainstream popularity (see Gjelsvik and Schubart 2016, 3–4): those published after the television adaptation have each made the *New York Times Bestseller List* (Orr 2011). The viewership of the series finale was just under 20 million, with an estimated 40 million streaming the episode after its initial release. Yet the viewership is probably larger, as the series has been the most pirated television show since 2012; the premiere episode of season eight was pirated almost 100 million times (Muso 2017). Alongside these staggering numbers, *Game of Thrones* was also well received by critics for its first seven seasons, scoring extremely highly (over 90 per cent) on review websites such as Rotten Tomatoes and Metacritic, and winning the most Emmys of any television drama (Nickalls 2016). *Game of Thrones'* success plummeted in its final season, which was criticised for its rushed and inconsistent character development and story arcs; an anticlimactic final battle; a simplification of the series' complex female characters; and errors in continuity and universe logic (especially the infamous Starbucks coffee cup). After the final episodes aired in May 2019, two million people signed an online petition to "Remake *Game of Thrones* Season 8 with competent writers," and thousands of angry blog posts and Reddit threads appeared across the internet. Several planned spin-off series were subsequently cancelled by HBO.

Game of Thrones and *A Song of Ice and Fire* are part of a larger Westerosi textual universe which includes video games (Schröter 2016), graphic novels, wikis, internet memes, companion texts—including *The World of Ice and Fire* (2014), *A Knight of the Seven Kingdoms* (2015), and, most recently, *Fire and Blood* (2018)—a spectacular amount of fan art (Howe 2015) and fan fiction, online fan forums and websites (Young 2014), merchandise, an online petition to remake the final season, and events like "Fire and Ice Con: A *Game of Thrones* Fan Convention." At least one *Game of Thrones* prequel series is still currently being produced

INTRODUCTION 5

based on the Targaryen family. The novels and television series are the two main texts around which the rest of this universe is oriented and provide a clear starting point for analysing masculinity in this narrative world. While both *Game of Thrones* and *A Song of Ice and Fire* have lost their prominence in the cultural landscape at the time of writing, they remain a fascinating case study through which audiences can understand masculinity and violence in the real world.

Masculinity and Violence

Throughout this book I trace ambivalent formations of "masculine violence" in *A Song of Ice and Fire* and *Game of Thrones*, by which I mean violence that is textually positioned as masculine. But how does this positioning occur? And how is violence linked to masculinity in popular fiction and television? These are two questions that this book begins to answer. In Martin's novels, stylised gendered acts are often represented as masculine through interior monologue, as characters make reference to their father/brother/masculine lover and so on as a means of making and making sense of their actions. The television show likewise makes use of this referential masculine coding, though it does so through costume, music, *mise en scène*, and dialogue. In addition, *Game of Thrones* presents acts of violence as masculine through phallic symbols, from strategically placed swords to weapons in the background. These textual cues range from the nuanced to the heavy-handed, although just because audiences are invited to view certain acts as masculine or enabling characters to enact masculinity does not mean that this is how they are interpreted. But considering that there is a very real and harmful connection between masculinity and violence in the real world, and that it is repeated in this hugely popular television series and its source novels, it is critical to ask how these texts are encouraging their audiences to understand masculinity, violence, and bodies.

Game of Thrones and *A Song of Ice and Fire* reflect and shape the dialectic between masculinity and interpersonal violence in the real world, and their high levels of violence are often criticised. For many of the series' detractors, the violence is gratuitous (Hughes 2015). *Game of Thrones* has been referred to as engaging in "the glorification of violence for violence's sake" (Morrison in Thistleton 2015) and many public figures have boycotted the series because of its depictions of sexual violence (Lee 2015). Academic scholarship has generally echoed this assessment, particularly in relation to sexual and sexualised violence: for instance, Debra Ferreday (2015) claims that the series reproduces rape culture even as the online fandom resists normalising sexual violence. Many scholars and critics reject the series because of its violence, but they see its violence in simple terms, stemming from an assumption that violence in cultural texts leads to real world violence, a notion that is disputed by media violence scholars (Barker and Petley 2001; Carter and Weaver 2003; Docherty 1990). In Westeros, violence is far more complicated than its detractors suggest.

The critical concerns about violence in *Game of Thrones* and (to a lesser extent) *A Song of Ice and Fire* produce and are produced by a growing concern with violence, gender, bodies, and popular cultural representation in the early twenty-first century. For many years scholars have questioned whether and how violence in popular media relates to violence in the real world. Some commentators are eager to blame seemingly increased levels of violence, especially gun violence, on first-person-shooter video games and gory television shows, while other critics point to a more complex relation between texts and reality. Popular culture, including popular cultures of violence, shape and are shaped by the real world. Stories save lives, and they can open or close possibilities for personhood in ways that range from the mundane and everyday to the spectacular and radical.

Stories about violence and bodies, whether coming from popular texts, news media, or crime statistics, offer a picture that is alarming and alarmingly consistent: it is men who are most likely to be the perpetrators and survivors of violence. The correlation is often blamed on testosterone, on natural aggression, on "boys will be boys." But these are all the social interpretations of masculinity: that it is natural, rooted in chemical truths of the body, and must be managed and explained by others (usually women). Masculinity and violence become naturalised.

But gender is nothing if not incoherent and contradictory, so even as masculinity and violence are normalised, men who are violent are separated from normative masculinity through a process of Othering, spectacularisation, or narrativisation. The young men who commit mass-shootings become loners, outsiders, misfits rather than the subjects of bullying. Men who commit rape become predators lurking in the shadows of alleyways and bushes rather than their far-more-frequent identities as boyfriends, husbands, or friends. And people who commit murder become celebrity monsters with their own dedicated docu-drama or reality television show rather than real people who are complex products of systems and structures of power.

Popular media perform a kind of magic by papering over these contradictory ideas about masculinity and violence: masculine people are naturally violent and society must learn to live with it, and "normal"

INTRODUCTION 7

men are not actually violent but are at the mercy of pathological, deranged, violent criminals like the rest of us. Scholars of gender and violence, myself included, argue that neither is true. Neither violence nor for that matter masculinity is naturally connected to cisgender male bodies (bodies that were assigned male at birth [AMAB] and are understood by the self and society as masculine, and present as such). Instead, our culture views the capacity for violence as being one way in which masculinity materialises on and through the body, and assumes that the body in question is cisgender, straight, able, white, and middle class. Part of the problem here is a narrow and restrictive understanding around what masculinity is and the acts that a person can do to be perceived as masculine. In some contexts, violence is one of few options for intelligible masculinity because other limited options, like a heterosexual relationship, money, or employment, are unavailable (DeKeseredy and Schwartz 2005, 353–366). This connection leads to violence against women, children, and minorities, but it is also deeply destructive for masculine people who must live with the emotional, social, and juridical consequences of their aggression, as well as a higher likelihood of being the victims of other men's violence. The dominant view of masculinity and violence is discursively produced in a wide range of cultural sites, including popular culture. But it is also negotiated, resisted, reworked, and challenged in these spaces, and often in ways that are deeply ambivalent.

The way that audiences experience these ambiguous depictions of violence depends upon the medium-specific ways in which they are consumed, and this is especially true of *Game of Thrones* and *A Song of Ice and Fire*. While the book as medium is increasingly digitised and interactive, it generally remains a private and intimate experience between reader and page (at least during the act of reading). The page of a novel is also capable of offering significant insight into its characters' internal worlds through different narration options and internal monologues, a device Martin uses to provide knowledge about his characters' memories, thoughts, and motivations. If the reader finds these challenging, they have the option to pause their reading, skim or skip a paragraph, page, or chapter, or to lean into an alternative reading such as refusing to imagine a scene or reading it against the grain.

These possibilities take different forms in the television format. Television can be private and/or public at different times and at the same time: from the way we interpret scenes to who knows what we are watching, television forces our viewing into the open. I watched the final three seasons of *Game of Thrones* for the first time with friends, and I have seen on social media that many viewers around the world made similar arrangements. The experience of watching with others fundamentally changes the viewing experience, opening some affective possibilities and closing others. Notwithstanding whether audiences watch television alone or with others, there are different interpretive possibilities because a different range of the imaginative work has been done. With so much laid out on the screen, there are different options for refusing or reworking troubling content. It is more difficult to reach for the remote and press pause than it is to lift your eyes from the page. Even if you look away from the screen you are still assailed by sound, and the narrative speeds on without you.

Because of these different consumption contexts, *Game of Thrones* and *A Song of Ice and Fire* offer potentially different narrative experiences in relation to the representation of violence and bodies. The immediacy of the television screen is one reason why *Game of Thrones* has been so heavily criticised. It is very different to read about a man's skull being crushed than it is seeing and hearing it in the intimate space of your home. I keep these differences in mind while delving into examples from each text, often focusing on each medium's strengths as I demonstrate how they achieve a particular discursive effect. Because the novels and television series share a common narrative there is often considerable overlap, though they sometimes go about this work in different ways. When they diverge, such as when a character from the novels is written out of the television show or when the show overtakes the novels, I signal the difference and consider its implications where relevant. There are aspects of the story from the books that are elided in the television series and, similarly, practical issues around the visual display of violence in the television programme. I discuss these differences where they are relevant to the series' depiction of masculine violence, although my focus is less on adaptation and the adaptation of violence than on how violence is being presented to audiences. For the average person, seeing bodily violence of this magnitude is disturbing, and some of the key questions this book answers are what disturbs us about the violence in Martin's books and their adaptation, why we are disturbed by it, and what the political value of these troubling feelings may be.

While there has been little substantial research on masculinity in either *A Song of Ice and Fire* and *Game of Thrones*, several scholars have recognised the importance of masculinity to the series, and its critical engagement with normative masculinity. Stéphanie Genz (2016, 248) observes that "these sudden male deaths also underline that here, masculinity is in crisis, and, more broadly, that patriarchy—as a political, cultural, economic, and sexual/sexist institution and discourse—is as damaging and dangerous for men, as it is for women." As a result of

INTRODUCTION 9

this treatment of male characters, Genz argues that the series reveals "the fragility, hollowness, and vulnerability of a paternalistic gender order in which male rule is based on acts of gendered strength—and, therefore, at least to some extent, performative" (248). This reference to the performative "acts of strength" and their connection to weaknesses within patriarchal masculinity are continually emphasised in ways that highlight the inability of individualistic violence to produce anything but destruction. In the same vein, Joseph Young (2017, 48) notes that when a warrior "dismisses a minor injury as 'only a new scar to boast of to my son' [GoT 647] [...] the wound festers and reduces him to a flyblown wreck who will not be telling his son anything." The warrior's rejection of his own vulnerability ironically stops him from entering the system of reproduction, whether of his own body through hetero-sexual kinship or through teaching his son to adopt this masculine performance. Writing specifically on *Game of Thrones*, Susan Johnston (2021) and Dan Ward (2018) argue that the show offers a highly complex representation of masculinity. Johnston suggests that the television series "critiques" hypermasculinity while showing that abjection can be a path to redemption via self-sacrifice. While existing research is limited to the scope of book chapters or journal articles, it highlights the complex critiques of normative masculinity within *A Song of Ice and Fire* and *Game of Thrones*, which I explore in relation to violence. The series' narrative structure and focus on "cripples and bastards and broken things" (GoT 237) forces the audience to consider a diverse set of ideas and practices relating to power and gender, and by that means constitutes a textual space in which destructive masculine norms are often criticised and non-normative masculinities are foregrounded.

Masculinity is by no means the only relevant lens for exploring Martin's series and its adaptation, as gender is continually negotiated alongside other identities such as race and class. The vast majority of major and/or perspective characters in *A Song of Ice and Fire* and *Game of Thrones* are white and of Anglo-coded descent, and *Game of Thrones* has received particular criticism in regards to its tendency to evoke a white saviour narrative. The representation of non-white characters in both the novels and television series, such as the Dothraki, has been linked to an ongoing disdain for racial others within the fantasy genre (Young 2015). In addition to a clear privileging of white characters, the series' perspective characters are overwhelmingly "upper-class" (Frankel 2014), indicating that the series privileges a high-class perspective. I recognise with respect to *A Song of Ice and Fire* and *Game of Thrones* that, as Judith Butler (1993, 18) argues, "these vectors of power require and deploy each other for the purpose of their own articulation." I would like to acknowledge fully that this book does not sufficiently examine how race and class shape the texts' depictions of masculinity and violence. Despite the undoubted importance of considering this deployment, for reasons of scope I focus on how masculinity and violence are negotiated in the series, including by normative masculine bodies as well as by characters who were assigned female at birth (AFAB), as well as those that are disabled and queer.

A Song of Ice and Fire troubles the idea that masculinity is natural, that cisgender men are better at it, or that acting in a hegemonically masculine way can lead to anything but failure and horror. When masculine characters in *A Song of Ice and Fire* and *Game of Thrones* use violence against less powerful subjects, they are linked to monstrous imagery and are shown to be part of a destructive cycle, whereas characters who use violence to empower others are able to maintain their constitutive borders and to reproduce their knowledges and beliefs through a system of queer kinship.

This book performs the first substantial analysis of masculinities as they are enacted and deconstructed in this major popular series and develops a critical framework for analysing two types of enactment of violence in this series and the embodied ways in which characters' monstrosity is expressed. To this end, I also break new critical ground by considering characters' violence in relation to their overall character arc, and how it leads to either a destructive cycle or a proliferation of their ideals and aspirations through queer reproduction, depending on whether the violence empowers others or reinforces patriarchal structures. Non-normative subjectivity offers a more flexible position from which to negotiate masculinity, but, as I will show, these negoti-ations take a variety of forms and are presented to audiences in multifarious and complex ways. My focus on masculine characters' entire story arc and their (mis)uses of violence and bodily autonomy builds on the work of scholars such as Johnston (2021), Charul Patel (2014), and Alyssa Rosenberg (2012), who argue that masculine characters become linked to the monstrous because of their violence.

I call this self-serving type of violence hegemonic violence because of its personal and structural relation to masculine power, drawing the concept from Raewyn Connell's work on hegemonic masculinity. Connell theorises hegemonic masculinity as a part of the hierarchy of masculinities she develops in her seminal book *Masculinities*; it is one of masculinity studies' major theoretical frameworks and has been for over three decades (Wedgwood 2009). Connell and Messerschmidt (2005) define hegemonic masculinity as: "the culturally most honoured way of being a man" (832) and emphasise that this gender configuration

INTRODUCTION 11

is not monolithic and ahistorical but actively adapts to maintain the oppression of women and non-hegemonic men. Connell postulates a masculine typology, which includes hegemonic, complicit, marginalised, and subordinated masculinities. Connell's hierarchy is historically variable and context specific; it is not a rigid structure intending to reduce complex gender relations into understandable categories (841). Connell's hierarchy, particularly the concept of hegemonic masculinity, is useful for connecting individual acts and the identities they correlate with intersectional gender systems, such as patriarchal reproduction. The theory is especially useful for considering how acts of violence may have a relationship to power, and additionally that this relationship is contextual: some of the violence I analyse is hegemonic or complicit within the world of the narrative but audiences are invited to view it as subordinate, and so on. I expand Connell's theory throughout this book to theorise hegemonic violence, which I define as that which empowers the self at the expense of others, reifies existing power imbalances (especially those between men and women and men and non-binary people), and is invested in the reproduction of the paternal law/family. It is a categorical tool necessary for clarity and scope, although I do not place hegemonic violence within a binary pair or typology, instead investigating many of the other acts that can be used to make the world a more livable place in the present and for future generations.

One of the other forms of violence I analyse is what I call "caring violence," drawing from the concept of "caring masculinity." "The central features of caring masculinities," according to Elliott (2015, 2), "are their rejection of domination and their integration of values of care, such as positive emotion, interdependence, and relationality, into masculine identities." The theory was originally developed to offer an insight into masculine carers and care workers (Hanlon 2012), and it associated "care" specifically with bodily care, from the perspective of everyday acts like toileting, washing, cooking, and cleaning. I expand the theory by applying it to fiction; by separating caring masculinity from the cisgender male bodies with which it is implicitly aligned in the original theorisations; and conceiving of care as something that can also occur outside the home, indeed something that can be performed through a wide range of acts including violence. Caring masculinity offers a practical way of illuminating this type of violence because it offers a theoretical framework that, like hegemonic masculinity, can speak to masculine performativity in relation to acts, identities, and structures.

When violence is used as an act of care, audiences of both *A Song of Ice and Fire* and *Game of Thrones* are invited to view it as acceptable, and it allows characters to maintain their constitutive borders and to share their knowledges and values through queer kinship. In Martin's novels and their television adaptation, violence can be a form of care, and when it is enacted in this way it is often (but not always) presented as alternately ambivalent and/or heroic. Caring masculinity, like hegemonic masculinity, is not a permanent or ongoing subject position; it is constituted through acts, and while it stems from an attachment of certain values, it does not offer a stable or coherent identity. Rather, characters can momentarily perform caring masculinity through acts of care. At the same time, the acts that constitute caring masculinity are, like hegemonic masculinity, always changing based on the political and social environment. Just as the conditions for maintaining the hegemony of cisgender men changes and so hegemonic masculinity changes, the conditions for caring for others change across time and space. This is why, in the violent neo-medieval world of Westeros, violence can be seen as an act of care, including teaching others to be violent so that they may better defend themselves and others. The characters who enact caring masculinity often perform acts of caring violence and do so, in part, because they recognise that their actions can help or harm others, rippling out into the narrative world in ways that can affect them and those they love.

But can violence be an act of care? Being forced to use violence can be considered an act of violence onto the self—and can we justify violence done to our own bodies as a viable means of caring for another? If the cost of protecting the Other is harm to the self, is that making a better world or simply reproducing a culture of violence? This is the question that this project grapples with and which is threaded through each chapter and each character's narrative arc. If we must reproduce harmful acts, identities, structures, in order to "increase[e] the possibilities for a livable life" (Butler 1999, xxviii), are we not inevitably reproducing those harms? This is the problem with working within and through the norms that make, bind, and harm us, because it is in them that we can also find community, self-knowledge, and pleasure. In the world of *A Song of Ice and Fire* and *Game of Thrones* bodies are forced to engage in violence (embodied, discursive, political) because this is the reality of the pseudo-medieval world, one of the conditions of survival. But that does not mean that this violence cannot be repeated differently, in this case through turning it against the heteropatriarchal structures that privilege individualism and flawless reproduction, and using it as a flawed tool to displace that order by caring for others. Caring and hegemonic violence offer a conceptual framework for connecting individual stylised acts, their motivations, masculinity, and larger power structures like heteropatriarchal reproduction and queer kinship.

INTRODUCTION 13

Queer Bodies in Westeros

What is queer about *A Song of Ice and Fire* and *Game of Thrones?* There is little same-sex attraction or gender diversity in the novels or show, but I suggest that the texts may be considered queer, and through the lens of queer theory. Both texts denaturalise gender and reproduction in its normative and non-normative forms. The queerness is built into the texts at the level of genre, narrative structure, adaptation, and themes. This is not uncommon in fantasy texts; Lenise Prater argues that "magical queering, symbolic or metaphoric queering made available by the conventions of the genre, are often more radical than the literal engagement with sexualities carried out by these texts" (2016, 32). The novels and television show invite audiences to (re)consider violent bodies from what we might call a queer perspective, imagining them and their attachments to patriarchal systems of reproduction in critical and subversive ways.

To make this argument I weave together insights from gender studies, especially Butler's notion of performativity, Elliott's concept of caring masculinities, Connell's work on masculinities and power, and from psychoanalysis, namely, Julia Kristeva's theory of abjection and Barbara Creed's notion of the monstrous feminine. This queer feminist psychoanalytic and poststructuralist framework permits me to explore how the novels and the television series negotiate relationships between masculinity and bodily boundaries in relation to acts of violence. While Butler's theory of gender performativity offers a basis for explaining how gendered acts are changeable, and that subversion can be used for numerous political projects, Connell's hierarchy of masculinities can illuminate how these acts actively legitimise, are complicit with, or challenge patriarchal power structures. Alongside Connell, Elliott's theorisation of caring masculinity provides a means of considering how violence can be put to more productive ends that allow characters to momentarily break free from the destructive cycle that hegemonic violence creates. Kristeva's account of abjection elucidates the mechanisms of the critique of patriarchal structures in *A Song of Ice and Fire* and *Game of Thrones* via the capacity of characters to negotiate and overcome (or be destroyed by) their loss of bodily and subjective borders.

The narrative world of Westeros, in both novel and television form, is obsessed with reproduction: of bloodlines and Great Houses, of rare and magical species, of codes of honour and religion. The most prized form of reproduction in the pseudo-medieval world is what I call patriarchal reproduction: a means of repeating the psychoanalytic law of the father through heterosexual biological reproduction, by which the son is

14   REIMAGINING MASCULINITY AND VIOLENCE

expected to perfectly reproduce the father's ideals, values, and masculine performance. The desire to reproduce perfectly is bound up with fears of racial and class miscegenation, as well as hegemonic violence. The only characters in *A Song of Ice and Fire* and *Game of Thrones* who successfully reproduce—by which I mean replicate their subjectivity to a new site and in such a way that it can be further replicated—are those that use violence for selfless reasons, namely, to help, honour, or empower others.

Both caring and hegemonic acts of violence are linked to the notion of reproduction, although only caring violence is shown to have any hope of allowing characters to reproduce. Caring violence leads to some of the series' only successful reproductions, though they are not the bio-familial kind that the patriarchal order venerates but one that is (often but not always) democratised, non-biological, and non-hierarchical. I find Butler's concept of queer kinship a useful term to describe these kinds of reproductive successes. Butler theorises queer kinship as "the resignification of the family" (1993, 95) and argues that "a cultural reelaboration of kinship"—such as that which occurs in drag balls when "men 'mother' one another, 'house' one another, 'rear' one another"—turns these normative terms "toward a more enabling future" that "binds, cares, and teaches, that shelters and enables" (Butler 1993, 95). Many characters in *A Song of Ice and Fire* and *Game of Thrones* similarly choose to embrace the Other, a process of undoing that allows them to withstand confrontations with "the abject," for they are already undone as individuals and remade in productive ways, as part of a community. Butler (2004, 19) notes, "we're undone by each other. And if we're not, we're missing something. If this seems so clearly the case with grief, it is only because it was already the case with desire. One does not always stay intact." Connection to others necessitates an undoing of the self, and yet embracing these connections allows certain characters in *A Song of Ice and Fire* and *Game of Thrones* to retain their subjectivating borders when they use violence and come face to face with abjection. The subversion of normative masculinity through abjection in *A Song of Ice and Fire* and *Game of Thrones* forces masculine characters either to accept a more open and connected body and subjectivity, and to foster queer kinship in those terms, or to refuse and be destroyed through their own circular violence. Queer kinship becomes one of few spaces in Westeros where it is possible to reproduce the self, in the sense that a character's values, knowledges, and practices can proliferate in the actions of others.

Queer theory offers useful tools for considering *A Song of Ice and Fire* and *Game of Thrones* in relation to reproduction, heteropatriarchal structures, gendered/sexual acts, and ambivalence. As a poststructuralist

INTRODUCTION 15

body of scholarship that grew out of lesbian and gay studies and proliferated mainly in the early 1990s, initially through the work of Butler (1990; 1993) and Eve Kosofsky Sedgwick (1990; 1993), queer theory offers a complex range of critical tools for examining identity, particularly compulsory heterosexuality, by revealing dissonances and instabilities between sex, sexuality, and gender. Queer theory offers ideas around the political implications of these dissonances and instabilities, which have been reflected in studies of gender performativity (Butler 1990), cross-dressing (Garber 1993), female masculinity (Halberstam 1998), locating queerness in literature (Sedgwick 1990; 1993; 2015), the relationship between sex and citizenship (Berlant 1997), queer culture building (Berlant and Warner 1998), and many others. More recently, queer theory has focused on questions of temporality (Halberstam 2005), geography (Binnie 1997; Hemmings 2013; Kazyak 2012; Oswin 2008), failure (Halberstam 2011), the figure of the child (Edelman 2004), prostheses (Preciado 2018), and archives (Drabinski 2013; Manalansan and Martin 2014). The diverse analytical possibilities within queer theory attest to its indeterminacy and its applicability not only to the specific concerns of the LGBTIQA* community but also to general concerns about the human condition (Berlant and Warner 1995, 349).

One of the key concerns in queer theory is denaturalising normative ideas about gender and sexuality, and I believe that this makes it a highly useful tool for analysing fantasy as a genre, which, by definition, is invested in troubling the real world through magic, especially as it relates to violence. The magical worlds in fantasy fiction are often highly violent, whether that violence takes the form of a supernatural conflict between characters, races, or armies representing the forces of good and evil or a more mundane "gritty realism" seen to represent a middle ages that had its own complex relationship to violence and its representation (Meyerson, Thiery, and Falk 2015). In both cases, a wide range of fantasy genre conventions are invested in orchestrating the protagonist's encounters with violence. However, these encounters often destabilise the normality of hegemonic violence by showing characters who excel at violence but actively dislike its use. "The kind of world the novels are set in demands its heroes to be strong fighters," argues Ulrike Horstmann (2003, 94), but the characters in fantasy fiction often find themselves "hating to kill and being aware of the moral dubiousness of depriving anyone of life." The connection between masculinity and violence is repeated in the fantasy genre, but it is also denaturalised as "sensitivity towards a person or a situation and the ability to empathise may be more important than aggressiveness or skill with weapons" (Horstmann 2003, 100). Violent hegemonic masculinity becomes strange within

16   REIMAGINING MASCULINITY AND VIOLENCE

fantasy narratives where the narrow understanding of masculinity that dominates in the West is expanded. Thanks to fantasy conventions like magic, characters have more options for connection, community, and care, and this allows them to embrace relationality and interconnectedness and in turn (re)imagine the relationship between feelings, violence, and masculinity.

Queer theory, especially ideas like Butler's theory of gender performativity, offers a means of seeing how *A Song of Ice and Fire* and *Game of Thrones* repeat masculine violence in critical ways. Butler (1993, 95) views gendered acts (including violence) as "not a singular 'act' or event" but instead as "a ritualized production" and "a ritual reiteration under and through constraint." Masculinity is subject to policing and freedom, which can function in ways that repress or empower us, and gaps and ruptures in what we expect of masculinity can be used to disrupt the gender regime. For Butler, that regime is the "heterosexual matrix," the system of power in which heterosexuality is enforced and gender and sex are discursively produced (47–106). Butler (1990, 25) argues that "gender is always a doing, though not a doing by a subject who might be said to preexist the deed. [...] There is no gender identity behind the expressions of gender; that identity is performatively constituted by the very 'expressions' that are said to be its results." There is no doer behind the deed, or no "sovereign self" behind gender (1999, 149): we become subjects *through* gender and cannot be intelligible as human without being sexed and gendered (22). Gender is produced through gendered acts that are seen as the reality of gender, but for Butler they are one and the same. The concept of performativity has been hugely influential in feminist theory and criticism; if gender is constructed rather than essential, there can be no support for claims to a natural patriarchy or women's natural inferiority (Petersen 2003, 56–57). Furthermore, as Butler notes, if gender is constructed it may well be constructed differently (Butler 1999, 140). I pursue these differences in Martin's novels and their television adaptation by reading caring and hegemonic masculine violence through Butler's theory: the acts are performative in the sense that they constitute the identities they are seen to reflect, and it is only when they are denaturalised that the possibility for subversion arises.

The question of whether violence can be a subversive act is raised continually throughout this book, and I find Butler's theorisation of gender subversion useful for tracing its tenuousness as a strategy for resisting the law. Butler's notion of gender performativity highlights the law's importance, which we as subjects can never evade or escape because our subjectivity, our being, and our capacity to resist come from

INTRODUCTION 17

within the terms of that law. From Butler's perspective, we must work from within the terms of the law and turn it against itself to make a world that is more open to the diversity of human experience. Butler claims that it is only because deviations occur *within* the normative frame that they can challenge that frame. Subversive acts are those that reveal gender to be tenuous, imitative, and malleable; subversion is "the occasion in which we come to understand that what we take to be 'real,' what we invoke as the naturalized knowledge of gender is, in fact, a changeable and revisable reality" (Butler 1999, xxiii). *Gender Trouble* (107–193) sees Butler theorise gender subversion at length, using drag performances as an example in which the signs of femininity are displaced onto the cisgender male body, rendering gender unnatural and revealing its contingency. In *Bodies That Matter,* Butler (1993) returns to the question of subversion, where they clarify that drag is neither the only form of gender subversion nor gender subversion par excellence. They explain that "drag is subversive to the extent that it reflects on the imitative structure by which hegemonic gender is itself produced and disputes heterosexuality's claim on naturalness and originality" (85). While films such as *Mrs Doubtfire* (1993) and *Some Like It Hot* (1959) may suggest that gender is performative, Butler argues that they maintain the heterosexual matrix and do not challenge or attempt to reformulate the current gender order. In other words, drag is not necessarily subversive, but has the capacity to be so. Subversion is more fully achieved when gender performativity is not only revealed but reconstructed or critiqued, offering a potential transformation. Subversion is found in "the arbitrary relation between such acts, in the possibility of a failure to repeat, a de-formity, or a parodic repetition that exposes the phantasmic effect of abiding identity as a politically tenuous construction" (1990, 192).

For this reason, Butler (1990, 93) argues that subversion occurs "when the law turns against itself and spawns unexpected permutations of itself." In other words, subversions come from within the psycho-analytic law of the father and as part of the exercise of the law. This is why particular models of masculinity in *A Song of Ice and Fire* and *Game of Thrones* are enacted in the context of a law—of unmitigated or unconstrained patriarchy and of constrained and "good"/legal patriarchy—and both are rejected, whereas other models of masculinity are able to work by reference to the same constraints: repeating the link between masculinity and violence through reference to phallic weapons but using this violence to forge connections to others.

In addition to untangling the subversive violence in *A Song of Ice and Fire* and *Game of Thrones,* Butler's theory also offers a way of understanding another "unexpected permutation" with which these texts are embedded: adaptation. As I chart the ways that the narrative in the novels, advance chapters, and television series twist the adaptation process, I use Butler's work on gender performativity paired with Linda Hutcheon's (2012) work on adaptation, following on from scholars such as Mansbridge (2017) and Handyside (2012). Hutcheon claims that every text is an adaptation, and Butler's work complements Hutcheon's view through their claim that there is no real or original gender, but rather "a set of repeated acts" (1990, 45) that creates the "illusion of an interior and organizing gender core" (186). Butler's arguments have been applied to the study of queer adaptation: as a means of abandoning the fidelity debates among adaptation scholars and as a means of thinking through adaptation as a process that is not linear but multidirectional.

A queer adaptation approach such as this is perfect for *A Song of Ice and Fire* and *Game of Thrones*. The television show has been overtaking aspects of the narrative in *A Song of Ice and Fire* since its fourth season, and as of season six it completely passed beyond the novels. While the television series concluded in early 2019, the novels are yet to be completed, meaning that the arguments I make are in relation to the book series as it stands at the end of *A Dance with Dragons* and in some cases sample chapters from *The Winds of Winter* that have been published on Martin's website. The dizzying adaptation movements between *A Song of Ice and Fire*, *Game of Thrones*, and the sample chapters has political value according to queer adaptation scholars. Writing on adaptation and queer theory using Butler and Hutcheon, Handyside argues that "a subversive repetition can call into question the regulatory practice of identity itself," as opposed to "the desire of the media and the State to promote a 'heritage cinema' that imagines repetition as perfect reproduction and in which adaptation works to help reproduce the nation" (54). The parallels between the reproduction of the nation/patriarchal law and the "perfect" adaptation, on the one hand, and the inevitable failure of all repetitions (be they gendered or textual) and their potential for destabilising the process of repetition and creating new meanings on the other, can illuminate the political stakes in adaptation and in public discourse around adaptation, as well as the adapted texts themselves and the ways in which they may reproduce (or fail to reproduce) patriarchal systems of reproduction. Combined, *A Song of Ice and Fire* and *Game of Thrones* make a fascinating adaptation case study, and one that is uniquely suited to a queer adaptation studies approach.

Butler's theory is useful for my reading of adaptation and gender, although it has been accused of being more interested in the discursive body than the material one, and for this reason I support their theory

INTRODUCTION   19

with psychoanalysis, namely, Julia Kristeva's theory of the abject and
Creed's work on the monstrous feminine as a means of illuminating the
mechanism of the critique and subversion of patriarchal violence in *A
Song of Ice and Fire* and *Game of Thrones*. Like poststructuralism, psychoanalytic approaches encourage exploration of both text (internal world/
unconscious) and structure (phallocentric culture/stages of development),
and thus map well onto Butler's theory while allowing me to place
emphasis upon bodies within the series: its focus on corpses, blood, and
vomit, as well as magic ice zombies, bestiality, and auto-cannibalism.
Many of these disruptions take place when bodies come undone, and
their value can be illuminated through Butler's politicisation of the
abject—the process of rejecting the Other through which the subject
comes into being—because it emphasises how the act of repudiation is
often ideologically motivated but that these motivations are not static
and can be changed.

Bodies regularly come undone, are re-made, contract, and/or expand
through prostheses based on their relation to violence in Martin's novels
and their adaptation. Normative masculinity depends upon borders that
are formed through a rejection of the body's own fluids and openings
(Thomas 1996), especially the anus (Thomas 2008; Bersani 1987), and it
is through these rejections that the "symbolic male body is [or becomes]
discrete, firm, closed and classical" (Creed 2005, 128). The "firm, closed
and classical" masculine body is revered in pseudo-medieval Westeros,
but when it is tenuous and in the moments when it becomes open,
disgusting, and/or undone in *A Song of Ice and Fire* and *Game of Thrones*,
these bodies can be used to contest both patriarchal claims about the
superiority of normatively masculine men and to broaden the existing
discourses around what it means to be masculine.

Kristeva's arguments about abjection are useful for making sense
of the horrific and graphic deaths that characters meet when they
use hegemonic violence. For Kristeva, abjection refers to that which
is expelled to produce the subject and allows them to move from the
mother to the father and the symbolic order: it is a process that contests
stable systems and binaries between, for example, the self and Other,
inside and outside, human and animal, masculine and feminine. Kristeva
(1982, 4) defines the abject as an object, a place, or process that "disturbs
identity, system, order [and] does not respect borders, positions, rules.
The in-between, the ambiguous, the composite." It is "a terror that
dissembles" (4) the distinctions between the meanings that sustain a
sense of self and order, such as the binaries "self/other, me/not me,
living/dead, male/female, infant/child, and citizen/resident" (Goodnow
2010, 6). We are, for example, often disgusted by faeces, blood, vomit,

and so on, and Kristeva claims that this is because these things cross the border between the inside and outside of our bodies.

Kristeva's treatment of the body as a site, experience, and process of abjection makes her formulation relevant to analysing how hegemonic violence in *A Song of Ice and Fire* and *Game of Thrones* is enacted on and through the site of the body and is mobilised in ways that reject this discourse. The desire to expel the abject and restore the borders of the "clean and proper body" (Kristeva 1982, 71) is a powerful force, although in Martin's novels and their adaptation it often leads to further horror because it is achieved through hegemonic violence. By contrast, characters who embrace the Other are, as Butler (2004, 19) would say, undone, but in *A Song of Ice and Fire* and *Game of Thrones* this undoing means that they are re-made through connections to others and can therefore withstand new unravellings as they come into contact with the abject. For this reason, it is useful to merge Kristeva's abject with Butler's, in which experiences with the abject can be political and productive, ideological ambiguity can be enabling, and gendered acts, genre conventions, patriarchy, and fantasy structures can be considered concurrently.

There is more to the gore in *A Song of Ice and Fire* and *Game of Thrones* than just boundary-crossing. The hegemonic violence and the circular deaths to which it leads are made uncomfortable for audiences through a distinct set of imageries both in text and on screen. These tend to revolve around mouths, fanged animals, dark and cavernous tunnels, literal and symbolic castrations, and cannibalism. The set of images feels at once disjointed and familiar and can be explained through Barbara Creed's concept of the monstrous feminine. For Creed, the monstrous feminine is a set of images in horror films that recalls the female reproductive system, its cultural interpretation as motherhood, and/or women's sexuality. Creed politicises the visceral abject in her study of femininity in horror films, where she uses Kristevian abjection to theorise the monstrous feminine as the prototype for all monstrosity. She argues that while women have conventionally been viewed as the victim in horror films, their boundary-crossing abilities, particularly in relation to reproduction and castration, are behind all figures of the monstrous. For Creed (1993, 166), images of monstrous femininity "provide us with a means of understanding the dark side of the patriarchal unconscious, particularly the deep-seated attitude of extreme ambivalence to the mother." In other words, the abject has ideological utility for revealing the patriarchal views behind film representations of femininity and untangling their embeddedness within horror genre conventions: it can be applied to gendered acts, as well as patriarchal structures. Integrating

INTRODUCTION 21

Creed's theory with Kristeva's and Butler's also highlights the ways in which the abject is gendered and, specifically, operates because of a psychic attempt to banish the feminine. In tandem, the three theories offer a way of elucidating the way that masculinity and violence are negotiated in *A Song of Ice and Fire* and *Game of Thrones* with attention to the relationship between gendered acts and the structures that inform them, namely, violence and the patriarchy. Creed focuses on film imagery, arguing that monsters such as the archaic mother, the witch, and the Medusa represent fears of the female reproductive body, especially the toothed vagina or *vagina dentata* and the womb. When characters use hegemonic violence against women in *A Song of Ice and Fire* and *Game of Thrones*, the feminine is often turned against them, and the monstrous feminine is useful for illuminating their descent into abjection and monstrosity as specifically feminine.

I will note that I read this dynamic optimistically—the feminine comes back to haunt the violent subject with satisfying results—though it is equally possible to read this as a homophobic or transphobic manoeuvre, as the (usually) cisgender masculine character is punished and made horrifying as they become feminine-coded (which here might mean gay or transfeminine). A critique that involves homophobia and/ or transphobia as its mechanism is not worth celebrating, but it does highlight two useful things: the ambivalence within the texts even at their arguably more subversive moments and the fact that these queer identities are horrifying specifically for the characters who use hegemonic masculine violence, that is, those who seek to maintain the heteropatriarchal order. The position of domination and exclusion fuels the need for monsters to abject.

So here we have the method of violence and its critique: certain characters use hegemonic masculine violence to dominate the Other (often women), and readers and viewers alike are invited to feel uncomfortable about that type of violence because it is realised through visual and filmic imagery that connotes the abject and, specifically, a monstrous feminine mode. The imagery works within the terms of the law (the heteropatriarchal system in which the feminine and the queer are to be rejected) but it is turned against the perpetrators of violence as their bodies become feminine and queer. An attachment to hegemonic masculine violence is revealed to offer nothing but a destructive cycle, and indeed the ultimate desire of patriarchal law—to reproduce that law perfectly from father to son—is regularly cited and thwarted amidst these violence encounters.

In *A Song of Ice and Fire* and *Game of Thrones*, monstrosity is not necessarily bad, and nor is masculinity. The series offers a way of thinking about masculinity that does not begin by assuming that it is a problem to be overcome, a crisis to be averted, or an epidemic to be treated. Rather, it is the way that masculinity interacts with other subjects and structures that determines whether it is criticised or valorised in Martin's novels and their adaptation. Fantasy fiction is uniquely suited to creating a context for moving away from patriarchal structures because it provides generic technologies such as magic that can be used to defamiliarise and radically privilege interpersonal connections by imagining them as taking place through an array of magical entities and acts. When masculine characters find their violence turned against them, they are forced either to embrace or to reject the Other. Integration with others provides connections that allow characters to secure their borders, whereas rejection leads them to become temporarily borderless and to be killed later in moments of narrative circularity. The textual echo suggests that despite its short-term benefits, hegemonic violence produces nothing but destruction and devastation, regardless of its legality, moral intent, or legitimacy. By contrast, when violence is used to challenge oppressive discourses and empower other characters, the destructive cycle is broken and replaced with queer reproduction of these new methods of masculine performance.

The Chapters

I begin with violence perpetrated by normatively masculine men: that is, cisgender, white, heterosexual, and able-bodied characters. Chapter 1 focuses on some of the most evil characters in *A Song of Ice and Fire* and *Game of Thrones*—Gregor Clegane and Ramsay Bolton—and how the violence they inflict on women is turned against them and mirrored in their deaths as they are unable to reproduce the paternal law, become abject, and are linked to images that connote what I refer to as the "queer monstrous feminine." This concept enables me to explore the queer as a mode through which monstrosity arises, a reflection of heteropatriarchal fears about femininity and queerness that can be utilised by conservative and progressive ideologies. I am not the first to link monstrosity to queerness, but I make a unique contribution to theorising a specifically queer monstrous feminine because Creed's work has rarely been used to illuminate these debates. Incorporating queerness into Creed's theory allows me to show how masculine characters retain their male bodies and masculine gender performance while simultaneously being linked to feminine imagery, with the implication that hegemonic violence is criticised without losing its ties to masculinity or maleness. At the same

INTRODUCTION   23

time, the monstrosity makes space for the men to be distanced from patriarchal power structures and presented as outliers who legitimise the need for a patriarchy in the first place. Their relation to a patriarchal hegemonic masculinity leads to a tension between the internal and external dramaturgy: in the narrative world their acts of violence are hegemonic and complicit but audiences are invited to view them as grotesque and hence subordinate. What emerges from these multiple tensions is an ambivalent depiction of hegemonic masculine violence in relation to monstrous men.

Hegemonic violence is also turned against the characters who use it in ways that are legally sanctioned in the narrative world. Eddard Stark and his sons Robb and Jon and his ward Theon attempt to replicate or reproduce legal and legitimate sovereign violence but fail because they use it as a result of individualistic (especially affective) motivations. Each character chooses to perform an execution to deal with a minor problem that is unacceptable according to the system of inflexible reproduction (patriarchy) that constitutes them, but in each case they lose their bodily borders through abject signifiers. They also face dire political consequences and are later killed in ways that echo their sovereign violence. The aggression is turned against itself, a reversal of the law from within the terms of the law, a process that Butler (1990; 1993) claims is also key to gender subversion. In charting how hegemonic acts of violence follow this trajectory regardless of whether they are perpetrated by antagonists or protagonists, I show that in *A Song of Ice and Fire* and *Game of Thrones* it is violence that is used to empower the self at the expense of others that are criticised and exposed as the source of monstrosity.

The same is true for characters who do not fit within the cisgender, white, able-bodied masculine norm that the monstrous and sovereign men strive to uphold. Turning to masculine characters who were AFAB, I show that Cersei Lannister also reproduces these existing power structures through hegemonic violence, and like the cisgender men I have examined, is criticised as she becomes monstrous. Cersei's violence is narrated in ways that connote queer monstrous feminine imagery, and she enters into a queer kinship with the reanimated corpse of one of her cronies, exposing both the positive and negative potential of this form of reproduction. But it is in relation to female masculinity that alternatives also become intelligible: the knight Brienne of Tarth uses violence to perform chivalrous and honourable deeds out of a fundamental respect for others who are less powerful than herself. When she comes into contact with the abject during her quests, she resists becoming grotesque because characters who recognise her honour intercede by restoring her bodily borders on her behalf. Instead of becoming grotesque, she builds alternative kinship bonds that have generative rather than destructive outcomes, first with Jaime Lannister, and later with Podrick Payne and Arya Stark. While these kinship bonds often develop in unexpected directions, they allow her to share her skills and knowledge with others: to reproduce queerly, that is, apart from heterosexual reproductive practices that privilege biology.

Heteronormative patterns of reproduction are similarly displaced for the disabled masculine characters I examine. Bran Stark, Jaime Lannister, and Tyrion Lannister begin the series citing patriarchs who inform their masculinity and lead them to enact or attempt to enact forms of hegemonic violence. But these characters learn that patriarchal models cannot be fully mapped onto disabled bodies. As a result, they reject dominating violence and undergo symbolic rebirths whereby they adopt different points of reference for their masculinities and learn to embrace the Other. At the same time, these rebirths are ambiguous, as the characters never fully abandon hegemonic violence. This ambivalence reflects the difficulty of resisting the matrices of power that we rely upon for our articulation as subjects.

Masculine women and disabled masculine characters provide a means of offering alternative bonds that can create a more livable world. But Westeros and Essos are vast and composed of many characters who do not fit the category of masculinity, or its supposed opposite, femininity. The implications of these queer characters in relations of violence and kinship point to further questions for exploration. I examine how the hegemonic and other-centred violence is restaged by queer characters, including those who are masculine some of the time, as well as those who shift between masculinity and femininity so quickly and with such overlap between the two supposed opposites that they could more accurately be described as gender fluid, non-binary, or post-gender. My final chapter, on gender fluidity and magical violence, claims that some of the genderqueer characters in the series can be seen to restage the acts of hegemonic and caring violence I have examined and to rework them in ambiguous ways. Magic enables characters like Varamyr Sixskins, Arya Stark, and Daenerys Targaryen to enact spectacular violence, dramatising their capacity for violent domination and abjection as well as their ability to critique and intervene in the patriarchal systems of reproduction. Throughout my readings of the violent bodies in *A Song of Ice and Fire* and *Game of Thrones*, I stress the tension between the subversive possibilities that are to be found when the law is turned against itself, and the need to reference those laws in order to act and hence repeat them. I suggest that the ambivalence that these tensions

INTRODUCTION   25

create can be put to a number of political uses, and that those I have charted are one of many interpretations. My final chapter emphasises this ambivalence, especially as it relates to the complex adaptation process between Martin's novels, their television adaptation, and the advance chapters of the final two novels. Within these texts, we are no longer invited to see either masculinity or adaptation as natural and perfect processes in which the patriarchal law is repeated with fidelity; rather, the texts invite their audiences to critique these systems of reproduction by showing how hegemonic violence leads to horror and failure, and how queer subject positions make space for negotiating masculine violence. These negotiations fail as often as they succeed, and we are repeatedly shown that it is only by embracing the Other and the relationality and interconnectivity of all beings that we can hope to escape the cycle of destruction and begin to repeat in ways that make the world a more liveable place.

The importance of masculine subjects caring for others in both *A Song of Ice and Fire* and *Game of Thrones* is significant to our cultural understanding of masculinity because it reverses dominant discourses in the real world that encourage a lack of emotion and discourage close personal relationships and suggests that these can have beneficial results for individuals and for society. Fantasy genre conventions create the space for challenging the normativity or naturalness of the gender performances of masculine characters; for characters where their birth-assigned sex or disability disrupts the assumed naturalness of their performances of masculinity, these genre conventions often contribute additional layers of subversion.

Chapter 1

Some Knights Are Dark and Full of Terror

In many ways this book is about transforming bodies, as the violence they perform changes their embodied subjectivity for better or worse. The present chapter investigates how hegemonic violence changes cisgender men in *A Song of Ice and Fire* and *Game of Thrones* into monsters, and specifically monsters who are coded as feminine. I call this temporary and unwanted shift "the queer monstrous feminine."

What is the queer monstrous feminine? Put simply, the queer monstrous feminine is a queer theory that accounts for a monstrous mode in which a masculine body becomes discursively coded as feminine through monstrous feminine imagery. I analyse queer monstrous femininity and cyclical patterns of hegemonic violence through a psychoanalytical, feminist, and queer reading of constructions of monstrous masculine violence as it is perpetrated by some of the series' most abhorrent characters: Gregor Clegane and Ramsay Bolton. Each character's role in the dynastic, familial, and geopolitical unfolding of the text varies, although they are all Westerosi. The representation of these characters indicates how hegemonic acts of masculine violence are critiqued by association with the queer monstrous feminine, imagery that materialises in a different way for each character and is informed by their class and geographical status and actively prevents men from reproducing the symbolic law and patriarchal family. This critique involves a circularity of horror in which these monstrous men both enact abjection and are subjected to it, a process that reveals the inability of heteropatriarchal violence to produce anything but destruction. Neither the monstrous feminine/queer nor the abject is inherently conservative or damaging for the representation of marginalised characters, even though they are often assumed to be so in popular culture and among scholars. Rather, they are two modes through which characters are undone, and what emerges from the incoherence can be put to productive, ambivalent, and/or destructive ideological uses.

28 REIMAGINING MASCULINITY AND VIOLENCE

Creed's description of the forms of the monstrous is useful for illuminating the imagery that surrounds hegemonic masculine violence throughout *A Song of Ice and Fire* and *Game of Thrones*: the unstable reproductive body, the archaic mother, the *vagina dentata*, the bloody mouth, and birth, all of which are coded as disgusting and terrifying. In both the novels and television show, attempts to banish the Other expose the unnaturalness of the subject by forcing a revisitation of the Other upon the monstrous male characters in a similar way to Butler's concept of gender performativity (1990) and their argument that drag is a confrontation with the citational and performative basis of what we take to be natural.

Accordingly, when symbols of monstrous femininity such as the *vagina dentata* and the archaic mother (or prostheses that signify them) are projected onto male bodies in *A Song of Ice and Fire* and *Game of Thrones*, hegemonic acts of violence—not the feminine or the queer—are presented as monstrous and as part of a destructive cycle through the repetitive structures within the text. Certain characters use hegemonic violence to dominate the feminine, but they end up being linked with and then consumed by it. Gregor is visually coded in ways that link him to pregnancy and childbirth, and he is reborn as a Frankenstein's monster, enslaved in *Game of Thrones* to the Queen Regent (and later Queen) Cersei Lannister in a bastardised form of queer kinship. Ramsay uses dogs as prosthetic toothed vaginas and is eaten by them in turn in the television series. I expand Creed's concept by viewing these images of feminine monstrosity and male bodies as queer and by arguing that the specific visual forms in which the queer monstrous feminine materialises for each character are informed by their differences within the text's narrative and cultural logics. However, regardless of the characters' specific geographical, class, and familial position, the narrative circularity asserts the horrific consequences of characters using hegemonic violence to bolster their own masculinity and legitimise the patriarchy. In *A Song of Ice and Fire* and *Game of Thrones*, acts of hegemonic masculine violence never take place without taking a pound of flesh. The horror is double-edged, for it also makes space for audiences to view the monstrous violence as separate from, rather than symptomatic of, normative masculinity and patriarchal structures. As I will show, the monstrosity leads to an ambivalent textual construction of hegemonic violence.

Hegemonic violence is often visually coded as masculine through phallic imagery, and when some of the characters I analyse have their violence turned against them, they become a prosthetic phallus for another character. In Lacanian psychoanalysis, the phallus is a

SOME KNIGHTS ARE DARK AND FULL OF TERROR 29

privileged signifier, the symbolic and imaginary representation of the erect penis (Lacan 1977). Men "have" the phallus, a symbolic position that links masculinity to heterosexuality, in contrast to women who "are" the phallus and signify their own alleged lack. Returning to these arguments, Butler (1993, 52) argues that the "lesbian phallus is a fiction, but perhaps a theoretically useful one, for there are questions of imitation, subversion, and the rearticulation of phantasmic privilege that a psychoanalytically informed reading might attend." Butler focuses on this rearticulation, claiming that "the phallus is a transferable phantasm, and its naturalized link to male morphology can be called into question through an aggressive reterritorialization" (53). The phallus can be seen as a text and phallocentric culture as the structure that enables it, but the relationship between them is flexible and can be reworked on both levels. For Butler, the reterritorialisation can take the form of phallic body parts or "purposefully instrumentalized body-like things" (55), and I would add that in the fantasy genre, conventions such as swords, knives, hammers, dragons, and direwolves as well as other characters can be read as phallic "things" that may disrupt the phallocentric logic of hegemonic violence.

The prosthesis—in the form of prosthetic phalluses and prosthetic *vaginae dentatae*—adds to the queerness of the monstrous feminine when it is projected onto male bodies and illuminates the horrifying implications of hegemonic violence in both the novels and television series. I understand prostheses to be objects, characters, or animals which allow a character to perform acts that they would not otherwise be able to achieve. Patel (2014, 238) argues that in Martin's books Cersei uses men as prostheses that allow her to access a knightly body: "her lovers become a political prosthesis, a prosthetic phallus: the armouring of her 'vagina dentata' or 'purse', a literal weapon through which she can control them and rule the throne." Prostheses allow characters in *A Song of Ice and Fire* and *Game of Thrones* to perform both masculinity and femininity simultaneously: to be prosthetic phalluses and/or *vaginae dentatae*, and to move between these positions with a fluidity that increases their abject potential. Monstrous masculine characters use or become prostheses in ways that initially allow them to subordinate the feminine and the queer through violence, but ultimately have the queer monstrous feminine projected onto their bodies and later are destroyed by it.

Baker's (2010) argument that when male bodies become monstrous they become queer offers a way of conceptualising monstrosity and maleness that can include femininity and masculinity concurrently. For Baker, "it is the effeminate male that is chosen as the template for the monster [...] because he refuses traditional masculinity; because he is somehow not a man at all [...] he signifies an abject (queer) desire; he transgresses the border between normal and abnormal genders and sexualities" (5–6). Baker uses Kristevian abjection to bridge the gap between the monstrous feminine and the queer monster: "queer and gender ambiguous individuals resemble—in that they share certain aberrant characteristics—the abject figures of discourse that much of Kristeva's work attempts to define" (7). In other words, the queer is a monstrous mode because it disrupts the binaries that inform gender and sexuality. Baker focuses on the latter, which allows him to demonstrate how antagonists in fairy tales are often informed by stereotypes about lesbian, gay, and bisexual subjects, but prevents him from considering how gender ties into monstrous queerness. For this reason, his theoretical framework does not account for the ways that the symbols of monstrous femininity that Creed describes (and that are highly useful for analysing the images in *A Song of Ice and Fire* and *Game of Thrones*) remain relevant and maintain their intelligibility as feminine even as they are transposed onto male bodies. I expand Baker's and Creed's work by theorising a mode of monstrosity that emphasises queer enactments of gender, which will help to illuminate the feminine imagery that is projected onto male-bodied and masculine characters as a subversive reversal of their acts of hegemonic masculine violence.

Depictions of masculine monstrosity in *A Song of Ice and Fire* and *Game of Thrones* are often ambiguous and are intimately bound with images that signal the monstrous feminine, such as the various bloody mouths and births with which hegemonic violence is aligned. I build on Baker's insight that feminine monstrosity does not necessarily make male or masculine monsters feminine. I argue that it can produce a queer monstrous feminine in which the forms of feminine monstrosity that Creed outlines can be projected onto masculine and/or male characters who retain their male body/masculinity but also become temporarily or partially feminine. In the same way that Butler (1993, 95) describes the structures of gender subversion, the queer monstrous feminine resignifies "the very terms which effect our exclusion and abjection" and becomes "an appropriation of the terms of domination that turns them toward a more enabling future." In *A Song of Ice and Fire* and *Game of Thrones*, the queer is presented as a solution to acts of violence that shore up the patriarchy: both as terrifying because of the imagery with which it is associated, and as a satisfying punishment for these evil characters, an instance of subversion coming from within the terms of the law. The dynamic is key to disrupting the simple and problematic equation of queerness with monstrosity.

Monstrosity has subversive potential for critiquing hegemonic masculine violence in *A Song of Ice and Fire* and *Game of Thrones*, but it also leaves space for audiences to separate the masculine characters who perform sexual violence from normative masculinity and patriarchal structures. Popular cultural texts have often followed this pattern, presenting "a hegemonic picture of rape. The offenders were depicted as antisocial 'monsters' who preyed on innocent [victims]. [...] These types of rapes do happen, but they do not represent more prevalent forms of rape in society, such as date rape and incest" (Bufkin and Eschholz, 2000, 1336). Sexual violence is often divorced from hegemonic masculinity in popular television even though the act is affirmed by the structures that produce and support hegemonic masculinity. *A Song of Ice and Fire* and *Game of Thrones* are in this way comparable to other contemporary texts that figure rapists as the masculine Other. For example, in the television series *Dexter*, viewers are invited to "explicitly map [the antagonist and Dexter's brother Brian's] violence onto and through his sexual identity and desires," a significant difference from the protagonist Dexter Morgan, whose "killing behaviors are largely devoid of sexual content, making his violence crucially distinct from his brother's, and Dexter crucially distinct from Brian" (Arellano 2012, 10). Sexual violence is likewise presented as a moral barometer in *A Song of Ice and Fire* and *Game of Thrones*.

A considerable amount of the existing scholarship on *A Song of Ice and Fire* and *Game of Thrones* focuses on how sexual violence is being presented to viewers and readers, which repeats a relationship between masculinity and violence even as sexual violence is punished and linked with monstrous men, as explored by scholars such as Alyssa Rosenberg (2012) and Caroline Spector (2012). With regards to the novels, Rosenberg (2012, 17) claims that "where the ability to kill is a sign of manhood and even honour, it's sexual misconduct that signals monstrosity." Scholars such as Anne Gjelsvik (2016) and Joseph Young (2017) agree; Gjelsvik notes that in both Martin's novels and their adaptation "rape is used to distinguish detested characters" (61) and identifies Ramsay Bolton and Gregor Clegane as two examples—an insight I extend in Chapter 2—and Young observes that in *A Song of Ice and Fire* "violence makes the Westerosi inhuman; sex encourages and guides speculation as to which of them might be salvageable" (52). Rosenberg (2012, 27) considers how masculine violence affects men within the narrative, commenting that sexual violence "serves as a powerful indication, and indictment, of corruption and inhumanity." While Rosenberg does not consider the relation between men, masculinity, and violence in depth, her comment highlights how the relation between masculinity and violence is a point of negotiation in *A Song of Ice and Fire*, an argument

32 REIMAGINING MASCULINITY AND VIOLENCE

that I would extend to *Game of Thrones*. Her focus not only on acts of violence but also on their consequences for masculine characters allows her to oppose the popular assessment of the series as unproblematically promoting violent content. In other words, her focus on gendered acts and dominant masculine discourses reveals a deeper level of complexity in both texts' depiction of violence. I take the same focus as Rosenberg, but with a queer feminist conceptualisation of masculinity—that is, I separate masculinity from male bodies and analyse the imagery that surrounds characters when they use violence, viewing it as instances where they come undone and/or become monstrously feminine. This approach reveals a complex dialogue between normative masculinity, violence, and the fantasy genre. The novels (and, I would add, their film adaptation) present a powerful critique of rape through the queer monstrous feminine, but the use of the monstrous also opens space for audiences to view characters who perform sexual violence as inhuman masculine others. What emerges is an ambivalent depiction of violence in which it is at once hegemonic and subordinate, an unacceptable patriarchal practice and an act performed by the Other that legitimises the need for the protection patriarchy offers.

The Monstrous Birth

Male birth is used to criticise the primary act of violence with which Gregor Clegane is associated in *A Song of Ice and Fire* and *Game of Thrones*, the rape of Princess Elia of Dorne, Rhaegar Targaryen's wife. Gregor is a minor character in both the novels and television show, and his main role in both narratives is as a horrifying bannerman for Tywin Lannister. While Gregor sometimes performs violence on Tywin's behalf, he often uses violence to dominate other characters, and this hegemonic violence is critiqued through birth imagery. Creed (1993, 58) argues that "the act of birth is grotesque because the body's surface is no longer closed, smooth and intact—rather the body looks as if it may tear apart, open out, reveal its innermost depths." The pregnant body giving birth is abject for both Kristeva and Creed: women's reproductive capabilities are understood as a mark of the natural world that defies "the paternal symbolic" (Creed 1993, 49). And yet Gregor's births are empty—they fail—because his hegemonic violence cannot produce anything but horror, and so he is unable to reproduce his subjectivity, as the law demands.

As a specific textual materialisation of the queer monstrous feminine, pregnancy and birth are attached to Gregor because of his class and

SOME KNIGHTS ARE DARK AND FULL OF TERROR   33

geopolitical position. Born the son of a minor house, Gregor won his knighthood through his bloody deeds rather than his bloodlines: he gave birth to himself. His middle-class status and his residence in the Westerosi capital, King's Landing, means that he is linked to specifically human births, although birth is abject according to patriarchal logics. Gregor's complex masculine violence is critiqued through its connection to birth from one of his earliest and most infamous acts of violence: the rape and murder of Elia Targaryen. The act is cited numerous times but never shown explicitly on screen or in text, inviting readers and viewers to imagine the scene through snippets of vivid dialogue. In the novels, Tyrion Lannister claims that Gregor raped and killed Elia with her infant son's "blood and brains still on his hands" (SoS2 337), and similarly in *Game of Thrones* Elia's brother Oberyn claims that Gregor "killed my sister's children and then raped her with their blood still on her hands before killing her too" (S04E07). The scene is retold in ways that evoke disgust but also draw attention to the horror of pseudo-medieval heteropatriarchy. The repeated descriptions of Gregor's bloody hands reflect his moral culpability in the violence—he is caught red handed—and the conflation of violence and sexuality that makes his aggression monstrous.

Gregor's acts of rape and murder are hegemonic and complicit within *A Song of Ice and Fire* and *Game of Thrones* while simultaneously inviting audiences to see him as subordinated because his violence is linked to sexuality and is thereby coded as monstrous. Gregor was ordered to kill the children by his liege lord Tywin Lannister during Robert's Rebellion, making the murder complicit violence because it passively reinforces patriarchal power structures, namely, the dominance of men over women and children. These dynamics are further bolstered when Gregor asserts his agency and chooses to sexually assault Elia, a form of violence that is constructed as masculine in the West (see Helliwell 2000) and can be viewed as hegemonically masculine because it naturalises the domination of the masculine over the feminine. Rather than bringing forth new life, Gregor's violence gives birth to horror as his own body is marked as a part of "the natural world of the mother" (Creed 1993, 49) because it is connected to children, sex/rape, and violence. The infant's blood represents Gregor's lack of futurity: he rapes Elia but murders her moments later, his own act of hegemonic masculine violence stopping him from accessing even illegitimate heterosexual reproduction. Within the narrative, and for audiences, Gregor's seminal act of heteropatriarchal violence is "the one act that defines his monstrosity [...] when he stepped over the line [...] into overt villainy" (Rosenberg 2012, 22). However, it is precisely this villainy that

34 REIMAGINING MASCULINITY AND VIOLENCE

encourages audiences to "symbolically expel" Gregor "from hegemonic masculinity" (Connell 2005, 78): to view him as an outlier performing hypermasculinity or an excessive toxic masculinity. Gregor's hegemonic-complicit violence is subordinated through its presentation in *A Song of Ice and Fire* and *Game of Thrones*, even as it also reinforces the idea that women are physically inferior to men. The layers within the texts and the interpretations that audiences are encouraged to make of them illuminate the ways in which a singular act of violence can be seen to occupy numerous positions within Connell's hierarchy of masculinities at once, especially in relation to the subject, the performative context, and the audience of the performance/text. I suggest that this ambiguity is linked to Gregor's connection to the queer monstrous feminine: his rape and murder of Elia is one of many instances in which the unstable female reproductive body is projected onto Gregor's male body, and in this way the queer monstrous feminine and its promises of terror and abjection are used to subordinate his hegemonic violence.

In *Game of Thrones*, Gregor becomes associated with the unstable female body through a conflation of birth and death, now cited through camera angles as well as his blood-stained body and complicated by camp aesthetics. The episode "Mockingbird" (S4E7) sees Cersei ask Gregor to be the state's champion during Tyrion's trial by combat. Her walk through the palace grounds to find Gregor is intercut with shots of him practising his deadly swordsmanship on prisoners, which highlights Gregor's prowess. Yet there is also an element of what Susan Sontag (1964) calls camp, or humorous excess, in this scene: Gregor kills men for no logical narrative reason and his violence is ridiculous because of his over-exaggerated yelling and unnecessary sword forms, such as stabbing a man through the torso and then lifting him up to the sky. The camp element of the violence makes it ideologically ambivalent, as in the scene with Elia. In this case, Gregor's hegemonic violence is denaturalised and becomes Other because it is so silly, making it subordinate for audiences. However, in the world of the narrative, Gregor's violence is hegemonic because it is entirely individualistic: he kills scores of men because he wants to hone his skills, and in so doing he reinforces the legitimacy of the patriarchy by showcasing his muscular and powerful male body. The violence also shores up the connection between masculinity and violence, for his strong, muscular chest and arms are emphasised, and low angle shots are used to make him and his body appear gigantic and powerful. Yet, as Ann Davies (2007) notes in her study of masculinity in Spanish horror films, "the assertion of overt, muscular masculinity always implies not only its possible dissolution but also the horror of the regression of virility into abjection" (142), because once it becomes spectacular, the masculine body is also "open to the possibility of decay and abjection" (143), an argument that has been widely made by film studies scholars and is applicable to Gregor in *Game of Thrones*.

Gregor's body succumbs to abjection because his hegemonic violence is linked with the monstrous feminine: as he slashes a man's stomach his entrails appear to fall from his groin in a medium shot of the lower half of his torso. The framing connotes childbirth as the man's bowels, like a baby, "pass from inside to outside" (Creed 1993, 49), seemingly from between his legs. But it is another empty birth, for nothing is produced but gore, as in Gregor's murder of Elia. Multiple layers of abjection work to code this moment as disgusting and terrifying: the blood, birth connotations, and the blurring of male and female reproductive capacities. The scene is presented as horrifying, although the camp theatricality tempers the critique by distancing "natural" masculinity from this unnatural spectacle. Part of this ambivalence also pushes the critique in a new direction by revealing that masculinity is performative and can become absurd in the fantasy genre—though, as I have noted, it becomes hard to pin this performativity to "real" men because of the camp excess. The ambivalent critique of Gregor's violence upon the body of his victim also spreads to his own body: by the end of the scene Gregor's chest is covered in blood. Through the alignment between Gregor's acts of hegemonic violence, birth, and blood, Gregor evokes an ambivalent absurd horror as his body becomes entwined with the queer monstrous feminine.

Another facet of the queer monstrous feminine, the bloody mouth as *vagina dentata*, is used to make Gregor's excessive violence monstrous during Tyrion's trial by combat in *A Storm of Swords* and the *Game of Thrones* episode, "The Mountain and the Viper" (S4E8). Creed (1993) contends that "fear of the castrating female genitals" (105) is part of the "iconography of the horror film, which abounds with images that play on the fear of castration and dismemberment" (107). She identifies "menacing, toothed mouths," "the barred and dangerous entrance," and the "animal companion with open jaws and snapping teeth" as hallmarks of the toothed vagina (107–108). Spaces, places, or animals that could be considered vaginal or womb-like in their form or function become *vaginae dentatae* when they are linked with violence, such as the bloody mouths that Gregor's hegemonic violence causes. According to Creed (107), "a trace of blood" on the lips connotes the toothed vagina but it also carries the added weight of abjection because the mouth represents one of the body's most mutable openings (Conrich and Sedgwick 2017, 103).

The *vagina dentata* is used to critique Gregor's violence when he represents the state and kills Tyrion's champion, Oberyn Martell, who volunteered to fight as a state-sanctioned means of avenging his sister Elia. Despite the battle's legitimacy, it is positioned as a masculine power play. Heterosexual horror becomes the scene's focus, with Oberyn repeating the phrase, "You raped her. You murdered her. You killed her children," in both texts (SoS2 397–399; S4E8). Oberyn's dialogue resurrects the feminine that Gregor sought to banish through hegemonic violence, a visitation that is partly enabled through his familial connection to Elia and partly through Oberyn's existing characterisation as Other because of his open bisexuality and marginalised Dornish ethnicity. When Gregor kills Oberyn, he punches his face and blood trails from his ruined mouth before Gregor crushes his skull in his hands. In *Game of Thrones*, Gregor says, "Elia Martell. I killed her children. Then I raped her. Then I smashed her head in like this" (S4E8), whereas in the novel he is more emotive, referring to Elia's children as her "screaming whelp" and smashing her "fucking head" (SoS2 401). The book emphasises the hegemonic nature of Gregor's violence to a greater extent by highlighting his domination of the child, whom he views as an animalistic Other, and his anger at Elia through his cursing. In every other way the scene is adapted faithfully from the novel, a repetition within a repetition that highlights Gregor's act of hegemonic violence as one that is part of the patriarchal system and its desire to perfectly reproduce itself.

In both texts, the statement is more horrifying in reversing the order of events, and the skull-crushing is extremely graphic, evoking visceral disgust while overlaying Oberyn's death with that of his sister. Elia's rape and murder, Oberyn's death, and the bloody mouth are conflated into a single narrative moment, revealing Gregor's violence as an act of hegemonic masculine domination that reinforces the legitimacy of white heterosexual men through banishing the feminine, infant, and ethnic Other. Gregor's hegemonic violence is presented as repulsive, although this very repulsiveness also marks Gregor as Other: it leaves room for audiences to separate him from hegemonic masculinity even as it embodies this gender performance. The sheer excess of his hegemonic violence leaves room for ideological ambiguity, as in the scenes where Gregor's murder of Elia is described and when he trains in King's Landing. Gregor's violence is specifically linked to bloody mouths as one manifestation of the queer monstrous feminine because he is acting on behalf of the head of state (in this case Tywin Lannister) and he performs the violence within the palace, the heart of high-class power in Westeros. Oberyn's death is shot in ways that foreground the bloody

SOME KNIGHTS ARE DARK AND FULL OF TERROR   37

mouth in the very centre of the frame in the show and are narrated in ways that emphasise the bloody mouth in the novel, and in that way link Gregor's ambivalent hegemonic violence to the queer *vagina dentata* and its classed and geographically inflected promise of horror, even as considerable ambiguity remains in both *A Song of Ice and Fire* and *Game of Thrones* because of the spectacular nature of the violence.

The figures of the monstrous feminine with which Gregor's hegemonic violence is aligned in life are cited and turned against him in the novels when he dies and his body becomes pregnant with abjection. Gregor is fatally poisoned in the battle with Oberyn, and as he dies his body transforms, revealing "the mutable nature" of his flesh, just as pregnancy does to women's bodies (Creed 1993, 50). However, unlike the female reproductive body, Gregor becomes heavy with abject fluids, another empty birth like the ones that were linked to his hegemonic violence. It is significant that Gregor's death is linked to the queer monstrous feminine in the form of pregnancy and birth rather than bloody mouths, for he reverts to his middle-class status when he is no longer the state's representative, and he is relegated to the dungeon of King's Landing even as he remains within the capital. The maester (doctor) who tends him, Qyburn, tells the royal council that Gregor's "flesh mortifies and the wounds ooze pus [...] Even maggots will not touch such foulness. [...] The veins in his arm are turning black (SoS2 425). Later in the series, Gregor's health further deteriorates: Qyburn reports that the knight's "veins have turned black from head to heel, his water is clouded with pus, and the venom has eaten a hole in his side as large as my fist" (FfC 124).

Gregor's bodily decay is presented as grotesque not only because of his rotting skin, but because of the specific acts of violence that caused it. In the lines before and after Qyburn's report, he and Cersei explicitly refer to the Martells: first through references to a magic "spell" that must have "thickened" the poison, and later when Cersei remarks that she must give Gregor's skull to the Dornish prince in belated compensation for Elia's death (FfC 124). Couched between these implicit references to Gregor's rape and murder are descriptions of his body expanding by oozing pus in his wound and urine, contracting as venom eats his flesh, and transforming as he festers and his blood darkens. Gregor's body follows "the great cycle of birth, decay and death" (Creed 1993, 47) that marks women's relationship to nature: just as his flesh was once covered in his victims' blood as a means of marking his connection to the natural world and the female body's generative power, so too he now generates filth and decay in death.

The reproductive body is further emphasised when Gregor is reborn in a bastardised form of queer kinship with Cersei, becoming her

38 REIMAGINING MASCULINITY AND VIOLENCE

prosthetic *vagina dentata* and phallus simultaneously, a patchwork of corpses, a disjointed body which threatens the phallocentric symbolic order. In the *Game of Thrones* episode, "The Children" (S4E10), Qyburn inspects Gregor's wounds and claims that he can save the knight's life despite the fatal poison. The maester begins collecting medical instruments from around the room, which is small, dark, and filled with tubes and vials: as in other films where a male scientist creates life, the laboratory "re-creates an intra-uterine mise-en-scène, a maternal landscape" (Creed 2005, 43). Just as Gregor's previous acts of hegemonic violence were made monstrous because they were presented as queer births, in *Game of Thrones* he is given life in a violent appropriation of women's reproductive power in Qyburn's prosthetic womb-laboratory, born into "a body without soul, a non-body, disquieting matter" (Kristeva 1982, 109), the ultimate form of abjection (Kristeva 1982, 4) and queer monstrosity. Gregor becomes a living dead monster, a fitting intertextual reference to Mary Shelley's *Frankenstein* (1818) that highlights his own failed attempts to reproduce through heterosexual kinship.

Gregor re-enters the narrative after a significant amount of time—almost two books have passed in *A Song of Ice and Fire*, and one season of the television series—and the scene is figured as a queer double birth for he and Cersei in which they become one in a terrifying version of alternative kinship. Butler (1993, 94–95) argues that non-normative kinship can have enabling effects, and I expand her idea to suggest that queer kinship—like the queer monstrous feminine—is a mode that can have numerous ideological functions, including destructive or enabling ones. In *Game of Thrones* and *A Song of Ice and Fire* Gregor and Cersei's kinship is queer in a number of ways: the lack of a boundary between their identities, the subversion of traditional gender roles, and the sense that Cersei's desire to inhabit a male body (see Chapter 3) has been magically fulfilled. However, the bond is not consensual or equal, and for this reason it is presented as monstrous. When Gregor next appears in *A Song of Ice and Fire* and *Game of Thrones*, visual signs that suggest birth are presented upon Cersei's body: she is naked, crying, and bloody, covered in filth and other abject fluids because she has just endured a walk of penance through King's Landing (Patel 2014). Cersei's body visually evokes the (re)birth that she and Gregor have experienced, particularly when she returns to the palace, is wrapped in a blanket, and Gregor carries her away, his physical size making her seem like an infant and he a protective father (S5E10 "Mother's Mercy"). Similarly, in the novel, Cersei is presented as a newborn child: she feels "a pair of great armored arms lifting her off the ground [...] as easily as she had lifted Joffrey when he was still a babe" (DwD 1000).

Where Cersei's body is visually coded as newborn, Gregor's intellect and identity are wiped afresh in both texts and he is completely dominated by her in the same way that he once attempted to dominate the feminine and the masculine Other. Gregor is in effect a secondary site for Cersei to embody, and his dependence upon Cersei for his identity is signalled when Qyburn explains the knight's inability to speak as "a holy vow of silence [...] he will not speak until all of His Grace's enemies are dead and evil has been driven from the realm" (DwD 1001; S5E10). Qyburn's dialogue in the novel is adapted almost verbatim in the *Game of Thrones* adaptation, a repetition that speaks to Cersei's desire to repeat the nation and patriarchal order through the hegemonic masculine violence that she intends to perform through Gregor *and* to Gregor's new identity as a perfect reproduction of Cersei's subjectivity as he enacts her will. The dialogue is adapted with a fidelity that reflects the content of the text, highlighting the interrelation between the adaptation process and the textual meanings. In both *A Song of Ice and Fire* and *Game of Thrones*, Gregor exists only to serve Cersei, but he cannot consent to the bond and Cersei dominates him completely. She uses him as a prosthetic *vagina dentata* when her violence is incorporative and centres on the horror of the female body and she also uses him as a prosthetic phallus when she wishes to extend her power outwards and violently penetrate the Other. They are (re) born as one: a queer interconnection that turns the acts of hegemonic masculine violence Gregor used in life to a means of serving a different royal woman in (living) death.

In the novel, Gregor is (re)named Ser Robert Strong, delivered into a new identity that is subordinate to Cersei's (DwD 1001). The name Robert Strong is significant to Cersei: her deceased husband was named Robert Baratheon, a man renowned in his youth for his strength and skill with a battle hammer. While Robert and Cersei were married, he abused and sexually assaulted her on multiple occasions, performing a version of hegemonic masculinity in private (and occasionally in public) that reinforced his domination over his wife and, by extension, the patriarchal domination of women by men. Despite Cersei's frequent criticisms of Robert and his weakness for beautiful women, she holds him as an exemplar of masculinity and repeats his gender performance when she becomes Queen Regent and later Queen. Naming her prosthetic phallus Ser Robert Strong in the novels emphasises their connection: Cersei repeats Robert's acts of hegemonic masculine violence and Gregor acts out the repetitions.

In *Game of Thrones*, Gregor's hegemonic violence is further turned against itself through visual imagery that connotes the queer monstrous feminine, specifically birth, in his death scene in "The Bells" (S8E5). During Daenerys's sack of King's Landing, Gregor battles with his brother Sandor on the disintegrating palace stairs, and during the confrontation he breaks from Cersei and murders Qyburn. However, where Gregor's acts of violence are steeped in ambiguity in life, the ambivalence is seemingly resolved when Sandor sees Gregor's monstrous face without a helmet for the first time since his rebirth and says, "Yeah, that's you. That's what you've always been" (S8E5). Viewers are invited to accept Sandor's claim that his brother was always a monster, thereby designating his monstrous violence as Other. Viewers are invited to view Gregor as marginalised despite his violence being hegemonic within the world of the narrative. The scene is heavy with textual echoes. Daenerys's attack on King's Landing in the narrative present mirrors Tywin Lannister's attack during Robert's Rebellion in the past, when Gregor raped and murdered Elia Targaryen. In addition, the visual image of Gregor crushing skills with his bare hands (as when he murdered Elia and Oberyn Martell) is also repeated twice. Gregor crushes Qyburn's skull by smashing his head against a wall, and he attempts to push his gauntleted fingers through Sandor's eye sockets. The repeated bursting imagery connotes birth and links it to Gregor's hegemonic violence in life. The violence that is inflicted on Gregor's body is further presented in ways that evoke scenes of birth: Sandor stabs Gregor's in the torso with a sword but the undead man is unfazed and a full six seconds of screen time is spent on close-up images of Gregor slowly pulling the bloodstained sword from his stomach. The act of pushing (or in this case pulling) something out of the body troubles the same boundaries between inside/outside the body that childbirth does, and the specific physical location of the stab wound—the torso—heightens this connection. When Sandor finally murders Gregor, he does so by pushing the man through the already-crumbling palace wall, which the two men burst through as they fall to their deaths ("The Bells" S8E5). The violent border crossing, visual focus on the sword leaving Gregor's body, and the repeated acts of skull-crushing can be seen to signify a queer monstrous feminine birth, which is connected back to Gregor's hegemonic violence in life because these acts were also connected to the body bursting open. Birth and pregnancy continue to be central to Gregor's violence and his monstrosity at the conclusion of *Game of Thrones*, although now they signal his abjection and death as violence is turned against itself in his final moments in the same palace where he raped and murdered Elia.

The Hounds

An ambivalent critique likewise takes place in relation to Ramsay Bolton's hegemonic violence in *A Song of Ice and Fire* and *Game of Thrones*, although in his case the specific materialisation of the queer monstrous feminine is no longer human births or bloody mouths but animal and "savage," inflected by his being lower in class status than Gregor and performing violence well outside of the metropole. Ramsay was born a bastard son of a minor lord and only becomes legitimate as an adult. Even afterwards, he finds this position tenuous as his father marries and impregnates a younger woman with the hope of raising a more docile heir. In the novels he is mentioned in passing a number of times before he appears as Theon Greyjoy's torturer in *A Dance with Dragons*. In *Game of Thrones* he is present from season three and his narrative has been expanded: he has a lover called Myranda and he kills his father and stepmother to become Warden of the North, after which he battles with Jon Snow and the wildlings and is killed by Jon in hand-to-hand combat. Ramsay's specific dynastic and geographical position shapes the form of the queer monstrous feminine through which his hegemonic violence is critiqued: before he is deemed legitimate and while he is living at the Dreadfort, his family's ancestral home, the queer *vagina dentata* is projected onto his own body as he tortures Theon Greyjoy and is made to appear savage and animalistic through imagery that connotes cannibalism.

In *Game of Thrones*, the cannibalistic *vagina dentata* is used to highlight Ramsay's monstrosity when he attempts to punish Theon with queerness by pretending to eat Theon's severed and cooked penis as an exercise in psychological torture, but Ramsay's violence is turned against him when citations of the monstrous feminine are linked to his own male body. Theon is castrated in the season three episode "The Bear and the Maiden Fair" (S3E7) after he is seduced by two of Ramsay's concubines, an act that is only hinted at in the novels. Ramsay chooses to castrate Theon because both men view the penis and phallus as defining features of heterosexual manhood: its violent removal makes a man feminine and queer, and these positions become part of the punishment. Ramsay's acts of violence shore up the connection between masculinity and violence as they simultaneously render it unnatural because of the numerous border crossings involved, especially the cannibalistic and queer undertones. Ramsay's violence is positioned as Other from hegemonic masculinity because of its excess, effectively legitimising the need for hegemonically masculine men to combat monstrous men. Viewers are invited to criticise Ramsay and view his violence as monstrous, but his monstrosity is so

42 REIMAGINING MASCULINITY AND VIOLENCE

spectacular that his masculinity is marginalised and the depiction of his violence becomes ambivalent.

While there is little doubt in *Game of Thrones* as to whether Ramsay went through with the castration, it is confirmed three episodes later in "Mhysa" (S3E10). The scene begins with a close-up of a plate containing a cooked sausage, a knife, and a medieval feasting fork. The sausage is focused on for seven seconds of screen time, giving the viewer the opportunity to make the connection with Theon's castration. Ramsay lifts the sausage to his mouth and the camera follows the motion of his hand, ending in a close-up of his face as he places the meat in his mouth. In the foreground of the frame, Ramsay chews with his mouth open. The sound of mastication is audible, along with subtle notes of Ramsay's theme music (see Misra 2015).

Both the chewing mouth and the implied cannibalism are coded as disgusting and shocking and are linked to the queer monstrous feminine as a critique of Ramsay's violence–a violence that is linked to his lower-class status and his geographically rural location. In the middle ground, Theon is visible, restrained in the centre left of the frame. Because Theon is in the middle ground and Ramsay is in the foreground, Theon's crotch is level with Ramsay's mouth, which looks large enough to consume his victim—a poignant framing decision that further evokes cannibalism. Ramsay's chewing mouth is also connected with Theon's penis through movement in the frame, as Ramsay's mouth and the fire in the background are the only things that move, creating a visual line that brings the viewer's eye directly over Theon's crotch. If these framing devices suggest that Ramsay is eating Theon's severed penis, it is soon confirmed when he says, still chewing, "those girls weren't lying. You did have a good-sized cock" (S3E10 "Mhysa"). The phrase "good-sized cock" can be read as either homosocial praise or mocking, highlighting Ramsay's awareness of, but lack of fidelity to, heteropatriarchal reproduction, for he severs and pretends to eat Theon's reproductive organ. Ramsay draws attention to the fragility of hegemonic masculine domination, but also polices it by removing a threat to it: the emasculated Theon.

Ramsay's words can also be read as expressing a homoerotic and sadistic pleasure in Theon's "good-sized" genitals: forcing Theon to become queer, as was Ramsay's intention in castrating him, but also inadvertently entering this category himself. This subversive reversal can also be seen in the next shot, in which the camera moves to a close-up of Theon's clothed crotch and then, at medium speed, pans up his muscular torso to his face. Theon is obviously distressed, but his half-naked body splayed on the rack and the camera's movement up his body nonetheless suggest a narrative rupture in which Ramsay and Theon may be read as having a queer relationship between their bodies. Homoeroticism is linked with horror for a full six seconds in which viewers are encouraged to believe that Ramsay is eating Theon's penis in an animalistic moment of cannibalism, but the horror that Ramsay intended to inflict is turned against him as he too becomes part of this queer scene.

As a terrifying *vagina dentata*/castrator/pseudo-cannibal whose male body is foregrounded, Ramsay's hegemonic violence is reversed and he is aligned with the queer monstrous feminine, which in this instance promises to threaten the patriarchal gender order by revealing that the borders between homosexual/heterosexual, queer/normative, human/animal, self/other, and male/female are easily breached. The framing and dialogue connote the cannibalistic *vagina dentata*, but it is a specifically queer and lower-class incarnation of this monstrous figure because it is linked to the male-bodied and masculine Ramsay, and because of the homoeroticism inherent in the image of Ramsay eating the phallic sausage. The latter is emphasised when Ramsay caresses Theon's chest and neck like a lover just before he renames him "Reek." The intimacy between the men is presented in such a way as to emphasise the sexualisation of Ramsay's act of violence and the intimacy between the men: unlike Gregor, who is separated from his violence in the eyes of the law, Ramsay's dynastic and class position mean that he must carry out most of Theon's torture with his own hands, and thus his own body becomes queer during, rather than after, the violence. In this moment and those that focus on the sausage, "the fragility of the law" (Kristeva 1982) is foregrounded and multiple borders are disrupted. Ramsay's act of violence is at once hegemonic and subordinate within the narrative and presented to audiences as a marginal Other apart from normative masculinity. The critique of a violent hegemonic masculinity is ambivalent, although the phallocentric symbolic order and the legitimacy of the patriarchy come under stress in *Game of Thrones* as the phallus is reduced to a fleshy and vulnerable penis that can be severed, cooked, and consumed.

The lens of the *vagina dentata* and the archaic mother are also useful for viewing the prosthesis-like relationship between Ramsay and his hounds as a critique of his acts of hegemonic violence that is shaped by his low class and geographical locale. Creed (1993, 108) argues that in paintings of beautiful women, the "animal companion with open jaws and snapping teeth" represent the toothed vagina: "the creature represent[s] her deadly genital trap and evil intent." When masculine characters are likewise linked with snarling animal companions, this

44   REIMAGINING MASCULINITY AND VIOLENCE

expands Creed's argument to reveal how masculine and male characters can be made horrifying through the monstrous feminine without becoming women, and how specific materialisations of the queer monstrous feminine are linked to the character's varying roles in the dynastic and geopolitical unfolding of the text, even though they are all Westerosi. In *Game of Thrones*, Ramsay's hounds are used as a prosthetic *vagina dentata*: they are the queer "genital trap" he uses to hunt, harass, and kill women. The shift from human to animal forms of the queer monstrous feminine reflects Ramsay's lower-class status and his geographical distance from the major political centres in Westeros. The act of murdering a woman is hegemonic because it legitimises men's supremacy over women, although the spectacle Ramsay makes of the violence—especially his decision to use hounds—makes the act marginal in the world of Westeros and for viewers, who are encouraged to see Ramsay as a monstrous Other rather than an agent of the patriarchy. The relationship between Ramsay and his hounds can also be seen to represent a bastardised form of queer kinship, like that between Gregor and Cersei, in which their relationship becomes monstrous because it is not consensual or equal. In "The Lion and the Rose" (S4E2), Ramsay, Theon/Reek, and his paramour Myranda hunt a peasant woman called Tansy in the woods, using the hounds to trace their victim's scent. Ramsay's choice of victim is significant, for Tansy is less powerful both physically and politically so that he can dominate her and thus perform hegemonic violence. The shift from Ramsay himself being the "savage" to the hounds is informed by the geographical shift from within the civilised human structure, the Dreadfort, to the woods: the realm of animals. The hunting scene is edited so that it consists of a series of very short shots, which work with Ramsay's eerie theme music to create an urgent and dangerous tone. These are combined with womb-like imagery during the chase: Tansy and the dogs run though a long dark tunnel, and each time she pauses to catch her breath it is within a muddy gully. When Myranda shoots Tansy through the thigh with an arrow, Ramsay orders his hounds to eat his victim alive, and her screams are audible over the sound of the snarling and barking animals. The imagery and sound evoke disgust and fear but direct them at Ramsay. It is he who leads the chase—he pulls Myranda along behind him—and controls the hounds: Ramsay yells "Rip her! Rip her! Rip her!" as a means of directing the animals to kill on his behalf. The dogs and the womb-like *mise en scène* within the forest promise the *vagina dentata* and the horror of death, castration, and blurred borders that it represents, and these are in turn projected onto Ramsay's hegemonic violence as a means of critiquing the act. However, the critique is rendered ambivalent because Ramsay's violence is spectacular in its horror, allowing audiences to view him as a monstrous Other rather than a symptom of the hegemonic gender order.

The queer monstrous feminine is similarly projected onto Ramsay's violence in season six of *Game of Thrones*, when he uses his hounds to murder his stepmother Walda Frey and his newborn half-brother in order to secure his patriarchal position as Lord Bolton after he murders his father. In this case, Ramsay's drastically higher-class status as legitimate heir and Lord of the Dreadfort means that he performs the act of violence entirely through a prosthesis (the hounds) rather than working with a prosthesis (as in the hunt) or with his own hands (as in Theon's torture). Ramsay unlocks the door and leads Walda and her son into the kennel where his dogs are housed, during which time his eerie theme music becomes progressively louder. Ramsay's theme plays when they enter the kennel, and his complete control over the hounds is foregrounded. As he enters the kennel, he silences the dogs with a verbal directive, and later commands them to kill Walda and her son with a high-pitched whistle. The whistle is an important shift in the representation of Ramsay's violence and his connection to the hounds as queer *vagina dentata*, for it suggests that he has more control over the animals yet is less clearly implicated in their violence than in the scene with Tansy, where he orders the animals to "rip her," or in the scenes with Theon, where he eats the sausage. Moreover, the hounds take on a new and higher-class significance in Winterfell because it is the ancestral home of the upper-class Starks, whose sigil is the direwolf. In Winterfell, the kinship between humans and canines is celebrated, and so Ramsay's connection to the hounds as prosthetic *vagina dentata* continues despite his higher-class status. And yet while Ramsay's violence bolsters this class system because it is patriarchal—it is entirely self-serving and thus reproduces the patriarchal system—it also deforms this same system because the son repeats the violence his father taught him but uses it to usurp his position as patriarch. In this way, Ramsay both succeeds and fails in reproducing the law of the father and the legitimacy of the patriarchy, and this ambivalence is reflected in his violence. The hounds function as Ramsay's prosthesis, allowing him to secure his status as the male heir to House Bolton while inadvertently evoking the monstrous feminine. Ramsay and the patriarchal system of reproduction become nightmarish in *Game of Thrones* as this geographically informed form of the queer monstrous feminine is projected onto his male body.

Ramsay's violence is positioned as terrifying in a different way in *A Song of Ice and Fire*, where he uses the hounds as a prosthesis that allows him to perform a failed version of patriarchal reproduction and is made monstrous through association with the archaic mother. Theon/Reek explains that the "peasant girls Ramsay had hunted, raped, and killed" get to "come back as bitches" if they are entertaining prey: "the next litter to come out of the Dreadfort's kennels would include a Kyra, Reek did not doubt" (DwD 492). The hounds incorporate Ramsay's victims by eating them and giving birth to puppies that carry the women's names. Ramsay creates a cycle of birth and death in which the peasant women become part of his prosthetic *vagina dentata* and are forced into a relation of queer kinship with him, but this attempt at (illegitimate) patriarchal reproduction fails. Ramsay rapes and potentially impregnates the women, but, like Gregor and Elia, he kills them before they can bear his children. Unlike Gregor, Ramsay does produce something—the puppies—but even these are marked as a failure because they are named after women, and he inadvertently creates a deformed matriarchy. Ramsay becomes what Creed (1993, 23–25) calls a "cannibalistic maternal figure [...] from which all life comes and to which all life returns."

Ramsay's hegemonic violence is also positioned as monstrous when he uses his hounds to sexually abuse his wife in *A Song of Ice and Fire*, but this act evokes the *vagina dentata* and prevents him from replicating the paternal law through heterosexual reproduction. In *A Dance with Dragons*, Ramsay marries Jeyne Poole, who grew up at Winterfell with the Stark girls. The Lannisters capture her in King's Landing, claim that she is Arya Stark, and send her back to Winterfell to be married to the newly legitimate Ramsay as a means of securing Roose Bolton's status as Warden of the North. Jeyne implies that she has been forced to have sex with the dogs: "I'll do what he wants ... whatever he wants ... with him or ... or with the dog or ... please ... he doesn't need to cut my feet off" (DwD 794). Jeyne's offer to perform bestiality is horrifying, and this horror is directed towards Ramsay and the acts of heteropatriarchal terror he has inflicted upon his wife. Soon thereafter Theon/Reek observes that "her small pale breasts [are] covered with teeth marks" (DwD 795), although it is unclear who or what bit her. Ramsay uses the hounds as a prosthetic *vagina dentata* that allows him to satiate his own individualistic desire to abuse women and reinforce his power over them—an attempt to violently banish the feminine Other and defend patriarchal power structures—but this violence inadvertently mocks his duty to reproduce the symbolic law/patriarchal line of succession because he forces his wife to engage in bestiality. The blurring of human and animal through the ambiguous sexual "bite marks" on Jeyne's flesh invites a specific materialisation of the queer monstrous feminine, the animalised *vagina dentata*, that is informed by Ramsay's dynastic failure and his geopolitical location in Winterfell, which reveres direwolves. Ramsay's violence forecloses his ability to reproduce the law, as it does

SOME KNIGHTS ARE DARK AND FULL OF TERROR   47

in the scene where he names his hounds after peasant women and those featuring Gregor's deformed births, but it takes on a less intimate and animal form of the queer monstrous feminine because of his geopolitical and class location in the pseudo-medieval world. At the time of writing, Ramsay's narrative remains unfinished and he remains at Winterfell, although his story has been expanded and concludes with his death in season six of *Game of Thrones*.

In the television series, Ramsay's death is highlighted as a reflection and condemnation of violence because of the narrative tension coded within the queer feminine monstrosity that surrounds him. In "Battle of the Bastards" (S6E9), Ramsay is eaten by his own dogs, starting at his mouth. The scene begins with Ramsay tied to a chair in the dog kennel in a position of abjection and submission, beaten bloody by his nemesis, Jon Snow. Ramsay appears in a close-up, his skin making a squishing sound as he wriggles in his bonds, with alternating shots of his face and fingers showing his bloody, filthy flesh: his own body has become abject matter. The dialogue in the scene emphasises Ramsay's death as a permanent failure to reproduce the law or legitimise the patriarchy and its family structures, an extenuation of the failures I have already noted. He tells his wife, the real Sansa Stark as opposed to the fake Arya in the novels, "You can't kill me. I'm part of you now," alluding to the psychological and physical scars he has given her and the possibility of her being pregnant with his child. But Sansa rebukes his desire to reproduce: "Your words will disappear. Your house will disappear. Your name will disappear. All memory of you will disappear." Ramsay attempted to banish the feminine and the queer with his acts of hegemonic violence, but they ultimately prevent him from perfectly—or imperfectly—reproducing the symbolic order and patriarchal law. Ramsay's violence is deployed against him in a subversive reversal, one which is highlighted throughout the rest of the scene. The hounds growl and Ramsay's theme music plays—just as it did when he fed people to the dogs. The textual echoes connect the scenes together and in so doing suggest that hegemonic violence only ever produces destruction for those who use it. The circularity is foregrounded on multiple fronts: Ramsay's death is heard, in the same way that it was when he killed Tansy and Walda, and his mouth is centralised, similar to when he tortured Theon. One of the animals walks up to Ramsay and sniffs his bloody visage, moves back for a moment, then attacks him, biting his face. The dogs turn on their master: Ramsay is incorporated by his own queer *vagina dentata* as the narrative comes full circle, confirming his monstrosity while revealing his violence as part of a destructive cycle. The graphic scene is presented as disgusting and horrifying, as well as satisfying, as Sansa enacts her revenge. Ramsay, like Gregor, uses acts of hegemonic violence to bolster his own power and banish the feminine, but he is ultimately aligned with and then consumed by a form of the queer monstrous feminine that is informed by his classed, dynastic, and geopolitical location, and he is unable to fulfil his part in the reproduction of the patriarchal law.

Conclusion

Violence is one of the stylised acts that constitute and legitimise patriarchal masculinity in society and in fiction. However, in *A Song of Ice and Fire* and *Game of Thrones*, acts of hegemonic masculine violence become grotesque and unsettling through the imagery that surrounds them. Creed's popular horror film application of Kristeva's concept of the abject, specifically her work on the monstrous feminine, helps illuminate how hegemonic violence by embodied male characters is rendered monstrous in Martin's novels and their television adaptation. However, following Baker's concept of the monstrous queer, I have explored how this occurs in a specifically queer mode in which male bodies are aligned with symbols of monstrous femininity including the *vagina dentata*, birth, and bloody mouths, and where the specific materialisation of the queer monstrous feminine is informed by the characters' geopolitical and class status. Ramsay and Gregor use violence to gain personal power and/or pleasure over women and less-powerful men to repudiate the feminine and to repeat the heterosexist patriarchal law, but this violence is turned against them. Their violence ultimately stops them from being able to reproduce the law/patriarchal family: Gregor is continually linked to empty or failed births and Ramsay is explicitly told that all signs of his life will "disappear" (S6E9). Hegemonic masculine violence is shown to be the true horror in a brutal world.

Chapter 2

Undoing Sovereign Violence

In the first chapter of *A Game of Thrones* and the first episode of *Game of Thrones*, a young boy called Bran watches his father execute a man for desertion, an act described in the novel as "the king's justice" (11). As I explore in this chapter, the deed is not simply "justice." While it is easy to condemn the monstrous acts of violence discussed in the previous chapter, violent punishments exerted for the purpose of "justice"— particularly in the king's name—might seem sequestered from that critique in the pseudo-medieval context of *A Song of Ice and Fire* and *Game of Thrones*. On the contrary, this most legitimate, legal, and seemingly acceptable form of violence is critiqued via the same mechanisms as the horrific monstrous violence in Chapter 1 because it is often (but not always) hegemonic or complicit in the sense that it legitimises the patriarchal order and reifies class power structures and naturalises the domination of some men over others through the law. In the case of the execution that Bran watches, there are negative consequences at the level of plot in both the novels and television show: although in killing the man Bran's father reactivates his power as the king's representative by performing sovereign violence, he loses valuable political information that could have readied the kingdom for an oncoming invasion. But those consequences also extend to Eddard's own death, and the death or abjection of the sons that imitate his performance of sovereign masculinity. In disclosing imitation as the means by which subjects are constituted and society is reproduced, performances of sovereign violence such as Eddard's also become sites for critiquing these constructions by revealing their contingency and flaws. Moreover, within this world, male-embodied masculinity is more explicitly and frequently connected to sovereignty than femininity.

As with the monstrosity of the "evil" men discussed in Chapter 1, acts of sovereign violence expose the citationality of the act and the structures that constitute subjectivity, which opens up a space in which

50   REIMAGINING MASCULINITY AND VIOLENCE

the male symbolic order and the law are revealed to be fragile and subject to revision. However, the characters I analyse in this chapter are an inversion of the monstrous men, not only in terms of their strict lawfulness but also because readers are given access to their thoughts through interior monologue for all but one of the four men I analyse. The insight into how these masculine characters think about their violence directs the audience's attention to the proliferation of sovereign violence, in which the act leads to parodic and/or flawed repetitions that disassemble the structures they are intended to support: a firm and closed male body and a prosperous kingdom. Masculine characters may use sovereign violence to reinforce their own power and legitimise the patriarchal order at others' expense, but the repetitive structures in the texts show that these acts are part of a disastrous pattern that harms the perpetrators as much as their victims.

I find Michel Foucault's theorisation of sovereign power (1977) useful for thinking through sovereign violence as a technology of power wielded by the monarch over the body of the subject. Via the technology of sovereign violence, the monarch punishes a criminal with torture or death as a means of redressing symbolic injuries against the sovereign's "two bodies," namely, the "transitory element that is born and dies" and "the physical yet tangible support of the kingdom" and the law (Foucault 1977, 28). In both the real medieval period that Foucault discusses and the pseudo-medieval fantasy universe in *A Song of Ice and Fire* and *Game of Thrones*, sovereign violence often supports the project of hegemonic masculinity. Sovereign violence is a technology of power that legitimises one group of men over others; as Connell (2005, 214) writes: "part of the struggle for hegemony in the gender order is the use of culture for such disciplinary purposes: setting standards, claiming popular assent and discrediting those who fall short." In *A Song of Ice and Fire* and *Game of Thrones*, the act of sovereign violence both sets the standard for masculine performativity and legitimises the domination of high-class men over the subjects of their laws, especially those of marginalised ethnicities and class backgrounds. The concept of "justice" glosses over the workings of the patriarchal order, making violent punishment seem like a natural response to crime.

While sovereign violence is practised by many characters in *A Song of Ice and Fire* and *Game of Thrones*, I focus on four: Eddard Stark, patriarch and Warden of the North, and his three eldest sons: his heir Robb Stark, his ward Theon Greyjoy, and his ward and supposed bastard son Jon. In both the novels and television series sovereign violence is comprised of a series of acts, promises, and intentions that the author and reader are aware of and which inform the narrative, including familial, affective, and phallic in the novels and elements of *mise en scène* and costuming in the adaptation. Both iterations of the series explicitly represent the imitative nature of sovereign violence through specific scenes showing a boy being trained to be a man through his exposure to hegemonic violence. The father–son relationships foreground the connection of sovereign violence to patriarchal legitimisation and reproduction. My combination of Judith Butler's, Raewyn Connell's, Julia Kristeva's, and Barbara Creed's theories of performativity, masculinity, abjection, and monstrous femininity allow these characters' repetitions of sovereign violence to be understood as acts through which a particular feature of male-embodied masculinity is (re)produced, as well as the site where it may be undone when the repetition is flawed. The practice of citing past performances of sovereign violence to justify or inform those in the present is similar to the practice of judicial sentencing: "the judge who authorizes and installs the situation he names invariably cites the law that he applies, and it is the power of this citation that gives the performative its binding or conferring power" (Butler 1993, 171). Sovereign violence is haunted by narrative circularity in which men are killed in ways that echo the sovereign violence they used in life, which leads to a critique of hegemonic masculine violence. These moments of disgust and the repetitive structures within the narrative point towards violence as part of a destructive cycle in which individual masculine identities and patriarchal society more broadly are undone. Investigating sovereign violence in *A Song of Ice and Fire* and *Game of Thrones* involves tracing the relation between repetition, failure, abjection, and circularity to demonstrate how these acts are presented as unable to support a coherent masculine identity or functioning society.

Sovereign Initiation

Sovereigns are not born knowing how to enact appropriate violence, and the processes through which it is taught—the acknowledgement that its familial, affective, and phallic promises are not natural—are key to disclosing its imitative function. While teaching violence can be an act of care when the learner is centralised and active in the process, sovereign violence is taught through demonstrations that reify the patriarch's power rather than share it. Sovereign violence is presented as an initiation into adult hegemonic masculinity in both *A Game of Thrones* and "Winter is Coming" (S1E1). As noted earlier, the initiate is Bran, Eddard's second-youngest son. Eddard is a protagonist in season one and *A Game of Thrones*, with one of the central narratives revolving around his becoming Hand of the king and travelling to King's Landing where he manages the kingdom and seeks to discover why his predecessor was killed. Eddard follows a rigid moral code that ultimately leads him to be betrayed and killed at the end of the first novel/season, much to the surprise of audiences. Eddard executes a deserter from the Night's Watch—a character called Gared in the television series and Will in the book—in front of his sons as an instruction in masculinity and sovereign violence. Placing his violence within the domain of the family, itself a self-reproducing system intrinsic to patriarchal systems, Eddard begins by also tying that violence to a broader tradition in the novel, stating that while other rulers hire a headsman, "our way is the older way. The blood of the First Men still flows in the veins of the Starks" (GoT 14). Similarly, in *Game of Thrones*, Eddard asks Bran why he thinks Eddard himself had to execute Gared. Bran responds, "Our way is the old way" (S1E1 "Winter is Coming"). Sovereign violence is presented as an "older" practice, an acknowledgement that the act and the restoration of order that it promises works to the logic that one "good" man—that is one who is cisgender, white, able, and heterosexual—can make the world "good." In other words, "good" men must take positions of leadership to protect the world from the forces of evil, even if that protection comes at the expense of the subordination of women and less-powerful men. Dan Ward (2018) makes a similar point, arguing that in the television show, "notions of chivalry and honour are integral to the images of normative masculinity that children of both sexes grow up with in Westeros" (110), particularly in this scene, as it emphasises "the weight of history and tradition on the Stark men" (111).

Bran's access to sovereign violence is dependent upon his successful repetition of specific positions and acts—including those that relate to genetics, class status, blood, gender, and the body. Repetition is signalled early in the initiation, disclosing sovereign violence as a practice that proliferates through the knowing citation of previous acts. In the novels, this is emphasised in an exchange between Bran and his half-brother Jon, who guides his initiation. Jon says, "Keep the pony well in hand [...] And don't look away," dialogue which is repeated back by the narrator: "Bran kept his pony well in hand, and did not look away" (12). Learning sovereign violence is comprised of repeated acts: controlling one's steed and watching the execution without revealing fear or disgust. Through Jon's instruction the reader receives the first building blocks of sovereign violence: imitation and domination.

The reproduction of patriarchal systems through violence is implied in *Game of Thrones* through the characters' costumes, which reflect the repetition through which classed subjects and the patriarchal feudal society are reproduced. Almost all the characters wear one of two near-identical outfits: that of the garrison (helmets, brown hauberk, and grey boiled leather) and that of the nobles (black cloak with a light brown fur stole and brown leather jerkin with straps crossed over the chest). In one long shot, Eddard's sons, Robb, Jon, and Bran, appear as miniature reproductions of their father as their faces are obscured by distance and only their identical costumes and height are visible. The multiple levels of repetition in the genre conventions, costumes, and setting place Eddard's act of sovereign violence within a world of imitation. Although these repetitions work to effect a sense of naturalness, violence is not natural or inevitable, and for this reason its repetitions can be determined and turned against their originating aims in subversive ways.

In the novels the performance of sovereign violence also involves particular emotional constraints. Eddard tells Bran that when he has to carry out "justice" himself, "you must take no pleasure in the task, but neither must you look away" (GoT 14). Sovereign violence promises objective and engaged perpetrators: it should not be motivated by individualistic feelings or desires, such as revenge, power, love, or honour. The importance of enacting the violence in the correct emotional register is of particular importance within the fantasy genre because, as I have noted, the acceptability of violence is powerfully mediated by affect. Through the fantasy genre expectations that Eddard reflects, sovereign violence is embedded within the masculine domain, and emotional repression is further linked to manhood.

One of the ways in which acts of sovereign violence are shown to be concerned with power rather than justice is through the promise of the phallus. One of the main fantasy genre conventions that attaches to violence—the sword—can be read as both a generic image and a denaturalised gendered act. When acts of sovereign violence take place in *A Song of Ice and Fire* and *Game of Thrones*, the sword is seen as a phallic image during certain executions as a means of representing the sovereign's personal desire for phallic power at the expense of safeguarding the realm, that is, its patriarchal elements.

"Swinging the sword" is one of many acts that produce the fantasy genre, and it is through the sword as genre convention that sovereign violence is revealed to be an act of power above all, and generative in multiple senses: it links masculinity with violence and judiciary power, sustains the family as a unit of social control, reinforces the able body as essential to all of these practices, and produces phallic power while making it essential to all of the aforementioned forces. In both the novel and television episode, Eddard says that "the man who passes the sentence should swing the sword" (GoT 12; S1E1 "Winter is Coming"),

54   REIMAGINING MASCULINITY AND VIOLENCE

indicating that sovereign violence should only be performed by elite and able-bodied cisgender men. Because execution and judgement are so tightly wound, judiciary power and, by extension, morality are gendered as masculine, reflecting the patriarchal pseudo-medieval world that is often reproduced in the textual and televisual worlds of Westeros. And because judgement and morality become masculine domains, the responsibility for fair sentencing must logically be assumed by men, and so the law becomes a paternal law through the operations of sovereign violence.

Bran's initiation in *A Game of Thrones* provides a useful illustration of phallic sovereign violence through his observations of Eddard's sword, which encourage the audience to see that the act is imperfect because it is about dominating less-powerful men and legitimising the patriarchy rather than protecting the realm. Eddard uses Ice to perform the execution, citing familial legacy, class power, the fantasy genre, and the male sovereign as critical to producing phallic sovereign violence. Bran observes that the sword "was as wide across as a man's hand, and taller even than [Bran's fourteen-year-old bother] Robb. The blade was Valyrian steel, spell-forged and dark as smoke. [...] [Eddard] took hold of Ice with both hands" (GoT 12). Bran's narration creates an image of Eddard as the ultimate sovereign and righteous enactor of sovereign violence: the "spell-forged" weapon is linked with classical fantasy heroism, and the "wide," "tall," "dark" sword that requires "two hands" indicates that Eddard's phallic power makes him an exemplar of masculinity. But it is also all-consuming: it is the focal point of the scene. When Eddard makes the "single sure stroke" (GoT 12) that severs the deserter's head, his confidence in his own sovereign power, moral judgement, and phallic skill are entwined in a ceremony that produces sovereign power as much as it does hegemonic masculinity. Here the scene focuses upon the majesty of Eddard's sword, betraying the moment of deformity in his sovereign violence: he is motivated by a desire to re-establish his own phallic power and the patriarchal gender order by enacting the law.

Eddard's phallic motivation becomes more visible in the *Game of Thrones* adaptation (S1E1 "Winter is Coming"), further demonstrating that his violence is a means of demonstrating his phallic domination of others via the law. The camera shows a low-angle shot of Eddard and his sword, where Ice and the loose end of the sword belt are in a phallic position. The shot occupies a full two seconds of screen time and is repeated moments later before Eddard severs the man's head. Between these frames is a long shot of Eddard in the middle of the lower third of the screen, his silver sword again suggestive of the phallus because of its placement near his groin and the visual contrast between the light silver sword and Eddard's black cloak. When Eddard and Bran speak after the execution, the pommel of Eddard's sword becomes visible at an acute angle from his groin, reminding viewers of his phallic power. In *Game of Thrones*, the phallus is the central element of sovereign violence, as demonstrated through the repeated visual motif of the phallic sword/sword belt. As in the novels, the phallus–sword's visual centrality reveals Eddard's act of sovereign violence as being flawed because one of his motivations is to reassert power over the criminal's body rather than protect the realm.

Contact with the abject is an inevitable part of hegemonic sovereign violence and the structure through which it functions. Criminals are abject because they challenge the law's stability, and this state is reflected upon their bodies through abject signifiers. Kristeva (1982, 53) contends that "the body's inside" breaks through the skin "in order to compensate for the collapse of the border between inside and outside." Crime represents such a collapse "because it draws attention to the fragility of the law" and "premeditated crime, cunning murder, hypocritical revenge are even more [abject] because they heighten the display of such fragility" (4). The men whose executions I examine experience bodily abjection because of the way their crimes disrupt the law. Sovereign violence is intended to resolve this fragility by restoring the monarch's power, the force of the law, the patriarchal gender order, and the kingdom's borders—restoring the boundaries of the sovereign's body which is also the body politic—but because the execution is clearly an act of domination, the criminal's abjection is not contained but spreads. In other words, sovereign violence produces abjection as the act of execution forces the criminal's body to become fragmented, unstable, penetrable, and permeable. But successful performances of hegemonic sovereign violence promise to resolve the blurred boundaries of the criminal's body instantly because they reactivate the kingdom's borders and the sovereign's power.

The performance of hegemonic sovereign violence by Eddard seems to be successful and later there are suggestions of deformity, and they lead him to become temporarily abject because of his contact with the criminal's body. However, in flawed repetitions of sovereign violence such as Eddard's, the sovereign body is shown to be fragile: he comes into contact with the abject and becomes a threat to the male symbolic order. The physical manifestation of the criminal's threat to the law upon the criminal body reinforces the urgent need for sovereign violence and in so doing makes it appear moral. In Eddard's case, this promise is realised in the novels through descriptions of Will's physically incomplete body. Bran observes that "he had lost both ears and a finger

56 REIMAGINING MASCULINITY AND VIOLENCE

to frostbite" (GoT 11), and Will's corporeal vulnerability becomes the key feature of his characterisation: Bran describes him as "the ragged man" on three separate occasions (GoT 12, 13, 18). Will's "ragged" body is abject because he lacks the closed, firm, and impermeable body that the male symbolic order demands. Bodily fragmentation is further evoked when Bran claims that "his father took off the man's head" (12) and, on the next page, when Robb says, "The Others take his eyes" (13). The sword and the supernatural Others—the army of living dead that is invading Westeros—suggest that Will's body is unstable and open. It is "in-between, the ambiguous, the composite" (Kristeva 1982, 4), which is unacceptable according to the dominant masculine discourse because it threatens the legitimacy of the patriarchy and must be remedied with sovereign violence.

Eddard's negotiation of the multiple forms of abjection that Will/ Gared represents through his ragged body and abject criminal status reveals a flaw, in that he privileges sovereign violence to the detriment of the kingdom in his desire to reactivate his power as the sovereign's representative and reinforce the existing patriarchal power structures in the pseudo-medieval world. If the white walkers that Will/Gared forewarns Eddard about are corpses, the pinnacle of Kristevian abjection, then living corpses push this abjection even further, blurring all of the boundaries that define and safeguard the self and culture. In *Game of Thrones*, Gared mutters: "white walkers ... I saw them ..." as soldiers escort him to the tree trunk, and when he explains his crime, he says, "I saw the white walkers. People need to know" (S1E1 "Winter is Coming"). Gared is cadaverous as he makes this warning, with chapped lips, frostbitten white skin, and dark eyes sunken into his skull. His liminality is highlighted when the close-up of his ravished face is interspersed with contrasting shots of the other characters in the scene, all of whom look healthy and alert.

Eddard's enactment of hegemonic sovereign violence in both *A Song of Ice and Fire* and *Game of Thrones* can be seen to fail because he refuses to listen to Will/Gared—to embrace the Other—in order to maintain the current class system, and he cannot face the idea that the white walkers have already invaded the kingdom. That Eddard—who is characterised as reasonable and sensible—will not listen to these warnings suggests that he views Will/Gared as unreliable because of his marginalised masculinity. In addition, Eddard cannot face the societal threat represented by the white walkers' penetration of the kingdom's boundaries. The realisation that the self is abject, when the subject "finds the impossible within [...] finds that the impossible constitutes its very being, that it is none other than abject" (Kristeva 1982, 5), is

UNDOING SOVEREIGN VIOLENCE   57

an unsettling experience, and Eddard empowers himself by ignoring the threat. He focuses on repudiating the micro-abjection before him: Will/Gared and the idea of the living dead. Executing Will/Gared is lawful and Eddard trusts the law completely, so he executes Will without pause. Sovereign violence is used to expel Will/Gared and symbolically reject the presence of the white walkers, as Will's/Gared's experience and decaying body herald their attack. Yet, as Eddard speaks in "Winter is Coming," non-diegetic sounds hint at his folly as eerie music plays in the background, hinting towards a looming threat. Eddard's refusal to listen is one of the reasons his sovereign violence is faulty.

Signifying this fault in the novel, Eddard's body takes on the fluidity of the criminal he executes, as when Bran observes that "his father peeled off his gloves" (GoT 12). The word "peel" conventionally describes the act of removing the skin or outer covering as from a fruit, and so speaks to the performativity of the scene, whereby Eddard's act of hegemonic sovereign violence is produced by many layered acts. But it is also a potential moment of abjection: for Eddard to "peel" off his gloves suggests that he is removing his outer skin to expose the porous (and potentially edible) membrane beneath. The skin is "the essential if not initial boundary of biological and psychic individuation," "a fragile container" (Kristeva 1982, 101) that promises to maintain one's subjectivating borders. Whether Eddard's act of peeling off his gloves is read as the removal of his skin in the novel or the signal of the performative through repeated costumes in the television show, he now diverges from the stable, natural, and closed male body demanded by the symbolic order and so has the potential to become abject.

In Eddard's mandate, the sovereign should use a "single sure stroke" (GoT 12) to end the criminal's life. The clean death reflects sovereign violence's major promises: that the execution will reify the patriarchal feudal system and restore justice to the kingdom by removing the threat of abjection that takes place when the criminal demonstrates the law's fragility. Conversely, in both *A Song of Ice and Fire* and *Game of Thrones*, the audience is thereby encouraged to associate blood and abjection with an improper performance of sovereign violence because a "single sure stroke" produces the least amount of blood and is less likely to spray the sovereign with gore. Eddard manages the "single stroke," but the resulting blood and abjection are emphasised. In "Winter is Coming," Gared's sanguination is audible for a full five seconds of screen time as the blood spouts from his neck and onto the grass. The other characters respond to the sound with the visceral disgust that the abject evokes: Bran, Robb, and the master-at-arms visibly clench their jaws in distaste over the five seconds where the blood is audible.

58   REIMAGINING MASCULINITY AND VIOLENCE

Similarly, in *A Game of Thrones*, "Blood sprayed out across the snow, as red as summerwine [*sic*]. [...] Bran could not take his eyes off the blood. The snows around the stump drank it eagerly, reddening as he watched" (GoT 12), with this personification of the snow furthering the sense of boundary transgression. Alongside blood, the corpse becomes linked with hegemonic sovereign violence. The cadaver is abject because it violates multiple boundaries and reminds the subject of what they must forget at all costs: their own death. Yet death is brought to the fore when Eddard decapitates Will in the novel and "the head bounced off a thick root and rolled. It came up near Greyjoy's feet. [...] He laughed, put his boot on the head, and kicked it away" (GoT 12–13). Even though Theon is rejecting the abject, his jovial dismissal is unsettling. His decision to laugh and kick the head away is a miniature re-enactment of Eddard's own disregard for Will's warning about the white walkers and, by extension, his life as a working-class man. Combined with the visible distaste that the characters display in *Game of Thrones*, Theon's casual interaction with the corpse in *A Game of Thrones* links Eddard's sovereign violence to the feeling of repulsion. In this way, *A Song of Ice and Fire* and *Game of Thrones* critique hegemonic sovereign violence after disclosing it as a performative act that is unable to support a coherent masculine identity or functioning society.

Eddard's lawfulness is critiqued in both the novels and television series because it is used against him and brings about his death: his hegemonic violence is "repeated in directions that reverse and displace [its] originating aims," as Butler (1993, 83) says of gender subversion. Eddard adheres strictly to the law and uses it to justify sovereign violence, believing in the patriarchal system that sovereign violence supports. He gains political power in the short term through lawful sovereign violence when he is named Hand of the King. However, he is later executed for treason by Joffrey Baratheon and a headsman uses Eddard's own greatsword, Ice, to carry out the deed. Right before Eddard is executed Joffrey tells onlookers, "So long as I am your king, treason shall never go unpunished" (GoT 702; S1E9 "Baelor"). Joffrey's statement and actions, repeated perfectly from novel to television show, are coded as dishonourable because he promised to spare Eddard but (it is implied) kills him because he dislikes the Starks and fears that Eddard will reveal that he has no legitimate claim to the throne. Joffrey's phrasing and his decision to have Eddard executed with Ice cite Eddard's own unflinching application of the law and inflexible moralism. Joffrey executes Eddard to dominate him and maintain his own sovereign power within the patriarchal feudal system, an act of hegemonic violence that parallels Eddard's execution of Will/Gared at the beginning of the series and demonstrates that the patriarchal order cannot lead to anything but destruction.

Joffrey's enactment of sovereign violence is one of the "repetitions of hegemonic forms of power which fail to repeat loyally and, in that failure, open possibilities for resignifying the terms of violation against their violating aims" (Butler 1993, 84). When Eddard's past act of sovereign violence returns to the narrative present during his own execution, Eddard's and Joffrey's acts of hegemonic violence are placed in dialogue and both are shown to be flawed. Sovereign violence is uncovered as "a copy, and an inevitably failed one, an ideal that no one can embody" (Butler 1990, 138–139). The circularity between Eddard's deployment of hegemonic violence and Joffrey's creates a queer rupture in the narrative: equating Joffrey's unnecessary and egotistical brutality with Eddard's strict lawfulness demonstrates that patriarchal violence in any form is destructive. The critique is reinforced at the intertextual level because the execution scene, especially Joffrey's dialogue, is adapted with absolute fidelity from the novel. Joffrey's words are repeated perfectly between texts, foregrounding sovereign violence as an act of masculine violence and a moment of adaptation that enables the "perfect reproduction" (Handyside 2012, 54) of the neo-medieval patriarchal feudal system. However, both Eddard and Joffrey are killed as their violence is turned against them. Strict adherence to sovereign violence leads to an inflexible worldview that cannot survive the coming winter—a form of abjection for the kingdom in the return of the dead. The only way to prevent the long night is to work together and recognise the interconnectedness of all living beings, which self-centred stylised acts such as hegemonic violence fail to acknowledge. Where Eddard began the narrative using sovereign violence to demonstrate his phallic power and dominance over working-class men by destroying Will's/Gared's abject criminal body, his last appearance in *A Song of Ice and Fire* and *Game of Thrones* is reduced to pure abjection as a severed head on display in King's Landing (GoT 723; S1E10 "Fire and Blood"), an exercise in the hegemonic sovereign violence he once (mis)performed.

Sovereign Repetition

A sequence of repetitions, the most faithful being Robb's, evokes the features of the father's performance, including its phallic dimensions and repetitions, while also failing to fulfil the promises of hegemonic sovereign violence. In both the novels and television series Robb is the heir to Winterfell, and when his father is arrested he gathers armies to save his father, which later become part of his efforts to attack the Lannister army when Eddard dies and Robb establishes the North as a separate kingdom and is named king. Robb's military ventures are successful, but he chooses to uphold his father's rigid moral code and this causes him to lose multiple allies and lose the war and his life.

When Robb cites Eddard as he decides to execute one of his own men after he becomes King in the North, sovereign violence is revealed as a "politically tenuous construction," and hence open to subversion (Butler 1990, 192). Robb is faced with a difficult moral decision in both *A Song of Ice and Fire* and *Game of Thrones* after one of his bannermen, Rickard Karstark, murders two political hostages in revenge for his own sons' deaths. In a consultation with his advisors in *A Storm of Swords* Robb ponders how best to punish the man and says, "I told myself ... *swore* to myself ... that I would be a good king, as honorable as Father, strong, just, loyal to my friends and brave when I faced my enemies" (SoS1 280; original emphasis). Robb's criterion for being "a good king" is to repeat his father's actions because he believed him to be the epitome of morality and masculinity. Robb evokes moral goodness and his father in order give himself a performative pattern to follow, but the notion of "good" also legitimises the patriarchy and conceals its logics of production, as in Eddard's execution of Will.

The performativity of the decision is indicated through the crown and the act of placing it upon one's head. Right after Robb cites his father, his mother Catelyn observes that "Robb reached down with both hands, lifted the heavy bronze-and-iron crown, and set it atop his head, and suddenly he was a king again. 'Lord Rickard dies'" (SoS1 280). As Robb makes the decision his sovereignty is reinforced. He is constrained by norms of masculine sovereign violence ("I told myself ... *swore* to myself ...") because he must adhere to them if he intends to be intelligible as a "good king." The crown is a physical object that signifies the feudal patriarchal power structures in the real world, especially as they pertain to class, gender, race, and sexuality. By donning the crown as he makes the decision to enact sovereign violence against Karstark, Robb's violence is shown to be hegemonic because he ignores the relationality and interconnectedness of his subjects and intends to dominate the other man and maintain the existing power structures in his world. By placing his crown on his head when he makes the execution order, and by citing his father, the way in which Robb's decision-making process is narrated in the novels illustrates how sovereign violence in fantasy fiction is comprised of repeated acts.

Robb's explicit citation of his father, specifically the notion of the "good king," connects his violence to Eddard's and implies that his

UNDOING SOVEREIGN VIOLENCE 61

violence is moral, even though all he achieves is momentarily restoring the feudal patriarchal order. The desire to be "strong, just, loyal to my friends and brave when I faced my enemies" (SoS1 280) reflects Robb's affective attachment to an imagined version of kinghood that does not exist. *A Song of Ice and Fire* and *Game of Thrones* feature many kings but none of them is "good." Robb's reluctance to embrace this reality reveals that the pseudo-medieval patriarchy offers promises that can never be fulfilled, and that its systems of organisation are copies, and inevitably failed ones. Moreover, he privileges his own desire to be a "good king" over his kingdom's need for a large army with which to defeat the Lannister forces, and this attempt to empower the self at the expense of others makes his sovereign violence hegemonic. The fantasy genre and its depiction of masculinity are both denaturalised through this moment, as in Eddard's case. And, like his father, Robb's violence is the first in a series of honour-bound decisions that lead him to lose the war and his life. After Robb gives the execution order in the novel, his mother observes, "Outside the thunder crashed and boomed, so loud that it sounded as if the castle were coming down about their ears. *Is this the sound of a kingdom falling?*" (SoS1 277; original emphasis). Two kingdoms fail because of Robb's repetition of sovereign violence: his own kingdom in the North, and his own ability to legitimise the patriarchy through his sovereign status.

The act of hegemonic sovereign violence that Robb performs, like his father's, is shown to be more invested in power than justice through phallic symbolism when he decides to execute Karstark in the *Game of Thrones* episode, "Kissed by Fire" (S3E5). The props and blocking allude to the execution scene Bran witnesses in "Winter is Coming" (S1E1) and demonstrate how Robb repeats his father's imperfect act of sovereign violence through the phallic fantasy sword. When Robb discusses Karstark, the sword is framed in a way that suggests that it originates from Robb's groin as he sits at his desk in medium and medium long shots. The weapon's provocative angle and its placement at the edge of the frame cite the shot in "Winter is Coming" when Eddard speaks with Bran and the pommel of his sword is visible near his crotch. Eddard's pose and the placement of his weapon are mirrored when Robb stands before Karstark during the execution, sword facing downward and held with two hands in the middle of his body. Through the sword, phallic imagery specific to the fantasy genre, Robb's performance of sovereign violence is made visible as an attempt to gain phallic power and legitimise the patriarchy through an inflexible adherence to the law that serves his own desire to be a "good king" while harming his kingdom. *Game of Thrones* uses the visual imagery of the sword–phallus to signify Robb's violence as hegemonic where *A Song of Ice and Fire* uses references to Eddard and the crown, although both achieve a similar effect. By focusing on the phallus as the object around which repetitions are orchestrated and legitimised, hegemonic sovereign violence becomes more deeply imbued with, and capable of imbuing, masculinity.

Robb's inability to perform sovereign violence in the correct emotional register leads his normative masculinity to become incoherent in both the novels and television series. While convening with his council in *A Storm of Swords*, Robb is described as speaking "angrily" (SoS1 275) and having "cursed, in a fury of despair" (SoS1 280). After he severs Karstark's head, Robb "flung the poleaxe down in disgust" and his mother observes that he "stood shaking with his hands half-clenched and the rain running down his cheeks" (SoS1 282), descriptions more suggestive of a toddler having a tantrum than a powerful sovereign. In "Kissed by Fire," Robb snarls as he brings his sword down, and as he strides away he throws the sword to the ground, clenches his gloved hands, and snarls. Robb's sentencing and execution of Karstark are emotional, although his specific feelings are ambiguous. His mother's perspective frames the scene in the novel, which may be inflected with her own maternal feelings about his violence, but also positions Robb as a child once again. In the television series, the scene takes place quickly and in low lighting, making it difficult to discern Robb's interior state. The only emotion that is undoubtedly present is anger, and even though it is one of the few emotions masculine subjects are permitted to display, as established in Eddard's original performance, sovereign violence in Westeros promises a detached actor. Robb's intense affective experience during and after the execution deviate from the version of sovereign violence that he has been taught to repeat, and this fault becomes one of the reasons why he cannot contain the threat of abjection against his kingdom or even his own masculine body.

The deformed version of sovereign violence that Robb produces damages his sovereign masculinity and his kingdom, arousing abjection and disgust as he fails to enact the execution quickly and cleanly. The bloody scene is like gender subversion in that it shows that hegemonic violence is "structured by repeated acts that seek to approximate the ideal [...] but which, in their occasional *dis*continuity, reveal the temporal and contingent groundlessness of this 'ground'" (Butler 1990, 192; original emphasis). Robb's botched attempt to execute Karstark is one such "*dis*continuity." When Robb carries out the execution in *A Storm of Swords* he struggles to do so without gore: Karstark is killed "in a single blow, but it took three to sever the man's head from his body, and by the time it was done both living and dead were drenched in blood"

(SoS1 282). The word "drenched" speaks to the thorough and intimate contact Robb has with Karstark's blood: the abject fluid seeps through his clothing, to his skin. Robb causes the bloody scene through his refusal to compromise his strict morals, and cracks appear in his kingdom as the Karstark soldiers withdraw from his army. The abject surges forth because Robb is unable to make the "single sure stroke" (GoT 12) that is expected during acts of sovereign violence.

Robb's masculine body becomes temporarily abject in response to his de-formed repetition of sovereign violence, although in his case it is visibly self-inflicted. Bodily surfaces, Butler (1990, 200) argues, "can become the site of a dissonant and denaturalized performance that reveals the performative status of the natural itself." Robb's reaction to the execution is narrated in such a way as to suggest that he makes his own body a dissonant version of sovereign masculinity after he beheads Karstark. Continuing his intense emotional response to violence, Robb insists upon wearing the clothing he wore during the execution despite it being "drenched in blood" (SoS1 282). Robb forces abjection onto the surface of his body: he creates a spectre of the dead man through which the reader views glimpses of "the place where meaning collapses," the abject (Kristeva 1982, 2). Robb's refusal to change his bloody clothes points towards his horrified reaction to his violence, as well as its implications for his character: "to have blood on your hands is to be implicated in the blurring of essential boundaries of identity" (Halberstam 1995, 77). Robb dresses himself in remnants of Karstark, disturbing the fundamental border between life and death that is required for his own subjectivity. In taking on Karstark's bloody remnants, Robb also temporarily disrupts the class system by lowering his own status as he is covered in his bannerman's blood. Through Karstark's lingering blood and viscera, Robb's body comes into close contact with the abject and once again sovereign violence is shown to be unable to support a coherent masculine identity.

Just as Robb's body falls prey to abjection because of his imperfect repetition of sovereign violence, so too does his kingdom. By killing the Karstark patriarch in both *A Song of Ice and Fire* and *Game of Thrones*, Robb knowingly forfeits the Karstark family's political allegiance and the soldiers needed to secure the North, which leads him to release his hold on his own land. In so doing, his kingdom's fragility and that of the feudal patriarchy is exposed. Robb repeats his father's inflexible adherence to the law and focuses upon Karstark as an individual rather than compromising his morals and addressing the larger and more urgent threat that the Lannister army poses, much like his father Eddard did by executing Will/Gared rather than dealing with the threat of the

64   REIMAGINING MASCULINITY AND VIOLENCE

white walkers. Both characters sought to maintain and legitimise the pseudo-medieval patriarchy by dominating lower class men through hegemonic sovereign violence, and both lead their kingdoms and their own bodies to abjection.

Robb's hegemonic violence is critiqued in both *A Song of Ice and Fire* and *Game of Thrones* in a circular fashion like his father's, showing the law turned against itself with subversive effects. Robb is murdered at the "Red Wedding," an infamous scene in which many of the major Stark characters are killed on Walder Frey's orders when they are attending the wedding of Frey's daughter Roslin and Robb's uncle Edmure. This revenge happens because Robb has sex with a woman out of wedlock and chooses to prioritise her honour over his own by marrying her. In response, Walder Frey seeks to avenge the slight by dominating Robb and his party completely through hegemonic violence that is intended to restore his patriarchal status within his home of The Twins. After Robb is killed, his head is severed and replaced with that of his direwolf, Grey Wind, who has a crown nailed to his head. Kristeva posits that the cadaver and the animal corpse must be rejected to maintain one's subjectivating borders, but the opposite occurs in Robb's case. The desecration is emphasised because of the ways that the scene is recounted within the novels: it is purposefully theatrical, which gives away its performative dimensions. Rob Stanton (2015, 58) argues that "the music, the crossbows, the (doubly) empty insults, the locked doors, the gaudy display of Robb's corpse with his direwolf Grey Wind's crowned head stitched in place of his own" are "destined to forge a memorable narrative unity—fit, vivid subject matter for a chilling tale or song." And the Red Wedding does become a story within the story, repeatedly retold as a rumour in *A Storm of Swords*: "They swear Lord Frey had the boy's head hacked off, sewed the head of his direwolf in its place, and nailed a crown about his ears" (SoS2 151). The phrase "hacked off" belies the scene's violence, although the careful act of sewing head to neck reveals that it is not a random act of violence but "a piece of thymotic theatre" (Stanton 2015, 56), a carefully staged performance of Frey's (grotesque) sovereign power. Maureen Attali (2017, 189) contends that "the narrative importance of this performance is emphasized by the fact that the scene is recounted twice," disclosing its citationality. In some ways, the fact that readers must imagine this scene and only hear about it through rumours and gossip elevates its abjection, as Robb becomes a spectral ghost who blurs the lines between present/past, real/imagined, and present/absent.

The scene evokes abjection to an almost hyperbolic degree, but it is an abjection that is specifically linked back to Robb's flawed enactment of sovereign violence. The "crown [nailed] about his ears" echoes the real crown that Robb wore in the books, covered in tiny phallic swords. The action of nailing the crown in place critiques Robb's hegemonic violence, specifically its rigidity and anger. Robb's crown was repeatedly referred to as a symbol of his sovereignty when he chose to dominate Karstark through violence, and his mother described the "circle of iron swords" that decorate it (SoS1 278). The swords speak to Robb's unwavering repetition of phallic hegemonic violence as a centre point of his sovereignty. He was too rigid and insistent upon following the law and a binary moral code because this rigidity enabled him to empower himself and feel like a "good king"; and it destroyed his kingdom. Robb's positioning as a character who is selfishly attached to an impracticable and patriarchally based moral code, and his consequent failure to survive the game of thrones (like his father), indicates that hegemonic violence is incapable of supporting his masculine identity or kingdom.

Robb's abject body and kingdom are tied to his sovereign violence through audio and visuals in the *Game of Thrones* episode, "Mhysa" (S3E10). In contrast to the novels, viewers directly witness Robb's dehumanisation: the wolf head is attached to Robb's body with a large spear, and the corpse is tied to a horse and paraded through the Frey campsite as the soldiers chant, "King in the North!" The mantra parodies Robb's sovereignty and his kingdom, locating them within a repeated system of violence that is exposed as abject as the corpse appears to move through the yard of its own volition. As the wolf–king–corpse wanders through the camp, the boundaries between North/South, human/animal, alive/dead, and animate/inanimate are disrupted. The spear that joins Grey Wind's head to Robb's body critiques violence as the phallic and hegemonic thread running through his sovereignty: it is the tool through which Robb's corpse achieves animalised abjection.

The grotesque merging of human and wolf in the televisions series peaks in this larger criticism of the Starks, whose sigil is the fierce direwolf, and their role in reproducing sovereign violence as a means of maintaining order in the North through upholding patriarchal power structures. The Stark–direwolf corpse collapses the boundaries between human/animal and life/death, but also those between self/ Other, animate/inanimate, and inside/outside the body. The parodic amalgamation of the deceased Stark sovereign with a slaughtered direwolf presents Robb's problematic citation of sovereign violence, and its grotesque inversion after his death, as reflective of the larger system of cultural reproduction in which masculine subjects are constituted through violent technologies of power that bolster but also conceal the workings of the feudal patriarchy. Accordingly, exactly the same imagery

66   REIMAGINING MASCULINITY AND VIOLENCE

is repeated in season six of *Game of Thrones* when Jon takes up this mantle, named the "White Wolf" in another candle-lit room, to cheers of "King in the North!" ("The Winds of Winter S6E10).

Sovereign Failure

The repetition of sovereign violence becomes even more fraught in relation to Theon Greyjoy, Eddard's ward. Theon is my favourite AMAB character in the series because his body is so central to his character development and his violence is so thoroughly turned against him. I don't pity him, but I find him a fascinating limit case for intelligible personhood. Theon begins the narrative in allegiance with the Starks, but after returning to his homeland, the Iron Islands, he allies with his biological family and seizes Winterfell from Bran in an attempt to impress his patriarch father. Theon soon loses the castle and is captured by Ramsay Bolton, who tortures him and makes him his servant. Ramsay renames Theon as Reek, no longer deemed worthy of a human name but simply a gaseous odour. As of *Dance with Dragons* it is unclear whether Ramsay survives an escape attempt, although *Game of Thrones* has extended Theon's narrative to show him saving Sansa Stark and allying with the Starks once more. Theon is only a sovereign for a short time in the series, but his violence highlights the fragility of sovereignty and the potential for hegemonic violence to provide stable power.

As I have demonstrated through Robb's and Eddard's executions, crime is abject because it disrupts the law and the class system, and in both *A Song of Ice and Fire* and *Game of Thrones* this abjection is reflected on the criminal's flesh. Theon executes one of Winterfell's inhabitants: the master at arms Ser Rodrick in the television series and the kennel master Farlen in the books. Ser Rodrick enters the yard with blood streaming down his face from two gashes to his head, and spits on Theon in defiance. The fluids disturb the boundary between inside and outside the body, and the spit reflects a dangerous transgression as it is an act through which Ser Rodrick challenges Theon's fragile sovereignty in the television series. The repetition of criminal abjection challenges the classed and gendered power dynamics in the pseudo-medieval world and provides a loose justification for Theon's act of sovereign violence, although it is worth noting that no such abjection takes place in *A Song of Ice and Fire*, further highlighting Farlen's innocence and, more importantly, Theon's violence, as flawed.

In *A Song of Ice and Fire*, Theon's repetition of sovereign violence is represented in such a way as to emphasise the citation of Eddard. Theon becomes sovereign of Winterfell for a brief period in *A Clash of Kings* after he betrays the Starks and seizes the castle for himself and his family. He faces dissent from the castle's inhabitants and is manipulated into killing Farlen in punishment for alleged murder. Initially it appears that Theon will allow his Ironborn soldiers to perform the execution on his behalf, breaking one of the core promises that constitute sovereign violence—that is, until Eddard is cited as a means of critiquing Theon's decision. In the novel, Farlen tells Theon that "M'lord Eddard always did his own killings" (CoK 725), directly and unfavourably comparing Theon to Eddard. A similar tactic is used by Ser Rodrick in *Game of Thrones*, who snarls, "He who passes the sentence should swing the sword, coward" (S2E6), repeating, verbatim, Eddard's own words back as a means of "forcibly shaping" (Butler 1990, 155) Theon's actions so that he repeats sovereign violence in the way Eddard condoned. Repetition remains central to this form of violence, although it is shown to fail in its proliferation and become open to subversion.

Theon's act of sovereign violence is also flawed in the sense that it is used to reinforce his individual power rather than to protect the realm. The lack of justice is highlighted in *A Clash of Kings* when Theon explains his reason for executing Farlen: "He could not let the killings go unpunished. Farlen was as likely a suspect as any, so Theon sat in judgment, called him guilty, and condemned him to death" (CoK 725). Theon knows that the murders were committed by one of his cronies as a means of stopping them from betraying him by revealing that he killed two farm boys rather than Starks, but he blames Farlen instead. The injustice is highlighted through the specific phrasing in this sentence, specifically the words "called" rather than found, and "condemned" rather than sentenced. The fact that Farlen's crime was being "as likely a suspect as any" reveals a conscious role-assignment informed by class inequality within the apparently natural judiciary process. Yet Theon's actions, unlike Robb's or Eddard's, are presented as departing from the sovereign model because of their moral ambiguity rather than the failure of their enactment. For readers, Theon's violence is presented as hegemonic because it is used to dominate the lower-class man for his own advantage; it is also subordinate because the word choices reveal a critique of the injustice. Within the world of the novel, where other characters are not privy to Theon's interior monologue, the violence appears a perfect enactment of sovereign violence that restores order to the castle. The different interpretive possibilities reveal that there is a public and private dimension to gender performativity. Both are equally important, although in this scene in *A Clash of Kings* Theon's private reflections on his violence are privileged over the public interpretation. By unjustly murdering

Farlen, Theon fails to live up to the promise of sovereign violence—that it will bring justice—but temporarily secures Winterfell: "The killings stopped after Farlen's death." However, ambivalence remains, as the Ironborn soldiers "continued sullen and anxious" (CoK 726). Even though Theon's repetition of sovereign violence restores peace to Winterfell in *A Song of Ice and Fire*, his decision to use violence to dominate other men and as an attempt to secure his patriarchal authority means that the society over which he rules does not prosper.

In the *Game of Thrones* episode, "The Old Gods and The New," Theon's decision to use sovereign violence is framed in such a way that it directs the viewer's attention to his desire to use violence to make legitimate the patriarchy and his place within it, disclosing his sovereign violence as unnatural. Theon intends to imprison Ser Rodrick rather than use violence against him, but he is manipulated into doing otherwise. His first mate, Dagmer, tells him: "My prince, you cannot let that stand. He must pay. [...] He has to pay the iron price. They'll never respect you while he lives" (S2E6 "The Old Gods and the New"). The "my prince" address and the reference to paying the "iron price" appeal to Theon's assumption that, as heir to the Iron Islands, he is owed honour and sovereign power—a promise that is presented as being informed by classed and gendered power structures through the "my prince" title. Theon acquiesces, and in so doing he demonstrates that his sovereign violence is motivated by a desire for "respect"—which is shown as the deep urge to see his personal phallic power and dominance over others maintained—rather than any thought for Winterfell's laws and justice.

Theon's act of sovereign violence is marked as deformed in *Game of Thrones* because it is imbued with emotion. As I have noted, sovereign violence promises objectivity in relation to both sentencing and execution. The violence and its failure are shown to make Theon feel anxious, an affective response that is expressed through the weather and music in the scene. Rain is audible throughout the scene, but it only falls in visible torrents after Ser Rodrick places his head on the block, after which the audience sees a medium close-up of Theon's face and shoulders with rain pouring down behind him. The weather heightens the scene's sombre mood, and Theon's emotional turmoil, as he is about to murder Ser Rodrick. The music also adds to this effect: the song "Pay the Iron Price" plays quietly after Dagmer's dialogue and soon thereafter thunder rumbles in the background. The music swells, expressing Theon's mixed emotions as he decides to heed Dagmer's words and murder Ser Rodrick. Through the music and weather in the television series, Theon's sovereign violence is revealed as flawed because it is intended for domination rather than the good of the kingdom.

UNDOING SOVEREIGN VIOLENCE 69

Theon's repetition of sovereign violence is further emphasised as imperfect in both *A Song of Ice and Fire* and *Game of Thrones* because he, like Eddard, is motivated by a desire for phallic power and a secure position within the pseudo-medieval patriarchy. Brooke Askey (2018) argues that Theon has internalised his phallocentric culture in the television show, and I would add that in both texts this desire for phallic power was learned from Eddard and from the social structures that inform his identity and is manifested when he decides to use sovereign violence. During the *Game of Thrones* scene in which he executes Ser Rodrick, almost every shot of Theon features an Ironborn soldier in the background holding a Greyjoy banner or spear, linking Theon's enactment of sovereign violence to phallic imagery that gives away his attempt at hegemony. A similar connection is made in *A Clash of Kings* through the narration: the story of Farlen's death is told as Theon is walking to meet his sister Asha. He feels threatened by his sibling and attempts to display his phallic power through his clothing. As he dresses, the narrator observes, "Around his waist he buckled sword and dagger, remembering the night [Asha] had humiliated him at his own father's table. [...] *Well, I have a knife too, and know how to use it*" (CoK 725; original emphasis). Theon's excessive use of phallic weapons, the "sword and dagger," discloses his desire to dominate his sister specifically through a display of his own phallic power, which she diminished when last they met. As the scene of Theon's flawed sovereign violence is recounted alongside his phallic struggle with his sister, the audience is encouraged to view the hegemonic violence as a repetition of Eddard's, whereby executions can be used to reactivate phallic power and legitimise the patriarchy.

Theon's act of violence fails to live up to sovereign violence's promises in either the book or television show because it is unjust, emotional, and is informed by a desire to wield phallic power to empower himself: it is hegemonic. For this reason, the execution produces abjection and the audiences are encouraged to link the hegemonic violence to disgust. As I have noted, successful enactments of sovereign violence see the criminal experience a swift and clean death, which will in turn secure the kingdom against the threat of the abject. Theon's violence further splinters, rather than resolves, the fragile law within his kingdom, and he becomes grotesque. In *A Clash of Kings*, Theon's "hands were sweating, so the shaft twisted in his grip as he swung and the first blow landed between Farlen's shoulders. It took three more cuts to hack through all that bone and muscle and sever the head from the body" (CoK 725). Likewise, in "The Old Gods and the New," Theon takes four attempts to sever Ser Rodrick's head, all of which result in blood spraying across

70   REIMAGINING MASCULINITY AND VIOLENCE

the yard. Despite all the gore, Theon's sword proves insufficient; in a degraded adaptation of the kick he gave to the head of Will after he was executed by Eddard in *A Game of Thrones* (GoT 12–13), in the television series he kicks the head from the body to detach it completely, and it then rolls across the muddy ground. Both versions of Theon's execution of Farlen/Ser Rodrick end with hyperbolic abjection, which the audience is encouraged to experience as intense disgust that, by association, attaches to hegemonic sovereign violence.

As in Robb's enactment, Theon's repetition of sovereign violence is further critiqued because of his own bodily responses to the practice. In the television series, the scene ends with a close-up of Theon panting, his face speckled with blood, and looking around the yard as if he is frightened. In the novel, Theon vomits and says, "He only wished he had killed him cleaner [*sic*]. Ned Stark had never needed more than a single blow to take a man's head" (CoK 725–726). As well as in his explicit memory of Eddard's actions, Theon's messy sovereign violence is placed in dialogue with Eddard's through the repetition of the phrase "single blow" (GoT 12), highlighting its imperfection by comparison with Eddard's performance. Theon's bodily response to the violence, panting in fear in *Game of Thrones* and vomiting in *A Clash of Kings*, highlights the contradictions within hegemonic masculinity: he must be capable of enacting violence with his own hands, but doing so makes him physically ill and unable to uphold the stoicism that is also expected of him as an exemplar of masculinity. The contradictions around Theon's act of violence are often present in hegemonic masculine discourses; writing about "iron men" athletes, Connell (2000, 84) writes that being an iron man actually forbids one particular athlete from doing "things that his peer group and culture define as masculine." "[S]ustaining the training regime that yields the bodily supremacy, giving him his status as a champion, is incompatible with the kind of sexual and social life that is expected by affluent young men." Being a masculine exemplar is rife with contradictions, and in *A Song of Ice and Fire* and *Game of Thrones* these are highlighted as a means of linking Theon's hegemonic masculinity to his own disgust at his actions.

Because Theon's act of sovereign violence fails in fulfilling so many promises, he does not contain the threat that the criminal poses to the kingdom and instead becomes abject himself, opening his own masculine body "to splittings, self-parody, self-criticism" (Butler 1990, 200). One such "splitting" is Theon's own physical rejection of the execution. In the novels, he remembers that "afterwards he was sick, remembering all the times they'd sat over a cup of mead talking of hounds and hunting. *I had no choice*, he wanted to scream at the corpse" (CoK 725;

original emphasis). Theon attempts to dispel the threat of abjection by vomiting, but he continues to engage with it as he "scream[s]" internally "at the corpse" (CoK 725), the pinnacle of abjection. In "The Old Gods and the New," Theon has an even closer encounter with the corpse as he kicks head from body to complete the execution, and by the end of the scene his face is splattered with Ser Rodrick's blood, as in the scene with Robb and Karstark. In both the novels and television series, Theon's aggression is conflated with the feelings of revulsion that are aroused by the abject. His misuse of sovereign violence reveals that the act blurs, rather than bolsters, his masculine identity as his body begins to unravel and he loses control over Winterfell. In the *Game of Thrones* adaptation, other characters' horrified emotional responses to Theon's botched execution are also used to critique his repetition of hegemonic sovereign violence. The execution is intercut with the sound of Bran screaming and the onlookers' faces, which show terror at the excessively bloody sequence (S2E6). Even Dagmer, who incites the violence, has a disgusted expression in a medium close-up. Rather than being cowed or impressed by his sovereign violence, Theon's subjects are terrified at the abject scene he has unleashed, and in this way this hegemonic violence is presented as repulsive.

Theon's performance of hegemonic sovereign power is critiqued in *A Song of Ice and Fire* and *Game of Thrones* when his sovereign status and phallic power are turned against him after he is captured, tortured, and castrated by Ramsay Snow (later Bolton). Ramsay's torture regime also repeats Theon's phallic sovereign violence "in directions that reverse and displace [its] originating aims," as Butler (1993, 83) says of gender subversion, through castration that limits, rather than aids, Theon's phallic power. The violence takes place explicitly in *Game of Thrones* and implicitly in *A Dance with Dragons* after Theon is taken prisoner. "Reek," the persona Ramsay gives Theon, describes himself in the novel as "docile as a dog," and thinks, *"If I had a tail, the Bastard would have cut it off"* (DwD 190; original emphasis). Theon's reference to the removal of a phallic appendage points towards his castration, and other references are made later in the novel. Theon says that Ramsay, *"has taken only fingers and toes and that other thing, when he might have had my tongue, or peeled the skin off my legs from heel to thigh"* (DwD 303; original emphasis). As Theon reflects on Ramsay's violent torture methods, it is implied that the unnameable *"other thing"* that was *"taken"* was his penis. Further confirmation of Theon's castration is given near the end of *A Dance with Dragons* when Ramsay orders Theon to sexually stimulate his new bride: "For a moment he did not understand. 'I ... do you mean ... m'lord, I have no ... I ...'" (DwD 583). Theon's confusion and reference to his

72   REIMAGINING MASCULINITY AND VIOLENCE

lack—"I have no ..."—suggests that his sexual organs have been removed, signalled by their disappearance from language. From the linguistic lack surrounding Theon's genitals, it is implied that "the castrated being has been mutilated into something "lacking" or less than a man" (Askey 2018, 2; see also Wassersug and Lieberman 2010). Ramsay disrupts the patriarchal logics that Theon reveres by highlighting his victim's bodily vulnerability while momentarily securing his own position as patriarch of the Dreadfort, much as Theon did to Rodrick/Farlen. Theon's masculinity, symbolised by his penis and achieved through his phallic sovereign violence, is taken from him in a moment of narrative circularity in which this form of hegemonic violence is again unable to support (and in fact, leads to the loss of) a coherent masculine identity.

In *Game of Thrones* Theon's castration is explicit from the moment it takes place in "The Bear and the Maiden Fair" (S3E7) and is linked to his hegemonic violence through references to the loss of his sovereign manhood and ability to produce heirs. In the season three finale, "Mhysa" (S3E10), Ramsay sends Reek/Theon's flayed penis to the King of the Iron Islands (Theon's estranged father Balon Greyjoy), calling it "a special gift: Theon's favourite toy. He cried when I took it away from him." Balon comments that Reek/Theon is no longer worth rescuing as "he cannot further the Greyjoy line" and is "not a man any more" (S3E10). While for some viewers this scene may suggest that masculinity is contingent upon fatherhood, the exchange is linked with class, sexual, and racial power. The Great Houses in Westeros are consumed with a narcissistic desire to reproduce and keep the family "pure"—often through killing those who fail to reflect their father's image (DeCoste 2015). Since Reek/Theon can no longer produce a Greyjoy heir, his sovereignty is forfeit and his ability to perform hegemonic acts of violence is psychologically curtailed. In response, Balon must remove him from the family so that his own masculinity is not questioned. Not only has Reek/Theon lost the symbolic power of the phallus and his cherished claim to sovereignty in both *A Song of Ice and Fire* and *Game of Thrones*, but the latter emphasises the fact that he cannot be a father and is "not a man any more"—unintelligible and lacking the power that he once used sovereign violence to maintain. By situating the castration as an act that removes Theon's phallic power and sovereign potential, it becomes clear that neither a prosperous society not individual masculinity can be supported or maintained through hegemonic violence, regardless of its legitimacy.

While Theon relinquishes sovereignty for the remainder of the series, the final season of *Game of Thrones* invites viewers to see Theon's embrace of caring masculinity as one way of regaining access to an intelligible

UNDOING SOVEREIGN VIOLENCE 73

masculinity. When the protagonists at Winterfell make their plan to lure the Night King out into the open by using Bran as bait, Arya objects to leaving him alone in the Godswood. Theon says, "I'll stay with you. With the Ironborn. I took this castle from you. Let me defend you now" ("A Knight of the Seven Kingdoms" S8E2). Theon performs caring masculinity by using violence to protect Bran's body. He aligns himself with the caring masculine values that Elliott (2015) defines, especially embracing emotion (his shame at his past hegemonic violence) and rejecting domination (for he seeks to empower Bran with the help of others). Theon's dialogue explicitly links his decision to sacrifice himself for Bran as an attempt to redress his violent claim to sovereignty in season one: his decision to take "this castle from [Bran]." Like Theon's castration and Eddard's and Robb's deaths, this moment highlights the narrative circularity between Theon's hegemonic sovereign violence and his death. However, Theon's death is unique in that his act of violence is motivated by a desire to care for the Other rather than dominate. Theon's embrace of caring rather than hegemonic masculinity disrupts the pattern of patriarchal repetition and creates an ambiguous opportunity for him to access an intelligible masculinity through violence.

Theon's act of caring violence is presented in phallic televisual imagery that denaturalises the connection between the penis, masculinity, and the phallus even as it simultaneously produces ambivalent meanings around violence. Throughout "The Long Night," Theon defends Bran with a large pike, the phallic weapon and the location in the Godswood echoing Theon's phallic sovereign violence in season one when he seized Winterfell from Bran and executed Ser Rodrick. However, Theon's caring masculinity has enabled him to embrace violence as an act of care. Right before Theon charges at the Night King with the pike, Bran tells Theon that he is "a good man. Thank you" (S8E4 "The Long Night"). The phrase "good man" raises the spectre of Theon's castration. His body became unintelligible as masculine after Ramsay severed his penis, especially in the context of his phallocentric Ironborn culture and its desire to perfectly reproduce the patriarchal order through biological heirs. By calling Theon a "good man," Bran's dialogue invites viewers to remember that Theon has spent much of his character arc feeling like he is neither a "man" in the pseudo-medieval world where phallic domination and heir-making are privileged nor a "good" person because he betrayed the Starks. Theon is only intelligible as a "good man" again, and one with access to acts of phallic violence, when he embraces caring masculinity by sacrificing himself for his community and embracing his shame as a means of empowering the Other whom he once sought to banish.

74 REIMAGINING MASCULINITY AND VIOLENCE

Theon's attack on the Night King is a recourse to the phallic violence that injured him and represents the ambivalent possibilities of reworking the norms that enable his intelligibility. Dealing with gender subversion, Butler (1993, 84) writes of "repetition as the very condition of an affirmative response to violation" and contends that "the compulsion to repeat an injury is not necessarily the compulsion to repeat the injury in the same way or to stay fully within the traumatic orbit of that injury." In *Game of Thrones*, Theon can be seen to have an "affirmative response to violation" in his embrace of caring masculinity after his castration, although in his death scene he is shown to remain "within the traumatic orbit" of phallocentric violence. Theon charges at the Night King holding the pike, and in a long shot the pike is suggestive of the phallus. The Night King breaks the pike and stabs Theon through the torso with it, "repeat[ing] the injury" that Theon's initial phallic sovereign violence wrought: his castration. His phallic pike is broken and quite literally turned against him in order to make him abject as he is killed by a living corpse. At the same time, Theon breaks free from this injury in the sense that the violence is now motivated by a desire to care rather than to dominate, and for this reason viewers are encouraged to see him not only as a "good man" but also as a heroic one. Multiple strategies are used to highlight Theon's heroism within his death scene. Theon is clearly the last man standing in the battle to protect Bran, highlighting his strength and perseverance. There are multiple shots of Bran before and after Theon dies, Bran alone has dialogue in the scene, and he is visible sitting in his wheelchair in the shots where Theon begins to charge at the Night King. The contrast between Bran's position, which audiences are invited to view as defenceless, and Theon's power further emphasises the sacrificial dynamic to Theon's violence. Theon maintains his attachment to the phallus as a source of power, but he also reworks phallic domination into phallic care. He is unable to escape the destructive cycle of hegemonic sovereign violence, but his recourse to caring masculinity allows him to "repeat the injury" in a way that allows him, unlike Eddard or Robb, to die as a hero helping others save the world.

Sovereign Resistance

Although multiple acts of hegemonic sovereign violence are exposed as failed copies that abject and destroy the subjects who enact them, in relation to one character—Eddard's alleged bastard son Jon—there are occasions in which the proliferation of sovereign violence is reworked

UNDOING SOVEREIGN VIOLENCE 75

and disrupted with ambivalent consequences for the patriarchal gender order. As such, they query the relationship between masculinity, power, and violence in the way that the question of repetition, in Butler's theory, has the capacity to *"displace* the very gender norms that enable the repetition itself" (Butler 1990, 203; original emphasis). In adopting, then reworking, sovereign violence, Jon *displace*s this form of masculine power from violence to pacifism, showing that masculine subjects can be intelligible if they refuse hegemonic violence and instead attempt to work with others to make the world safer and more equitable.

Jon is one of the main characters in Martin's novels and their adaptation and he plays a major role in all three of the central plotlines. At the start of the narrative, Jon has an uneasy relationship with his family, especially Catelyn and Sansa Stark. He chooses to join an ancient order called the Night's Watch, who guard the magical Wall that separates the south of Westeros from the icy and wild North. He rises to become Lord Commander of the Night's Watch, but he is betrayed and murdered by his men when he allows the wildlings to cross beneath the Wall and join in the fight against the living dead. *Game of Thrones* has expanded his narrative, in which he is magically resurrected by his allies and returns to Winterfell to defeat Ramsay Bolton in battle. Jon is named King in the North and discovers that he is not in fact Eddard's bastard but the heir to the Iron Throne. However, he does not want to contest Daenerys's sovereignty and fights alongside her to defeat the Night King and his undead army. Jon has a complex relationship to sovereignty, and his sovereign violence is highly ambiguous. His status as bastard in a high-class family gives him a greater awareness of difference and power, including how his subjects are interconnected and their well-being is relational to the rest of Westerosi society.

In both *A Song of Ice and Fire* and *Game of Thrones*, Jon gains sovereign status as the democratically elected Lord Commander of the Night's Watch, a position earned through merit rather than blood. Although Jon is likewise motivated to perform sovereign violence by the emotional desire for revenge, and thus also fails to enact sovereign violence successfully, in some ways he comes closest, restoring peace (temporarily) to the Night's Watch by executing the disobedient Lord Janos Slynt. Jon's actions demonstrate that there can be an enactment of sovereign violence that reinforces a version of masculinity that is other-centred and egalitarian. Jon's relationship to masculinity is complex; Ward suggests that in *Game of Thrones* Jon is "not quite so bound by codes of honor as the hegemonic archetype of the hero might typically connote, particularly as embodied in Robb or Ned" (Ward 2018, 117). Jon is certainly far from "the hegemonic archetype," although I would suggest

76   REIMAGINING MASCULINITY AND VIOLENCE

that he exemplifies a new formation of hegemonic masculinity. The most culturally honoured enactments of masculinity are, as Connell (2005, 76–77) notes, "not a fixed character type, always and everywhere the same. [...] it is the successful claim to authority, more than direct violence, that is the mark of hegemony (though violence often underpins or supports authority." Jon has successfully claimed authority as the Lord Commander of the Night's Watch, chosen by his comrades for his adaptability and his commitment to saving Westeros from the Long Night. After becoming Lord Commander, Jon demonstrates a willingness to embrace the Other, particularly the wildling people who live south of the Wall as well as the other misfits he encounters. Faced with the apocalypse that the Long Night will bring, Jon realises that he must reorient his masculine performance and that of the Night's Watch to what Elliott (2015, 17) describes as caring masculinity: he moves "away from values of domination and aggression and toward values of interdependence and care." Jon's caring masculinity makes his masculine performance "the currently accepted answer to the problem of the legitimacy of patriarchy" (Connell 2005, 77), although in this case it is humankind, rather than the patriarchy, that is being safeguarded. The Night's Watch is a patriarchal institution, but in both the novels and show Jon uses it temporarily to end the subordination of women and racial others by allowing them to fight alongside the Westerosi. These connections prove valuable as they save his life in *Game of Thrones*, even though his sovereign violence remains ambiguous.

Jon's performance of sovereign violence is located as a repetition through citations of Eddard, as with Robb and Theon, although in this case vengeance for Eddard's death is the true reason for the execution. Janos was Commander of the City Watch in *A Game of Thrones* and season one of *Game of Thrones* when Eddard attempted to contest Joffrey's claim to the throne, believing he had the military support of the Watch when the Lannisters had bribed the army. Jon repeatedly alludes to this betrayal in the novels: when he first gives an order to Janos, Jon admits in interior monologue that he mistrusts the man because he *"helped slay my father and did his best to have me killed as well"* (DwD 124; original emphasis). When Janos makes no move to follow his orders, Jon says, "I am giving you a chance, my lord. It is more than you ever gave my father" (DwD 125). Jon's decision to repeat sovereign violence is framed in such a way as to highlight the citations of Eddard, disclosing the act as performative rather than natural and highlighting its emotional motivation intersecting with its objectivity.

Jon's act of sovereign violence also repeats Eddard's, Robb's, and Theon's in *A Song of Ice and Fire* because the criminal he executes is

UNDOING SOVEREIGN VIOLENCE 77

described as having an abject body that represents his threat to the
law and kingdom. Jon describes Janos as "dribbling porridge down his
chest," sees his "jowls quivering," and watches as "his face went white
as milk" after the execution order (DwD 126). When Janos resists, Jon
sees "flecks of porridge spraying from his lips" and later observes that his
smile "had all the sweetness of rancid butter" (DwD 127). The "dribbling,"
"quivering," and "spraying" that Jon narrates mark Janos's body as
malleable and unable to maintain boundaries between the inside and
outside of the body. Janos's skin, the border that maintains his subjectivity, turns "white as milk" then to "rancid butter": bodily instability
becomes bodily decay. Janos's subjectivating borders break down and
he becomes, as Halberstam (1995, 1) says of the intense visibility of the
monster, "all body and no soul." His excessive and rotting flesh mark
him as neither human nor masculine.

Yet Jon's repetition of sovereign violence is narrated in ways that
highlight its ambiguity and difference from his father's binary moralism
and patriarchal individualism, specifically through his interior monologue
in the novel. In the instant before Jon sentences Janos to death, he
considers and rejects several other options:

> 'Please take Lord Janos to the Wall—'
> —*and confine him to an ice cell*, he might have said. [...] *And the
> moment he is out, he and Thorne will begin to plot again.*
> —*and tie him to his horse*, he might have said. [...] *It will only be a
> matter of time before he deserts, then. And how many others will he take
> with him?* (DwD 126; original emphasis)

Jon recognises that Janos is a versipellous coward and that the only
way to contain the threat he poses—his likelihood of plotting and
desertion—is to execute him for the minor crime of disobedience and
disrespect. The repeated sentence structure and the phrase "he might
have said" is a performance within a performance. Jon's explanations
and dismissals show that he is aware of his world and the fact that
noble decisions are rarely rewarded. The repetition also discloses Jon's
reluctance to use force, which emphasises the fact that his priority is the
Night's Watch and its continued operation, rather than Jon's personal
feelings. Unlike his father and brothers, Jon acts in the best interests
of his people because his enactment of caring masculinity allows him
to recognise their interconnectedness and relationality. In doing so,
Jon reinforces a patriarchal institution, but he also undermines the
broader mechanisms of the Westerosi patriarchy by rejecting domination
and privileging unity. Sovereign violence becomes the best choice for

78   REIMAGINING MASCULINITY AND VIOLENCE

empowering the Night's Watch because it ensures the outcome Jon needs in order to maintain peace, and in so doing to ensure the kingdom is protected. Jon's own liminal status as a bastard and the youngest Lord Commander in Westerosi history has forced him to face the harsh realities of a world of moral ambiguity and approach his sovereignty through this lens. Unlike his predecessors, he is the only sovereign whose decision to use violence is presented as brushing up against, but never privileging, patriarchal gender structures. Even though Jon's decision to enact sovereign violence is contextualised by his awareness, as an outsider, of the ambiguity of "justice," the act is imperfect because it is not performed objectively but is revealed to be partially informed by Jon's personal feelings about Janos. In the novel, this flaw is exhibited prior to the execution order, as Jon repeatedly cites his father's death when he deals with Janos—revealing the act's performativity and its emotional motivation.

The television series reverses this dynamic: Jon repeats sovereign violence flawlessly until Janos begs for mercy, for "all I've said and done" (S5E3 "High Sparrow"). Janos does not explicitly mention Eddard, but the reference to "all" of his crimes makes this clear. Jon responds to Janos's pleas with rage, even though it is unclear whether Janos's emotional display is feigned or marks genuine personal growth and is an appropriate response to the violence he has enacted, symbolically against the kingdom and literally against Eddard. It could be argued that feeling wrong does not excuse Janos's actions, but for the fantasy genre this rejection of one's own violence is critical: Janos's emotions suggest that he repents his crimes and should be spared from execution. Jon chooses to use sovereign violence anyway, and it is here that Jon's violence is shown to be ambivalent because it is motivated by anger and a desire to dominate Janos rather than a desire to protect the kingdom. In a close-up of Jon's face right before he executes Janos, Jon's veins stand up on his forehead, he makes a tense frown, and breathes rapidly before snarling as he swings his sword down. Jon, like Robb and Theon, is unable to perform sovereign violence successfully in either *A Song of Ice and Fire* or *Game of Thrones*, according to the model that his father encouraged, because his actions are informed by a desire to safeguard the kingdom as well as his own desire to express his anger.

While Jon's repetition of sovereign violence is not entirely successful because it is emotionally motivated, it does prevent the Night's Watch from political upheaval and for that reason the execution itself is quick and clean, minimising his contact with the abject. In the novel, the execution is given less than half a page: "Longclaw descended" and, as "Janos Slynt's head went rolling across the muddy ground," a man asks

UNDOING SOVEREIGN VIOLENCE

to keep his expensive boots (DwD 128). The rolling head is abject, but its motion means that it is immediately expelled from view. So swift is the head's rejection that the focus shifts to mundane matters: the (re)possession of Janos's belongings. The television series also features a brief moment of abjection: viewers see Jon's sword slice through Janos's neck, followed by three seconds of the bleeding stump as the camera pans up to Jon's face and then to an approving nod from King Stannis (S5E3 "High Sparrow"). Stannis's approval is highly ambiguous: he is characterised as cold and uncharismatic as well as an excellent leader and strategist. His respectful nod towards Jon after Janos's execution amplifies the ambiguity around the act. Jon retains his coherent masculine identity and receives approval from another sovereign for protecting the Night's Watch from dissent, though that approval is questionable and the protection Jon provides the Night's Watch is second to Jon's own feelings. His sovereign violence is not entirely in keeping with the idealised model because of its affective flaw in both *A Song of Ice and Fire* and *Game of Thrones*, but nor is it exposed as failed.

The circularity between Jon's life and death is as ambiguous as his sovereign violence, and this is especially true of the circumstances that prompt his murder. The coup initially confuses Jon in *A Dance with Dragons* and his attackers tell him that they are acting "For the Watch" (DwD 1064). The phrase is repeated when "Bowen Marsh stood there before him, tears running down his cheeks. 'For the Watch'" (DwD 1064). The brothers are destroying Jon's "two bodies": they stab his sovereign body and deactivate his power because they believe he has broken the law and injured the kingdom by choosing to leave the Night's Watch to defend Winterfell. However, just as Jon executed Janos because of his feelings towards him, the mutineers execute Jon because they are angry about his decision to work with the wildings and for abandoning his oaths even if he does so in order to protect them from another threat. The "tears running down" Bowen's cheeks gesture towards the emotive dimensions of the decision and subsequent actions. Bowen regrets having to kill Jon because they were once friends, but he is overwhelmed with feelings of betrayal and fear of the Other. The Night's Watch and its honour are only a secondary reason for his violence. It becomes difficult to see the abstract kingdom, "the watch," as a valid reason to execute Jon, or anyone else. Sovereign violence, and specifically Jon's flawed citation of it and the need to preserve the impermeability of the sovereign body, bring about his death. Whether Jon's death is final or temporary in *A Song of Ice and Fire* remains to be resolved at the time of writing, as his death scene constitutes the final chapter in the most recently published novel. Regardless of whether or

80 REIMAGINING MASCULINITY AND VIOLENCE

not Jon is magically revived, it is clear that hegemonic violence can only produce more violence.

The inappropriate emotion that informed Jon's act of sovereign violence is emphasised even more strongly in the *Game of Thrones* episode "Mother's Mercy" (S5E10). From the beginning of the scene, emotion plays a far greater role than in the novel: Jon is lured from the office by the (false) news that one of the wildings has seen his uncle, the First Ranger Benjin Stark, who was presumed dead. Jon's cautious optimism vanishes when he walks through the cluster of men and sees two crossed pieces of wood with the word "TRAITOR" written across the horizontal. The word indicates that Jon has betrayed the Night's Watch's mandate by allowing the wildlings to pass, and the cross's religious symbolism suggests that they have betrayed Jon. In biblical stories, Jesus is betrayed by his disciple Judas for money, and he is crucified, only to rise again days later. As the scene unfolds in *Game of Thrones*, the cross and its cultural meanings indicate that the brothers, like Judas, are betraying their leader for an ignoble reason. Indeed, the emotionality behind the decision is demonstrated by the first and last characters who stab Jon—his nemesis Alliser Thorne and his steward Olly. Thorne has a longstanding hatred for Jon, and when he stabs Jon and says, "For the Watch," his face is expressionless and his voice is contemptuous. "The Watch" is a thinly veiled excuse to release his loathing with violence.

In contrast to Thorne, Olly, the last character to stab Jon, airs the group's anger and fear about Jon's decision to aid the wildlings. Olly's character represents the majority of brothers in the Night's Watch: he loathes the wildlings and experiences anger, fear, and a sense of betrayal when Jon decides to forgive their past misdeeds and combine forces ("Kill the Boy" S5E5). As Olly walks through the other men, the song "Goodbye Brother" begins to play, a mournful string piece that heightens the emotion in the scene. Olly's facial expressions betray his mixed feelings: rage and grief, as well as sadness and regret. Olly stands directly in front of Jon, who implores, "Olly..." (S5E10). The boy frowns and stabs Jon in the chest before saying, "for the Watch." This last moment bears a striking resemblance to Jon's imperfect performance of sovereign violence. Janos, like Jon, begged for mercy, but Jon, like Olly, was acting because of his own emotional motives and chose to kill in vengeful anger. Olly, Thorne, and the other men who attack Jon do so as a means of challenging Jon's other-centred hegemonic masculinity; as Connell (2005, 77) notes, "new groups may challenge old solutions and construct a new hegemony." Jon solidifies his hegemonic masculinity by using sovereign violence against Janos, and this act is reversed and used against him as his men attempt to (re)establish a patriarchal and self-centred hegemonic masculinity. The entire society enacts hegemonic violence, attempting to banish the Other in order to reify the existing patriarchal structure, because they have seen from Jon's exercise of sovereign power as Lord Commander that this is acceptable. Jon's death, just like that of Theon, Robb, and Eddard, is circular: his deformed performance of sovereign violence in life is repeated to cause his own death.

Jon is murdered because of his radical embrace of the Other, but it is also these connections that allow him to come back to life in *Game of Thrones*, proving that the cycle whereby sovereign violence is enacted on the body of the sovereign can be broken because the act is a protection both of the body of the sovereign and of the borders of the kingdom: it is a protection both of the individual and of the community. Commenting on Jon's relationship to Daenerys in season seven, Ward (2018, 119) argues that "Snow's trajectory after resurrection suggests a more flexible embodiment of masculinity, one in which deference does not equate to weakness or subordination, and heroism is malleable rather than unyielding." I agree that Jon's masculine performance is less rigid than his father's and brothers', and I would add that it is his connection to others that allows him to be brought back to life and take on a more flexible approach to violence. As I have noted, Jon is brought back by Melisandre, but the priestess learns of Jon's death because of his relationships to others, which are a product of his caring masculinity. Jon's direwolf Ghost howls to alert Jon's friends, and they work together with the wildlings to send word to Melisandre. Jon is saved through a web of connections, and he continues to privilege these after he returns to life.

At first Jon appears to continue the pattern of sovereign violence when he executes four of his killers, including Thorne and Olly, in "Oathbreaker" (S6E3). The men are hanged—with Jon cutting the rope that releases the floor beneath them—and after they die, seven seconds of screen time is spent on a medium close-up of Olly's corpse swinging in the wind. The shot creates intimacy between the viewer and the corpse, and the terrifying confrontation is exacerbated by its duration, which is far longer than most others in the scene. While Olly's hanged corpse is less monstrous than Robb's desecrated body, or Eddard's severed head, because it is whole, it creates similar levels of abjection because the viewer is forced into inescapable intimacy with it. In *Game of Thrones*, Olly becomes the object by which Jon's flawed sovereign violence is critiqued; he stands in for the self-centred hegemonic aspect of sovereign violence that Jon continued when he executed Janos, and this is continued when he executes his killers.

82   REIMAGINING MASCULINITY AND VIOLENCE

Yet after the execution and abjection Jon ceases using sovereign violence. The execution is followed by a breaking rather than an aligning of the body of the sovereign and the nation. Jon hands his cloak to his friend Dolores Edd as a symbol of his sovereignty, telling him, "Wear it. Burn it. Whatever you want. You have Castle Black. My watch is ended" ("Oathbreaker" S6E3). This scene marks a break in Jon's repetitive use of sovereign violence. While he does take up a sovereign position as King in the North and a pseudo-sovereign position as true heir to the Iron Throne, he does not enact sovereign violence again, as such. After this scene, he uses violence solely to protect or defend others. When he uses violence (and the threat of violence) in future scenes, it is framed as violence that is intended to protect the Other, rather than the public, theatrical, and dominating shape that sovereign violence takes.

One of these scenes in the final season of *Game of Thrones* invites viewers to see sovereign violence as necessary, although these scenes are also bound up with Jon's hegemonic caring masculinity. When Jon visits Tyrion in his prison cell in "The Iron Throne," Tyrion attempts to convince Jon to murder Daenerys, the newly crowned Queen of Westeros, because she plans to dominate the entire world. Tyrion says, "You are the shield that guards the realms of men. You've always tried to do the right thing, no matter the cost. You've tried to protect people. Who is the greatest threat to the people now? It's a terrible thing I'm asking. It's also the right thing." Audiences are invited to accept Tyrion's notion that Jon must kill Daenerys to protect the world from her sovereign violence. A sense of continuity and justice is evoked through the reference to the Night's Watch, as this was the last time Jon performed sovereign violence, and when he relinquished it. Jon must use sovereign violence to defeat sovereign violence, but this circular pattern is concealed through Jon's ambivalent sovereignty. Tyrion raises the spectre of Jon's claim to the throne, asking, "Do you think I'm the last man she'll execute? Who is more dangerous than the rightful heir to the Iron Throne?" Viewers are reminded that Jon is the "rightful heir," but Tyrion falls back on Jon's caring masculinity, this time speaking specifically about Jon's family: "And your sisters? Do you see them bending the knee? [...] Why do you think Sansa told me the truth about you? [...] You have to choose now." Hypothetical threats are used to justify in advance Jon's "queenslaying," as in the scene where Sam asks Jon whether he would have burned Randyll and Dickon Tarly, as Daenerys did in the previous season (see S8E1 "Winterfell"). Audiences are encouraged to view a desire to protect the Other as a means of making morally acceptable decisions around sovereign violence.

Because Jon's hegemonic masculinity is justified by care for the Other and his sovereignty ambiguous, his violence against Daenerys is one of few successful enactments of sovereign violence in *Game of Thrones*. Throughout the scene audiences are reminded of Daenerys's crimes. She walks alone through the ruined Great Hall, the contrast between the dark grey bricks and the white snow and the light grey and white clouds highlighting the destruction. Jon joins Daenerys and they speak for several minutes, during which time he confronts her about the "little children" who were "burned" in the chaos (S8E6 "The Iron Throne"). The reference to children operates on multiple levels; as Lauren Berlant (1997, 21) notes, the child is often figured as an "infantile citizen whose naïve citizenship surfaces constantly as the ideal type of patriotic personhood in America, in ways that are both extremely simple and extremely complex." By murdering these perfect citizens, Daenerys is presented as a dangerous threat to the nation of Westeros and to the future of (straight, white, and able) humankind. For Daenerys, the reference to children takes on additional significance. Throughout *Game of Thrones*, she has been characterised as both the Mother of Dragons and as a mother or "Mhysa" to her people, despite being unable to bear children herself. Jon's reference to children in this moment invites viewers to remember these previous scenes and how Daenerys's heroism in earlier seasons was entwined with her desire to protect the Other. By becoming a child-killer, it is implied that Daenerys has abandoned the principles that made her a good leader earlier in the series. The reference indicates that Daenerys has become what she sought to banish.

Viewers are encouraged to view Jon's act of violence against Daenerys as moral and successful through music and the actor's emotive performance. Where other enactments of sovereign violence in the series fail because of the emotions that the sovereigns experience, Jon's emotions highlight his rejection of domination and his ability to embrace emotion, interdependence, and relationality. Right before Jon stabs Daenerys, he says that she is "his queen. Now and always." As they kiss, the song "Truth" plays, a sweeping string piece that is first heard in "The Dragon and the Wolf" (S7E7) in the scene where Jon's true identity is revealed by Bran at Winterfell, which is intercut with Jon and Daenerys having sex for the first time on board Daenerys's ship. The song connotes love and (to a lesser extent) truth, and for this reason its repetition in the moment Jon murders Daenerys invites viewers to see Jon's sovereign violence as an act of love rather than domination or revenge. Jon's own emotions offer additional weight to this suggestion; as Jon holds Daenerys's lifeless body, he cries, tears visible on his nose in a medium close-up. It is rare to see a masculine character crying

84 REIMAGINING MASCULINITY AND VIOLENCE

in *Game of Thrones*. Jon's tears are presented as a sign of a genuine display of grief and love. Jon's hegemonic sovereign violence becomes acceptable and successful because he uses violence to reject Daenerys's moral domination over the Other, embraces his emotions in a productive (rather than destructive) way, and recognises that people must depend on one another to construct societal moral principles rather than have them imposed by a singular monarch.

Sovereign violence necessitates an encounter with abjection, and the comparative lack of abject signifiers during Jon's violence further invites viewers to see it as acceptable. Daenerys's body takes on few abject signifiers; as she lies dying, blood runs in a thin stream from her mouth and then her nose, and soon thereafter her corpse is banished from Westeros in the claws of her dragon. Jon's interaction with the abject is minimal and his constitutive borders are not threatened, as in the scene when he executes Janos Slynt. The lack of abject signifiers indicates that Jon has successfully performed sovereign violence, even though his sovereign status is ambiguous. Hegemonic sovereign violence can be heroic in *Game of Thrones*, but only when the hegemony through which it is constituted as masculine is caring, as in Jon's case. Jon's story reveals that there can be acts of sovereign violence that are also acts of care, and that in some contexts, such as the dire environmental crisis that Westeros faces, the feudal and patriarchal model of hegemonic masculinity that prizes domination over others can be supplanted by a caring hegemonic masculinity that rejects domination and embraces feeling and the interdependence of all people. In the finale of *Game of Thrones*, this comes together as Jon and the Wildlings return beyond the Wall. As they march away from Castle Black and into the forest, viewers see a single green plant growing out of the snow, indicating that the environmental threat has been defeated and balance is returning to the world. As the camera moves into an extreme long shot of the wildlings disappearing into the forest, the main *Game of Thrones* theme plays, a slower version with a choir, indicating a moment of great significance. Jon's caring masculinity allows him to rework sovereign violence and to find kinship among the Wildlings, and in so doing displace the patriarchal feudal system that ostracised him for most of his life.

Conclusion

In the fantasy genre, sovereign violence is comprised of a wide array of often contradictory promises, even as it is also a practice through which masculinity materialises and the patriarchal order is legitimised and

UNDOING SOVEREIGN VIOLENCE 85

defended. When Eddard, Robb, Theon, and Jon enact sovereign violence in *A Song of Ice and Fire* and *Game of Thrones*, the act becomes visible as a repetition of phallic, affective, and bodily gestures. Sovereign violence is often presented in such a way as to evoke an attachment to a just and moral world, yet the ways in which such violence is enacted, and its effects, highlight its moral ambiguity.

Sovereign violence is comprised of so many contradictory or grandiose promises that failure is more likely than success, especially when it is enacted by characters who privilege a self-oriented hegemonic masculinity. This is especially true for Eddard and Robb, who refuse to compromise their personal ideals for the good of the kingdom. An inflexible attachment to moral absolutism leads each sovereign to fail to restore order. Through these flaws, the act is revealed, as Butler says of gender as a whole, "to be a copy, and an inevitably failed one, an ideal that nobody *can* embody" (Butler 1990, 189). This failure of embodiment is then demonstrated in the inability of these sovereigns to contain the literal and figurative threats of abjection presented by the criminals. Instead, the sovereign becomes subject to that same instability. The self-oriented version of hegemonic masculinity that Eddard, Robb, and Theon perform when they undertake acts of sovereign violence returns to destroy the subject. After making contact with blood and the corpse, an unavoidable facet of execution, the sovereign's own personal boundaries become blurred and unstable, and hegemonic sovereign violence is revealed as unable to support a coherent masculine identity.

Alongside abjection, sovereign violence is problematised through circularity: the way men use sovereign violence in life is reversed, parodied, or de-formed so that they are killed by the same version of sovereign violence that they enacted. After these circuitous demises, the association of sovereign identity and abjection is foregrounded as the men are reduced to horrifying corpses: mutilated and put on display as tools of horror. The sovereign body is punished with abjection beyond death, placed within a cycle of violence that can produce nothing but destruction. Through these textual resonances, each man is shown to be complicit in a dangerous cycle of subject constitution and patriarchal reproduction in which violence that is enacted for individualistic ends can only produce more violence for the self and society. Yet in *Game of Thrones*, Theon's decision to embrace caring values in order to become intelligibly masculine and Jon's reworking of hegemonic masculinity and sovereign violence show that this cycle can be subverted. As the legitimate son of Rhaegar Targaryen and Lyanna Stark, Jon is heir to the Iron Throne, a position that would logically encourage his return to sovereign violence. Yet, after momentarily adopting an ambivalent sovereign status as he kills Daenerys, he rejects this form of power, returning to the North and joining the wildlings. *Game of Thrones* provides a means of breaking from the destructive cycle of hegemonic sovereign violence through Jon.

Chapter 3

Vile, Scheming, Evil Bitches?

When Cersei Lannister, the Queen Regent (and later Queen) of Westeros, visits her daughter-in-law in prison halfway through the series, she is accused of being a "vile, scheming, evil bitch" (FFC 738)/"hateful bitch" (S5E7). She is certainly one of the major villains in *A Song of Ice and Fire* and *Game of Thrones*, and one of the most violent women characters. Violent women are a topic of fascination in popular culture and criticism. Feminist cultural scholars are especially divided on this issue. Representations of violent women can subvert harmful stereotypes that position women as victims and offer a way of challenging heteropatriarchal structures (Halberstam 1993). However, these same representations may also reinforce patriarchal values and the desirability of violence. Women's violence on screen is often trivialised and glamorised (Minowa, Maclaran, and Stevens 2014), and has fewer negative consequences than men's violence (Fernández-Villanueva, et al. 2009). When women become violent, their aggression is often constructed as a product of normatively feminine concerns such as romantic love or maternal instinct (Cecil 2007). Otherwise, the aggression is explained away through mental illness (Quintero Johnson and Miller 2016) or an individual woman's "deviant" sexuality, which is figured as lesbianism (Hart 2005), sexual dysfunction, or erotomania (Sjoberg and Gentry 2008). Many of these debates are underscored by a tension around whether women's violence is an imitation of men's violence or is uniquely feminine or female, a tension that is echoed in discussions around masculine women. Does being violent make a person masculine? No—but characters who feel more masculine than feminine may have increased access to violence because masculinity and violence are so tightly interwound in dominant Western cultural discourses.

In this chapter, I continue to investigate the relationship between violence and masculinity in *A Song of Ice and Fire* and *Game of Thrones* as it is negotiated through fantasy genre conventions, embodiment, and

88 REIMAGINING MASCULINITY AND VIOLENCE

abjection, but now turn to alternative forms of masculine embodiment, in relation to which both positive and negative interpretations of violence can be found. Violence is viewed as a gendered act (or series of acts) through which masculinity can be enacted because of cultural associations between men and violence, not because of any biologically essential link between male bodies and violence. The masculine characters I have analysed thus far, such as Theon Greyjoy and Robb Stark, are presented in terms of this performative dynamic through their citation of other patriarchs and are shown to make use of violence to bolster their own power and to legitimise the patriarchy in ways that consequently make them monstrous. Masculine characters who were AFAB are a non-normative subject position from which violence is also enacted. For these characters, as with the male-embodied ones, self-oriented hegemonic violence leads to a loss of subjectivating borders and their violence turned against them in death. However, from this non-normative subject position, other uses of violence and their consequences are also demonstrated. Specifically, forms of violence that are informed by a caring or other-oriented masculinity allow characters to maintain their constitutive borders and share their knowledge through queer kinship. In examining both of these outcomes, I argue that AFAB masculine characters in *A Song of Ice and Fire* and *Game of Thrones* make violence a visibly masculine act that can be coded as heroic or monstrous, depending on whether the violence legitimises and reproduces the patriarchal gender order or pushes them in more enabling directions. The Queen Regent (and later Queen) Cersei Lannister and the knight Brienne of Tarth represent the two most extreme examples of this dynamic.

I understand Cersei and Brienne as masculine, or embodying female masculinity, a gender configuration aligned with people who are AFAB and "feel themselves to be more masculine than feminine" (Halberstam 1998, xi) or are "mistaken consistently for a man" (57). I find Halberstam's terms and phrasing well suited to the pseudo-medieval world of Westeros, which straddles a space between an imagined medieval world with binary genders and the context of the 1990s to the 2010s in which Martin's books and their adaptation were created and in which queer, transgender, and non-binary identities were gaining cultural visibility. More-nuanced and less-morphologically centred language has since evolved and continues to be so, but the term "female masculinity" captures the spirit of Brienne's and Cersei's gender identities since it reflects scholarly thinking about transmasculine people at the time the books and show were created. The two criteria that Halberstam proposes reflect two of many different ways in

VILE, SCHEMING, EVIL BITCHES?   89

which female masculinity can be embodied: as a gender identification that may not align with physical appearance (as in Cersei's case at the beginning of the series) or as a personal or cultural interpretation of embodied gender presentation (as in Brienne's case). Masculine women and transmasculine people often appear in fantasy fiction; as Anne Balay (2010, 7) argues, the genre "isn't limited by genders as we know them, or even as we believe they might be possible" and therefore "offers a fruitful sight [*sic*] for investigation of female masculinities."

While I make use of Halberstam's earlier concept, Brienne and Cersei are also highly useful for placing transgender theories in dialogue with performativity. Both characters transgress the socially imposed boundaries of normative high-class Westerosi femininity because they are masculine people, though in different ways and with different results for their embodied and political gender performance. For this reason, Brienne and Cersei can be understood as transgender, as it is defined by Susan Stryker: "*the movement across a socially imposed boundary away from an unchosen starting place—rather than any particular destination or mode of transition*" (2008, 1; original emphasis). I do not mean to suggest that the characters are or should be viewed as transgender (I'll leave that to the texts' audiences), but that reading them in this light opens up new insights into their relationship to gender and violence. For Brienne, the "movement" Stryker describes is straightforward in both the novels and television show as she moves from the "unchosen starting place" of cisgender womanhood to a stable and intelligible knightly masculinity prior to the narrative present. Cersei's "movement across a socially imposed boundary" is in some ways more complex because it does not revolve around an intelligible masculinity *or* femininity, as does Brienne's, but rather oscillates between the two. Cersei's transgender characterisation bursts forth in private moments in *A Song of Ice and Fire* and is gradually hinted at through her increasingly androgynous costumes in *Game of Thrones*. In addition, her ability and willingness to pass as cisgender is entangled with her political power. It is no coincidence that in both the novels and television series Cersei's masculinity becomes more pronounced after she becomes Queen Regent (and later Queen) and is no longer beholden to the patriarchs around her. Both Cersei and Brienne undergo movement away from the assumed category of woman, but the way they transition and their desired gendered destination are not the same even as they both perform masculinity.

Female masculinities stage a complex (re)negotiation of the relationship between masculinity and violence in *A Song of Ice and Fire* and *Game of Thrones*. Cersei's violence is performed in ways that cite other patriarchs: her father, Lord Tywin, but also her deceased husband, King Robert

90   REIMAGINING MASCULINITY AND VIOLENCE

Baratheon. Cersei follows the same gendered patterns that these men enacted, using violence to dominate others and empower herself. Within the narrative some of Cersei's gendered acts are hegemonic, which sheds new light on Connell's theory by demonstrating that people with female bodies can temporarily become an exemplar of masculinity. Connell (2005, 77) notes that "individual holders of institutional power or great wealth may be far from the hegemonic pattern in their personal lives," noting that in the 1950s, "a male member of a prominent business dynasty was a key figure in the gay/transvestite social scene [...] because of his wealth and the protection this gave." In *A Song of Ice and Fire* and *Game of Thrones*, Cersei's class power within the feudal system gives her (some) protection from her world and its sexism, allowing her to rule and perform hegemonic gendered acts. At other times, her stylised acts are complicit or subordinate within the fictional universes, though for audiences her violence is often presented as subordinate. Cersei's hegemonic masculine violence is often oriented around the reproduction of the patriarchal order, whether through dominating the Other or expanding her Lannister line biologically, though all of her attempts at reproduction fail. Cersei's embodied masculine performance becomes horrifying through figures of queer feminine monstrosity and through bodily abjection during her walk of penance in the novel, and through her relationship with Gregor Clegane in the television series. The presence of the monstrous feminine as mode of critique does not make Cersei's violence feminine: as I will show, her violence is explicitly coded as masculine through citations of other patriarchs, costumes, phallic imagery. As Cersei's narrative has continued in *Game of Thrones*, her violence is trapped within a destructive loop: she repeats the violence that was used against her but fails to break free from the patriarchal models that inform it and is killed in ways that echo her own violence.

Cersei's female body does not make her masculine performances problematic; rather, it is the hegemonic violence that divides people, endangers society, and maintains a masculine hierarchy. It could be argued that the critique arises because Cersei transgresses the boundaries of intelligible femininity, or what women can say, rather than from her violent acts. Caroline Spector (2012, 182–183) takes the latter view, arguing that "Cersei wields power by adopting the strategies and behaviours of the patriarchy more often than the ones routinely available to women. It is telling that she is judged negatively while the men who use similar tactics are celebrated as legends." As I will show, the way Cersei uses violence in both the novels and television show is what makes her monstrous and abject, rather than her female-bodied performance of masculinity. While Cersei is empowered and operates

VILE, SCHEMING, EVIL BITCHES? 91

within masculine domains, her power is gained through acceptance of hegemonic masculine power structures. She makes individualistic efforts to succeed rather than advocate for social change. Cersei dons a masculine role but does not attempt to rewrite the Westerosi gender order.

By contrast, Brienne also occupies a non-normative gender identification but uses this difference to reject hegemonic masculinity, and uses a sword, which allows a way of bridging the critical divide between Judith Butler's performativity theory and transgender scholarship. Brienne is able to enter categories of her own choosing—to be as she identifies—while simultaneously collapsing those categories, especially as they attach to hegemonic violence. In both *A Song of Ice and Fire* and *Game of Thrones*, Brienne has no singular model of masculine reference and so cites the figure of the knight, which for her encompasses honour, chivalry, and oath-keeping and so allows her to forge an alternative form of pseudo-medieval masculinity. The knightly discourse enables Brienne to use violence as an act of care work, which challenges patriarchal structures that venerate domination and individualism. Because Brienne uses violence to empower others, she is able to maintain her personal borders when she comes into contact with the abject during her quest. In the novels, despite being covered in animal blood and having her face eaten, and in *Game of Thrones* killing several men, Brienne's subjectivating boundaries are never overwhelmed for long, a resistance that is explicitly tied to her connection to others and her honour, constructed with reference to the masculine figure of the knight. Brienne's violence demonstrates that it is possible to break free from destructive patriarchal structures and forge a masculinity that combines violence with care, which she does through queer kinship. Rather than passing her knightly violence down to biological children, Brienne's violence proliferates queerly, through her bonds with Jaime Lannister and Podrick Payne in both texts, and with Arya Stark and institutions like the Kingsguard in the television show.

This chapter brings these concepts of queer kinship and female masculinity together with the theoretical framework already used to investigate monstrous and sovereign male violence—that is, Butler's theory of gender subversion, Connell's hierarchy of masculinities, Julia Kristeva's theory of the abject, and Barbara Creed's work on the monstrous feminine—to argue that in *A Song of Ice and Fire* and *Game of Thrones*, masculine AFAB characters who reproduce hegemonic violence are criticised, whereas those who use violence to care for other characters are presented as heroes. In so doing, I progress Halberstam's (1998, 9) conclusion on female masculinity—that it is never ideologically resolved but may function in service of numerous political projects: "sometimes female masculinity coincides with the excess of male supremacy" and sometimes it represents "the healthful alternative to what are considered the histrionics of conventional femininities." By returning to Creed's theory of monstrous femininity, now with a focus on masculine AFAB characters, I reveal a new framework for understanding the queer monstrous feminine, which combines the female body, masculinity, and femininity to problematise self-oriented hegemonic violence. These forms of monstrosity do not feminise the masculine women, as their violence is coded as masculine through citation, costume, and music. Rather, the monstrous feminine works as a mode and draws attention to the horror that their hegemonic violence evokes in such a way as to critique its continued repetition.

"I Choose Violence"

Cersei is one of the most widely discussed characters in academic criticism of *A Song of Ice and Fire* and *Game of Thrones*. She is a major character and frequent antagonist who plays a crucial role throughout the series, as a wife, mother, lover, and ruler. Cersei is not a typical queen, good or evil: she manipulates several men, including her brother and cousin, through sexual favours; gets drunk on wine; and arranges dozens of murders of men, women, and, in the novel, Robert's bastard children. The novels see her rise and fall in power, and the television show has expanded her narrative, whereby she becomes queen in her own right, wages war against Daenerys's armies, and is killed when Daenerys attacks King's Landing. Despite being a sovereign through marriage and later in her own right, Cersei seldom enacts sovereign violence because she often acts through prostheses and/or in private, removing the public spectacle of sovereign violence that is venerated by Eddard and his sons. Scholars have analysed Cersei's walk of shame and ensuing abjection (Patel 2014), her relation to femininity (Frankel 2014, 72–75) and feminism (Spector 2012, 181–183), her moral judgements (Anglberger and Hieke 2012), medievalism and realism (Finn 2020), her connections to other women in history (Mares 2017, 148–150) and historical alchemical commisions (Runstedler 2020), and her Machiavellian practices (Beaton 2016, 199–203). In addition, scholars such as Finn (2020) and Jones (2012) have analysed Cersei through the lens of adaptation, the latter noting that much of Cersei's violence in the novels is removed or attributed to men in the early seasons of *Game of Thrones*. Phillips (2016, 164–165) notes that Cersei has additional violence performed against her in the

VILE, SCHEMING, EVIL BITCHES?   93

television series, especially the changed scene in which she is raped by Jaime at Joffrey's bedside (S4E3 "Breaker of Chains").

At first glance, Cersei's traditionally feminine beauty and her lack of masculine accoutrements appear to make her an unlikely choice for this discussion of female masculinity. Charul Patel (2014) suggests that Cersei enacts a monstrous femininity, yet while the character is monstrous, she expresses an explicit desire to be a man on multiple occasions. For instance, in the television show, Cersei's costumes increasingly incorporate armour and in the novels she says, "I should have been born a man" (CoK 291), and thinks, *"I am the only true son* [Tywin] *ever had"* (FfC 54; original emphasis). There is ambiguity around these statements because Cersei conflates power with manhood; saying that she should have been born male reflects both a desire to inhabit a male body so that she can access the power she deserves and an identification with Westerosi masculinity rather than femininity. In the terms of Halberstam's notion of female masculinity (1998), the fact that Cersei feels "more masculine than feminine" means that she may be described as a masculine woman. In both texts, Cersei's transgender subjectivity becomes more apparent as the narrative progresses, namely, when readers gain access to her perspective chapters in *A Feast for Crows* and after her walk of penance in *Game of Thrones*. Her identification as not-feminine, and her citation of patriarchs such as Tywin and Robert, mean that her violence is positioned as masculine. Just like the cisgender sovereign and monstrous characters I have analysed, Cersei's violence is presented as horrifying through the monstrous feminine. This monstrous mode is not affixed only to AFAB bodies or feminine people even as its visual vocabulary often draws on a cisgender female reproductive system and motherhood.

Cersei identifies strongly with her father and in *A Song of Ice and Fire* she regularly thinks of him as a source of model masculine conduct. When Cersei sees her advisor Qyburn torturing a man, she "felt ill. Part of her wanted to close her eyes, to turn away, to make it stop. But she was the queen and this was treason. *Lord Tywin would not have turned away"* (FfC 657; original emphasis). Similarly, before Cersei's walk of shame, she thinks, *"I am Cersei of House Lannister, a lion of the Rock, the rightful queen of these Seven Kingdoms, trueborn daughter of Tywin Lannister. And hair grows back"* (DwD 989; original emphasis). Cersei's interior monologue reveals that her masculine performativity is in imitation of idealised memories of her father and his patriarchal lineage, and this is what marks her gendered performance (including her violence) as masculine.

In *Game of Thrones*, Cersei cites Tywin by repeating his words in conversations with her family. When Cersei and Tyrion are discussing the Battle of the Blackwater in season two, Cersei mentions "rain[ing] fire down on them from above," and Tyrion says, "You're quoting Father, aren't you?" (S2E7 "A Man Without Honour"). Cersei notes that Tywin has an excellent mind for strategy—one, it is implied, that she is choosing to repeat in her own masculine performance. Likewise, in season seven, when Cersei discusses her strategy against Daenerys Targaryen, and reveals her pregnancy, she says, "If we want to beat her, we have to be clever. We have to fight her like Father would have. [...] Whatever stands in our way, we will defeat it. For ourselves, for our House, for this" (S7E5 "Eastwatch"). Cersei places her hands on her torso as she says "this," disclosing to Jaime and the audience that she is pregnant and tying her pregnancy into a larger system of patriarchal reproduction. She makes a similar reference to Tywin moments later, signalling that she plans to continue to proliferate Tywin's masculinity through her own acts of dominating violence and through her unborn child. It is these references to Tywin that highlight Cersei's violence as masculine and specifically as acts that are intended to be hegemonic.

Far more frequent than Cersei's dialogue is her costumes, which attempt to reproduce Tywin's attire. Beginning with a thin metal belt around her waist in season one, Cersei's dresses increasingly incorporate masculine armour, from a full breastplate at the end of season two to an armoured under bust corset in season three, and so on. The masculinity that the costumes evoke is compounded after seasons six: Cersei's long blonde hair is removed for her walk of penance at the end of season five and she chooses to maintain her short hair as queen. The references to Tywin are made explicit by costume designer Michele Clapton. In an interview about Cersei's coronation gown, Clapton says, "I wanted the cut leather that would mirror Tywin's—it was everything she always told her father she could do, and she can now do it" (Flaherty 2016, para. 24). Cersei's clothing cites her father, as her interior monologue does in the novel, achieving a similar effect of disclosing her violence as masculine. She imitates her father's enactment of hegemonic violence, much like the Stark sovereigns, and this imitation is part of how her violence is coded as masculine.

While Cersei models her idealised version of masculinity on her father, in *A Song of Ice and Fire* her violence is often narrated alongside references to her husband Robert. Robert was once a formidable warrior, but after he became king, his body and his morality fell into disrepair: when readers first encounter him, he is a fat, drunken womaniser who skirts his responsibilities and wastes the kingdom's coin. Robert's acts of sexual domination, alcohol consumption, and position within the feudal system make him an exemplar of masculinity, although these same acts

VILE, SCHEMING, EVIL BITCHES? 95

diminish his knightly honour and muscular body. Robert exemplifies the contradictory nature of hegemonic masculinity as he legitimises the patriarchy even as his body falls into poor shape. Cersei arranges Robert's death in *A Game of Thrones*, but his masculine practices continue to inform her own gendered conduct. One of the clearest examples is Robert's marital rapes, "assaults" in which "he would drink too much and want to claim his rights" (FfC 544), after which "those nights never happened. Come morning he remembered nothing" (FfC 543). Marital rape empowers the rapist by dominating the Other and their agency: it is an act performed through masculinity, and it is one that Cersei repeats as queen. In *A Feast for Crows*, Cersei has sex with her "olive skinned" friend Taena Merryweather, the wife of a courtier. When Cersei begins sexually stimulating Taena, she says, "I am the queen. I mean to claim my rights" (FfC 548). Cersei repeats the phrasing that she used to describe Robert's marital rapes and thinks about how he would have acted with Taena: *"Robert would have loved you, for an hour. [...] but once he spent himself inside you, he would have been hard-pressed to remember your name"* (FfC 548). In rewriting her position in her memory of Robert's marital rapes, Cersei shifts her position from being the phallus to having the phallus as the penetrator in this queer sex scene. Cersei is able to enter the category of her choosing as she realises her desire for power and masculinity through embodying the role of penetrator as she becomes the one with the phallus. The importance Cersei places on this positionality are important to her, for she refuses Taena's offer of reciprocation and repeats Robert's dismissal of the sexual violence after she brings Taena to climax: "It would be morning soon, and all of this would be forgotten. It had never happened" (FfC 549). By citing Robert in this way, it is clear that Cersei views her sexual experience with Taena as an act of dominating hegemonic violence rather than pleasure. In some ways, she is correct: the race and class difference between the Caucasian Queen and the dark-skinned noblewoman may mean that Taena felt pressured to acquiesce. Yet Taena appears to enjoy the experience, and tells Cersei, "Please [...] go on, my queen. Do as you will with me. I'm yours," and, on the next page, she "shuddered again and arched her back and screamed" (FfC 549). Taena's enjoyment can be read as submission to Cersei's power and an attempt to provide a theatrical orgasm that may stop the assault. However, if Taena's comments are taken to express a genuine desire and pleasure, then Cersei's insistence that she is raping Taena is an attempt to dominate the other woman's voice and colonise her experience.

Cersei's reproduction of self-oriented hegemonic violence is made grotesque and terrifying through imagery that evokes the *vagina dentata*.

96 REIMAGINING MASCULINITY AND VIOLENCE

Creed (1993, 105) understands the *vagina dentata* as reflecting a "fear of the female genitals," which may be manifested as a toothed mouth, a beautiful woman with a fanged animal companion, a barred entrance, or a mother consuming her young. When the *vagina dentata* is linked with male-bodied characters and their hegemonic violence, both become monstrous and the latter is rejected. A similar process takes place in relation to Cersei's sexual violence: the *vagina dentata* is aligned with her, and this link makes both Cersei and her violence terrifying. Cersei's violence is presented as masculine because her interior monologue clearly cites Robert as informing and motivating her actions, even as these actions are also horrifying and are linked to the monstrous feminine. The toothed vagina may be linked with either "symbolic castration" or "literal castration" (107), and Cersei imagines performing a mixture of the two on Taena. While the women are having sex, the queen "let herself imagine that her fingers were a bore's [*sic*] tusks, ripping the Myrish woman apart from groin to throat" (FfC 549). Cersei wants to destroy Taena's genitals and then her entire body, literally and symbolically, "castrating" her by "ripping" open her vagina and then dismembering her. At the same time, Cersei wishes for this destructive position through her desire to enter an embodied masculinity: the tusks she imagines for herself are also part of her transmasculine desire, even if that desire is centred on the violent destruction of the Other. It is not Cersei's desire to embody masculinity that makes her acts monstrous, but rather the desire to dominate the Other: Cersei goes from penetrating Taena to (imagined) murder, as the type of hegemonic masculinity she aims to embody is ultimately destructive for cisgender and transgender masculine characters alike. The boar as *vagina dentata* is significant because Robert was killed by a boar in a drunken hunting accident in *A Game of Thrones*, and it was Cersei who arranged his death. The boar becomes Cersei's "animal companion with open jaws and snapping teeth" (Creed 1993, 108), but it is linked to her enactment of hegemonic violence rather than to her female body because of the way she cites Robert before, during, and after the act. The horror that the boar evokes because of its connection to the *vagina dentata* and because of the abjection of the human/animal (Cersei/boar) crossing is projected onto Cersei's hegemonic violence, which also becomes monstrous.

Hegemonic sexual violence is further critiqued through Cersei's interior monologue during the same scene, in which she reveals that she rebelled against Robert's marital rapes by eating his semen—an act that evokes the evil queen and the monstrous feminine. When Cersei penetrates Taena, she thinks about Robert: *"Ten thousand of your children perished in my palm, Your Grace [...] I would lick your sons off my face and*

VILE, SCHEMING, EVIL BITCHES?

fingers one by one, all those pale sticky princes. You claimed your rights, my lord, but in the darkness I would eat your heirs" (FfC 549; original emphasis). Cersei presents Robert's sperm not as a bodily fluid but as "children" and "pale sticky princes," anthropomorphism that elevates her (stereo-typically feminine) consumption of his sperm to violence against his royal offspring. Yet Cersei is Robert's queen, which would make any of his "pale sticky princes" her own children: she gives symbolic birth to them by humanising them and imagining them as grown children—as queen she must be the mother of any royal offspring. Cersei becomes a figure of queer feminine monstrosity: a "cannibalistic mother" (Creed 1993, 109), who births and then consumes her own young.

The specific way in which Cersei describes the violence, "in the darkness I would eat your heirs," adds to her monstrosity by evoking the *vagina dentata*. While Cersei explicitly states that she does not allow Robert to ejaculate inside her, "the darkness" and oral sadism she alludes to conjure images associated with the monstrous female genitals, such as "sharp teeth and bloodied lips" and "a trap, a black hole which threatens to swallow [men] up and cut them to pieces" (Creed 1993, 106–107). Cersei's vaginal violence is also a symbolic castration in the sense that she removes Robert's phallic power by stopping him from producing legitimate heirs. "Cersei usurps the line of succession," argues Spector (2012, 182), by "substituting another man's child for Robert's own, an act that is both treason and the ultimate emasculation." Because that other man is Cersei's own brother, it could be argued that the horror comes from incest. However, because Jaime is Cersei's *twin* brother, the incest is also parthenogenetic: as Patel (2014, 142) argues, "not only has she substituted her own children into the line of succession so that a matriarchal rule will follow, but the children are a product of a relationship with her twin and thus Cersei enacts a form of self-replication or auto-impregnation." By eating Robert's "heirs" as a *vagina dentata*, Cersei swallows his future: she becomes a "black hole which threatens to swallow [men] up and cut them to pieces" (Creed 1993, 106–107). Robert's marital rapes failed to impregnate Cersei and in that way reproduce the patriarchal order, and when she repeats this hegemonic masculine act with Taena she replicates this form of hegemonic masculinity even as she fails to reproduce biologically because she has sex with a female partner. Cersei appears to disrupt patriarchal reproductive systems when she is disempowered through Robert's hegemonic violence and eats his sperm, but when the feudal patriarchy gives her power as queen, she maintains its logics by explicitly reproducing Robert's hegemonic violence in order to further empower herself and banish the feminine Other. The act of violence does not become feminine even though the monstrous feminine mode is used to encourage criticism because her insistent citations of Robert foreground the fact that she views the rape as specifically masculine. The horror that the *vagina dentata* and castrating mother evoke in *A Song of Ice and Fire* is projected onto Cersei's hegemonic violence in the narrative present in which she rapes Taena.

In *Game of Thrones*, Cersei's repetitions of this form of violence are also critiqued through the queer monstrous feminine, although in the film medium both her violence and monstrosity are made more spectacular and she is portrayed as pregnant in the final two seasons. In the season six finale, "The Winds of Winter," Cersei murders the majority of Westerosi nobility in a magical explosion. When Cersei does not appear at the sept where she is to be tried for crimes (including deicide, regicide, and adultery), her cousin Lancel, a member of the Faith Militant, is sent to find her and instead discovers barrels of magical "wildfire" that are about to ignite. The mass violence is reminiscent of Tywin Lannister and his conflict with House Reyne of Castamere, in which the latter house attempted to challenge the former and was entirely obliterated. Cersei makes use of wildfire as a means of repeating her father's hegemonic masculine performance, re-establishing her power, and banishing those who challenge her. She intervenes in the reproduction of the paternal law by destroying a patriarchal institution, the sept, but she does so in order to reproduce the symbolic law in a way of her choosing: through her son Tommen, and after his death through declaring herself as queen. Cersei wants to seize the means of patriarchal reproduction for her own ends, namely, empowering the Lannister family, but she ultimately fails to do so because her last living child kills himself in response to her violence. The violence only produces destruction and it is made terrifying through the tunnel in which the substance is stored, which evokes the *vagina dentata* through its shape and the explosives it harbours, like the "tunnels and caves" hiding "spiders, snakes or bats which attack the unwary" in horror films (Creed 1993, 108).

The image of the *vagina dentata* in *Game of Thrones* works alongside the archaic mother, which is cited in a way that is very similar to how this latter figure appears in the film *Alien* (1979), as Creed analyses it. In *Alien*, the crew of a commercial spaceship investigates the distress signals of another vessel. They find the ship abandoned but filled with rows of eggs. The "womb-like imagery, [and] the long winding tunnels leading to inner chambers" are, for Creed (1993, 19), images whose horror comes from a fear of the archaic mother. In "The Winds of Winter," the barrels of wildfire can be read as "rows of hatching eggs" (19), embryos of destruction that Cersei has planted beneath the city and which will give way to a monstrous birth. Like a woman in labour, the city's "surface is no longer closed, smooth and intact—rather the body looks as if it may tear apart, open out, reveal its innermost depths" (58). As green fire engulfs the city, King's Landing is torn apart literally as its infrastructure crumbles, and symbolically as the religious headquarters and the nobility are destroyed. Cersei's terrorism is not merely an explosion but one rendered abject through association with the female reproductive body. Yet even here, Cersei's masculinity is emphasised. After the explosion, the audience sees Cersei in her chambers watching the mayhem, but her breasts, normatively female morphology, are excluded from the frame for almost the entire scene, and her masculine garb is foregrounded because it takes up a quarter of the frame. These framing choices work alongside the narrative association between Tywin and mass violence to code Cersei's terrorism as masculine, even as viewers are invited to critique it through the monstrous feminine. The horror that Cersei's wildfire explosion inspires is linked to imagery that connotes the reproductive female body as well as her hegemonic violence, and consequently the latter is positioned as monstrous. Cersei's desire to reproduce the patriarchal order and Lannister legacy is reflected in the monstrous womb imagery, and both are shown to lead to nothing but failure and destruction.

Cersei also uses hegemonic violence to dominate those who have wronged her, acts which are similarly made terrifying in *Game of Thrones* through the monstrous feminine. In "The Winds of Winter" (S6E10) and "The Queen's Justice" (S7E3), Cersei tortures and murders Septa Unella, who oversaw her imprisonment by the Faith Militant, and Ellaria Sand, who murdered her daughter Myrcella Baratheon. When speaking with Unella in the dungeon, Cersei makes her enjoyment of violence clear: "I killed your high sparrow, and all his little sparrows, all his septons and all his septas, all his filthy soldiers, because it felt good to watch them burn. It felt good to imagine their shock and their pain. No thought has ever given me greater joy" (S6E10). Cersei enjoys taking her revenge, an act that she views as masculine because her father Tywin was notoriously vengeful, as I have noted. Cersei takes great pleasure in violent domination in this scene and (it is implied) in the one in "The Queen's Justice." Her affective response specifically to dominating the Other and her understanding of mass revenge as masculine marks her violence as hegemonic within the narrative while inviting viewers to view it as subordinate because it is coded as monstrous.

Because Cersei repeats her father's domination-based hegemonic masculinity, her acts of violence are critiqued through the queer monstrous feminine. Both torture scenes take place inside cavernous dungeon rooms that resemble wombs: the brown mottled walls give the space an organic quality, especially when they seem damp as the light shines on them. The dungeon evokes the horror of the abject womb: where Kristeva views the corpse as the epitome of abjection, Creed (1993, 49) contends that it is actually "the womb [...] for it contains a new life form which will pass from inside to outside bringing with it traces of its contamination—blood, afterbirth, faeces." Adding to the scene's abjection is Cersei's costume. In both scenes she wears jewel-encrusted shoulder pads that masculinise her frame and reflect the light from the torches, giving her regal garb a reptilian look that disrupts the binary between human and animal. The abject and the monstrous feminine work in concert to make Cersei's positive affective response to her hegemonic violence disgusting and terrifying: an unacceptable means of performing masculinity. The wombs are prominent as a part of the monstrous feminine mode not because of Cersei's female body but because of her desire for patriarchal reproduction. Both Ellaria's and Unella's torture scenes are tied to reproduction of the Lannister legacy: Cersei avenges Myrcella's death by using the same poison on Ellaria's daughter, and Unella's torture is linked to and takes place right after Cersei's mass murder at the Sept of Baelor. However, both of Cersei's attempts to use violence to reproduce the patriarchal order fail: Myrcella is still dead, and the scene in which Tommen kills himself takes place right after Cersei's terrorism and torture of Unella. Cersei enters into the same cycle of failed hegemonic violence as her cisgender masculine counterparts even as she succeeds in performing hegemonic masculine violence because she repeats her fathers' performative acts and dominates the Other. The violence does not become unacceptable because it is used by a woman; it is unacceptable because Cersei uses violence to empower herself and disempower the Other.

Cersei's violence reinforces patriarchal structures in both *A Song of Ice and Fire* and *Game of Thrones*, and for this reason she becomes trapped within the same cycle of bodily abjection as her male counterparts. In the novels, Cersei's abjection is highlighted in *A Dance with Dragons* when she is punished by the Church. Patel (2014, 144) argues that Cersei becomes abject during her walk of penance, as she has abject objects thrown at her: "they call her dirty names [...] and begin to throw rotten food and even a dead cat that explodes maggots and entrails all over her. The rotten food and dead cat are significant, as Kristeva identifies the corpse as a symbol of abjection." I agree that the walk of penance is where Cersei first becomes publicly abject in the novels but would add that her interior monologue can illuminate the ways in which she has internalised this abjection.

VILE, SCHEMING, EVIL BITCHES?   101

Cersei maintains the emotional repression she learned from Tywin until she imagines seeing an alleged witch from her childhood, Maggy the Frog, in the crowd. The narrator says, "Suddenly the hag was there, standing in the crowd with her pendulous teats and her warty greenish skin, leering with the rest, with malice shining from her crusty yellow eyes" (DwD 999). With her exposed breasts, sickly pallor, and infected eyes, the witch's body is overburdened: it spills forth across the boundaries of past/present, childhood/adulthood, public/private, and sickness/health. Maggy the Frog gave Cersei a prophecy before she came to court as a young noblewoman, and Cersei recalls the witch's words on this walk: "'Queen you shall be,' she hissed, 'until there comes another, younger and more beautiful, to cast you down and take all you hold most dear'" (DwD 999; original emphasis). It is here that Cersei loses her self-control and "there was no stopping the tears" that "burned down the queen's cheeks like acid" (DwD 999). Inner monologue is used to show that Cersei's abjection is not only external but internal, representing the "peak" of abjection: in Kristeva's words, the "subject, weary of fruitless attempts to identify with something on the outside, finds the impossible within; when it finds that the impossible constitutes its very being, that it is none other than abject" (Kristeva 1982, 5). Maggy the Frog's imagined re-emergence forces Cersei to recognise her own abjection, as demonstrated in the scene's narration. Tears, as a liquid that moves from inside to outside the body, are abject, especially for Cersei, who views hegemonic masculinity as unemotional. Tears are rendered horrifying as their border crossing is made explicit: they feel like "acid" corroding Cersei's flesh. Placing one hand across her breasts and the other "down to hide her slit," Cersei "scrambled crab-legged" to the castle (DwD 1000). The word "slit" to describe Cersei's genitals builds on the acidic tears that run down her face, inviting the audience to recognise how Cersei's body has begun to disassemble in her own mind. The particular form of public abjection that Cersei underdoes is also a moment where her assigned gender at birth is made public; she moves to cover her genitals *and* her femaleness, which she sees as being at odds with her masculinity. "Slit" suggests an undoing as well as an openness, a vulnerability, in the stable and closed body that the symbolic order venerates. Such is Cersei's abjection that she sees herself as becoming animalised, "crab-legged," and lacking the constitutive borders that grant her intelligible humanity.

In *Game of Thrones*, Cersei's abjection is expressed through her relationship with Gregor Clegane, a bastardised form of alternative or queer kinship. Like the alternative kinship Butler (1993, 95) discusses, Cersei "repeats in order to remake" the sexist pseudo-medieval system

102   REIMAGINING MASCULINITY AND VIOLENCE

and its violence into a space that allows for her existence by spreading her subjectivity across two sites as Gregor's body is integrated with her own. Gregor's body is tall, muscular, and famously strong: it allows him to access hegemonic masculine acts that Cersei cannot, and so complements her own ability to wield political and class power. From season four, Gregor has been played by Hafþór Júlíus Björnsson, an award-winning professional strongman. The decision to cast Björnsson as Gregor means that his character carries additional meaning in the show: in some scenes he is the epitome of hegemonic masculinity because of his muscular body. In *Game of Thrones*, Gregor functions as Cersei's prosthetic *vagina dentata* and a prosthetic phallus, performing acts of hegemonic violence on her behalf that are presented as penetrative and incorporative through cinematography. The fact that she chooses Gregor, whose body carries these cultural meanings, reflects her own desire to embody hegemonic masculinity however she can, including through a queer prosthesis. The relationship between Cersei and Gregor is queer in a number of ways: the radically fluid gender dynamic, the lack of boundaries between bodies and subjectivities, the way in which Gregor's body enables Cersei to transition from her female body to a hegemonically masculine body. In this case, the queer kinship is toxic because it is non-consensual, hierarchical, and Cersei does not share her power and knowledge nor encourage Gregor to do so. As Cersei enters the category of her choosing, hegemonic masculinity, through her queer kinship bond with Gregor, it is clear that transgender masculinities can be as destructive as cisgender masculinities, although it is not Cersei's transgender desire that makes her masculinity and their kinship monstrous but rather her acts of hegemonic masculine violence. Gregor perpetrates violence on Cersei's behalf, and for this reason their kinship only reproduces patriarchal logics. Cersei fails because she empowers herself regardless of the cost to others and so does not consider pushing her repetition in productive directions— such as "creat[ing] the discursive and social space for a community." Viewers see the monstrous kinship in action during Cersei's torture scenes: when she confronts Septa Unella and Ellaria Sand, she makes lengthy monologues about her violence, but it is Gregor who carries out or oversees the acts in silence.

Violence is the precise point where Cersei's identity is merged with Gregor's: he acts out her desires. Gregor's violence becomes terrifying through its association with the queer monstrous feminine, but Cersei too becomes a figure of horror in this arrangement. She becomes abject because her second body is used to reproduce patriarchal structures through its violence. Her attempts to reproduce this system are limited

VILE, SCHEMING, EVIL BITCHES?

and ultimately fail, as the non-consensual and hierarchical nature of her kinship with Gregor mean that she cannot proliferate her knowledge through him. In spreading her subjectivity to increase her capability for violence, Cersei purposefully disrupts identity as she enacts hegemonic violence. She uses Gregor to carry out these deeds, and the violence becomes the locus of terror because it is the site where their abject identities merge and are made horrifying.

Alongside abjection, Cersei's violence is critiqued in *Game of Thrones* because it is shown to be part of the destructive cycle of dominating hegemonic violence that I have explored in relation to monstrous and sovereign violence. Cersei's death in the final season of *Game of Thrones* echoes the hegemonic violence she used in life, demonstrating that any character, whether male or female, transgender or cisgender, can be critiqued through circular deaths that evoke the queer monstrous feminine and that the fantasy genre context extends this theory by contributing a new animal that can evoke the *vagina dentata*: dragons. When Cersei tortures Septa Unella and the Sandsnakes in "The Queen's Justice" and "The Winds of Winter," her hegemonic violence is critiqued through imagery that cites the *vagina dentata*, as I have noted. A similar process takes place in relation to cisgender masculine characters such as Ramsay Bolton and Gregor Clegane, which demonstrates that *vagina dentata* imagery is used to critique a range of masculine characters rather than only those with female bodies. The same imagery that is used to make Cersei's violence horrifying in life is foregrounded during her death as a means of highlighting the cycle of destruction that individualistic violence brings. Cersei and Jaime encounter a significant number of fossilised dragons as they attempt to flee King's Landing in "The Bells" while Daenerys sets the city ablaze. As Jaime leads Cersei through the warren of tunnels under the Red Keep, they pass through the rooms where the Targaryens' fossilised dragons are stored. The spiked specimens are visible in almost every shot as Jaime and Cersei run through dimly-lit chambers. The association between dark tunnels and dangerous animals is, for Creed (1993, 108), a means of signifying the horror of the *vagina dentata*, although where Creed discusses "spiders, snakes or bats which attack the unwary," it is instead dragon skeletons that make the "dangerous entrance or passageway" (108). While the dragon can also signify the phallus in other contexts, its presence within dark tunnels suggests the toothed vagina, and in that way links Cersei's violence to her death. As in previous scenes, the monstrous feminine operates as a mode: Cersei does not become feminine but rather her attachment to patriarchal reproduction (here signalled through the dangerous vaginal imagery) becomes a source of terror.

The non-diegetic music during Cersei's death scene contributes to the critique of her hegemonic violence by locating the cycle of destruction alongside her reproduction of patriarchal systems. Right before the extreme long shot I have discussed before, viewers see a medium shot of Cersei during which piano notes from the songs "Light of the Seven" and "The Rains of Castamere" are audible. As I have noted, when Cersei blows up the Sept of Baelor in "The Winds of Winter," the song "Light of the Seven" is featured. The musical repetition foregrounds and extends the link between Cersei's domination-based violence and her death. Audiences hear a few bars of the song before it transitions into "The Rains of Castamere," the House Lannister musical theme. As I have noted, in the narrative world the song was written about Tywin's violent revenge against House Reyne of Castamere, and it has since come to carry more general revenge connotations after being featured in the infamous "Red Wedding" scene in which the Freys massacred the Starks (S3E9 "The Rains of Castamere"). The song foregrounds Cersei's connection to Tywin as well as their shared obsession with reproducing the Lannister legacy through hegemonic masculine violence. "The Rains of Castamere" is traditionally played on string instruments, so its reprise on piano alongside "Light of the Seven" links these connotations specifically to Cersei and her own vengeful hegemonic violence. The connection and the musical transition between the two songs reflects the reproduction of the patriarchal system through violence and the destructive loop it creates; it is fitting that "The Rains of Castamere" plays as most of the living members of House Lannister and their unborn heir are killed.

The embodied nature of these destructive cycles of self-oriented hegemonic violence is foregrounded through repeated dialogue during Cersei's death scene. When Cersei realises that she is trapped, she says to Jaime, "I want our baby to live. I want our baby to live. [pause] I want our baby to live" (S6E5 "The Bells"). Cersei's reference to her unborn baby cites the heteronormative pseudo-medieval patriarchy, especially given that she has positioned her child as the future of the Lannister legacy ("The Dragon and the Wolf" S7E7) and later as a future prince/king ("Winterfell" S8E1; "The Last of the Starks" S8E4). The reproduction of the patriarchal Lannister family and the repetitive structures that support it are explicitly raised here, but they are also shown to have failed to produce anything but destruction in the long term. During her life, Cersei performed masculinity through repetition: citing her father through dialogue and costumes was a key way in which her hegemonic masculine violence was marked as masculine in her own mind and for viewers. As she dies, her reliance upon repetition is foregrounded. She repeats her next two lines of dialogue three times each: "Please don't

VILE, SCHEMING, EVIL BITCHES? 105

let me die" and "Not like this" (S6E5). Jaime attempts to soothe her by saying, "Nothing else matters ... nothing else matters ... only us" (S6E5), another instance of repetition that also echoes an earlier conversation in season six (S6E1 "The Red Woman") in which Jaime told Cersei that they would seek a violent revenge after their daughter Myrcella's death: "Fuck everyone who isn't us [...] we're the only ones who matter [...] we're going to take everything there is." The reference to this conversation connects Cersei's death to her individualistic violence throughout previous seasons. Cersei's final moments in the television series cement her reliance on a patriarchal system of reproduction while emphasising the notion that she is trapped within them.

The theme of entrapment is foregrounded through the repeated dialogue loops, non-diegetic music, imagery that connotes the *vagina dentata*, and through Cersei's cause of death: trapped and crushed to death under the weight of the Red Keep, the patriarchal seat of power in Westeros. Cersei's circular death demonstrates that masculine women characters have their hegemonic violence critiqued in exactly the same ways as the sovereign and monstrous cisgender masculine characters; the queer monstrous feminine can be cited during death scenes for female as well as male characters. While Creed's notion of the monstrous feminine is centred on cisgender women, the theory can productively be applied and expanded to cisgender male characters (such as the sovereign and monstrous characters I have analysed) and a variety of transgender and AFAB characters. In decoupling femininity from female bodies and the monstrous feminine mode from gender essentialism, I have demonstrated that the monstrous feminine need not innately be linked to cisgender women monsters but can instead be understood as a monstrous mode. While reproduction (and especially failed reproduction) is central to Cersei's violence and its critique, it does not make her feminine—rather, it highlights her attachment to the reproduction of patriarchal structures. The similarities between Cersei's circular death and that of the monstrous and sovereign masculine characters demonstrates that it is not Cersei's femaleness that leads her to be critiqued and killed but her repetition of a dominating and self-oriented hegemonic masculine violence.

Cersei's actions may be read as empowering or subversive in both *A Song of Ice and Fire* and *Game of Thrones* because she challenges patriarchal institutions such as the Church, marriage, and the feudal system even as she reifies them in new ways. An AFAB ruler is significant within the fantasy genre, even if she proves to be, as Margery Tyrell claims, "a vile, scheming, evil bitch" (FfC 738). Almost all of Cersei's decisions are hastily made and poorly considered, which may suggest to readers that female masculinities are poor imitations of male masculinities; or

106 REIMAGINING MASCULINITY AND VIOLENCE

worse, that women should be excluded from power because they cannot rule effectively. However, it is hegemonic violence that leads the queer monstrous feminine to be projected onto Cersei's body. Rather than contesting dominant and oppressive gender regimes, she retraces the steps of the patriarchy in both the novels and their television adaptation, and where the latter has overtaken Martin's series, she has achieved the same monstrous ends.

The Magic Sword

Brienne of Tarth, the tall and muscular warrior who is originally encountered serving King Renly Baratheon as a kingsguard during the War of the Five Kings in both *A Song of Ice and Fire* and *Game of Thrones*, enacts masculinity through knighthood, especially protecting others through chivalric violence. After leaving the island of Tarth, Brienne serves multiple characters: Renly Baratheon, Catelyn Stark, and Sansa Stark (and, in the television series, also Arya Stark). Because Brienne performs masculinity with a female body she is subordinated by other characters in Westeros throughout *A Song of Ice and Fire* and most of *Game of Thrones*. When the conditions for legitimising the patriarchy change because of the impending long night in the final two seasons of the television series, the self-oriented hegemonic masculinity is replaced by an Other-oriented hegemonic masculinity and the living/dead and warrior/non-warrior binaries become central and the masculine/feminine binary is played down. Under these conditions, Brienne's masculine acts can be understood as complicit with the new hegemonic masculinity, as demonstrated by her acceptance into institutions like the court at Winterfell, knighthood, and the Kingsguard.

While these quests dominate Brienne's narrative arc, her characterisation in *A Song of Ice and Fire* and *Game of Thrones* is intimately bound with her relation to knighthood and her sword, which are both fantasy conventions and symbols of her masculinity. Brienne identifies as masculine, and when she receives her sword Oathkeeper—a symbol of honour, phallic masculinity, and knighthood—this identity is positively affirmed. Brienne's position as a character who collapses categories even before she gains a magic sword is demonstrated when she uses the figure of the knight to move from one form of gender performativity, high-class femininity, to another, masculinity.

In both *A Song of Ice and Fire* and *Game of Thrones*, Brienne regularly denounces the title of "Lady" (here meaning high-class woman) and while she also notes that she is "no knight," she rejects this title because

VILE, SCHEMING, EVIL BITCHES?

she has not sworn knightly oaths or been otherwise officially interpolated into knighthood rather than because of the title's implied masculinity. In the television series, Brienne dismisses the title of "knight" purely on the grounds of "tradition" right before she is knighted by Jaime in "A Knight of the Seven Kingdoms" (S8E2). Yvonne Tasker and Lindsay Steenberg (2016, 176) contend that these "ritualistic denials [...] signal her uneasy and unsettling combination of both categories," and brush off Brienne's "assumption of knightly regalia" as "a complicated kind of cross-dressing; neither disguise nor burlesque, but an outward indicator of her inner commitment to chivalric ideals" (178). I agree that Brienne's clothing reflects her interest in chivalry and knighthood. But this interest shapes and is shaped by her identification as masculine. In *Game of Thrones*, Brienne claims on multiple occasions that she is "not a lady," and in the novels Jaime asks if Brienne has siblings and she says, "No. I was my father's only s—child." Jaime responds, "*Son*, you meant to say. Does he think of you as a son? You make a queer sort of daughter, to be sure." And the narrator says that Brienne "reminded him of Tyrion in some queer way, though at first blush two people could scarcely be any more dissimilar" (SoS1 155). In both texts Brienne makes it clear that she does not identify as feminine, while Jaime's repeated use of the word "queer" in the novels highlights Brienne's queer gender as well as her potential homosexuality.

Brienne's possible same-sex attraction is noted by Halberstam (2019, para. 7) in a blog post about *Game of Thrones*. Halberstam refers to Brienne as a "blue-ribbon lesbian," although they suggest that she has "given up" this "status" by having sex with Jaime Lannister in "The Last of the Starks" (S8E4). Putting aside the gatekeeping implication that having sex with a man once automatically and forever precludes one from lesbianism, I suggest that Brienne's insistent heterosexual pairings inadvertently highlight her queer gender. The novel and television series suggest that one of the cornerstones of Brienne's character is her love for the deceased (and implicitly gay) Renly. Rather than confirming Brienne's heterosexuality, her attraction to Renly may signal Brienne's transness: she desires a queer man because she is a queer man. In the television series, Brienne is subject to advances from a wildling man called Tormund Giantsbane, which are earnest though played for comedic value. Yet the comedy comes from Brienne's clear disinterest, which is hardly a convincing sign of heterosexuality. Finally, in *A Song of Ice and Fire*, there are some scenes which arguably point towards a budding romantic relationship between Brienne and Jaime Lannister, which have been expanded in *Game of Thrones* (Shaham 2015). Reading this relationship through a trans lens, the similarity in both texts between

108   REIMAGINING MASCULINITY AND VIOLENCE

Brienne's and Jaime's appearance (both tall, blonde, muscular) may signal a braided desire to *be* Jaime and to *be with* Jaime. In the television series, the relationship is acknowledged and consumated in season eight, and even this seemingly heterosexual scene may be read queerly. The scene begins with a drinking game between Brienne, Jaime, Tyrion, and Pod, in which Tyrion asks Brienne whether she "ever slept with a man? Or a woman" (S8E4). After a moment of silence Brienne excuses herself, but Tyrion's comment holds open a queer space for her character. Jaime follows Brienne and they speak in her chambers, and even here her queerness is emphasised. The scene begins with a close-up of Brienne's sword and chainmail, which pans to a shot of Brienne stoking the fire. When Jaime enters the room, the shot is framed so as to show that Brienne is the taller of the two. Right before they kiss, Jaime says, "I've never slept with a knight before" (S8E4). Brienne's masculinity ruptures the heterosexual consummation scene and pushes it in queer directions for both characters. This type of characterisation is not isolated to this encounter. For example, when Brienne is forced to wear a dress in season two, she looks visibly uncomfortable, and in the same scene in *A Storm of Swords*, Jaime observes that "Brienne looked more like a man in a gown" (SoS2 49): she retains her masculinity despite societal policing. Brienne is presented as a character who collapses categories, and this queerness is amplified when she gains Oathkeeper.

Brienne's characterisation as transgender in *Game of Thrones* is further complicated by casting decisions, namely, the fact that she is played by Gwendoline Christie, a cisgender model and actress. Casting has a significant effect on how audiences understand characters in film adaptations, especially when the casting runs antithetical to the source text in relation to race and/or gender (Knox 2018; Brodie 2014; Genovese 2019). The decision to cast Christie is in some ways part of a broader trend in *Game of Thrones* to make characters more conventionally attractive than they are described in the novel, as was also the case with casting the actor Peter Dinklage in the role of infamously unattractive Tyrion Lannister. However, in Christie's case the casting decision also has implications for the way viewers understand Brienne's gender and sexuality. Christie becomes a prosthesis through which the character Brienne embodies cisgender womanhood as she is adapted into the televisual medium. While Christie's Brienne is more masculine than most of the AFAB characters in the series, she is also slim and has a conventionally attractive feminine face. She is a far cry from the way Catelyn Stark describes Brienne in the novel: "her features were broad and coarse, her teeth prominent and crooked, her mouth too wide [...] her nose had been broken more than once" (CoK 312), with a body

VILE, SCHEMING, EVIL BITCHES?

"broad of hip and thick of limb, with hunched muscular shoulders and no bosom to speak of" (CoK 315). Even when Brienne wears feminine attire in the novel, characters like Jaime observe that she looks more like a man in a dress than a cisgender woman (SoS2 49). When Christie plays Brienne in *Game of Thrones*, the character embodies masculinity in a different and less explicit way. Audiences are still invited to view Brienne as a masculine character in *Game of Thrones*, but her masculinity is performed through props, costumes, and acts like chivalry and violence rather than through a masculine physique.

In both *Game of Thrones* and *A Song of Ice and Fire*, Brienne's knightly masculinity is revealed as performative through her use of prostheses, specifically the sword. The sword is a unique site through which to bridge the divide between performativity and transgender theory because it is discursive, embodied, and performative. Writing on swords and AFAB characters in fantasy, Jes Battis (2006, para. 17) argues that in Tamora Pierces' *Song of the Lioness* series (1983–1988), "Alanna's sword, the mythical weapon called Lightning, becomes the representation of her phallic power, the most important piece of artifice in her performance as a male knight." While Alanna quite literally performs her status as a "male knight" because she does not identify as a boy but pretends to be one for the purposes of receiving knightly training, the sword is the central prosthesis that allows her to convince others of her masculinity because its shape can carry phallic power for the owner. Attention is drawn to the phallus as "an idealization, one which no body can adequately approximate," which for Butler (1993, 53) makes the phallus transferable and open to a "aggressive reterritorialization" that disrupt its link to normative masculinity.

Such a reterritorialisation takes place in *A Song of Ice and Fire* and *Game of Thrones* when Brienne gains her sword. The sword's function as a performative act makes Brienne's violence intelligible, and it allows her "to be" (Prosser 1998, 32) in the sense that it gives her a means of entering the embodied category of knight. The sword empowers Brienne to enter her desired identity (a masculine body via a phallic prosthesis), but this entering is shown to be a process that is never complete. Moreover, the sword destabilises all of these categories because it is so saturated with meaning, denaturalising the violent domination with which the sword is commonly associated and making room for it to be re-forged. The sword is an icon of "knightly masculinity," an identification that is "a perpetual work of progress" (Larrington 2017, 269–270)—a point of similarity between Butlerian gender performativity and the notion of transition in transgender scholarship. Knighthood is a specifically phallic form of performativity and the sword is the object through which class, ability, and masculinity materialise. Brienne's relationship to Oathkeeper reveals that it also produces knighthood. When phallic swords are wielded by women who identify as masculine, the weapons can be understood as prostheses that allow characters to bridge the gap between transgender identification, performativity, and embodiment.

In *A Song of Ice and Fire* and *Game of Thrones,* the sword makes Brienne's violence intelligible as violence, and it provides an embodied way to enter knightly subjectivity. At the same time, the sword destabilises all of these categories because it is so saturated with meaning, denaturalising the self-oriented hegemonic violence with which the sword is commonly associated and allowing it to be remade by Brienne. She cites knightly masculinity as her model for gendered conduct, including as she reforges the relationship between masculinity and violence. Rather than reinforcing patriarchal structures, Brienne uses violence to care for others, including lower-class women and children. Brienne's ability to rework Westerosi masculinity to make the world more liveable is enabled by her characterisation as transgender, a non-normative subject position that both excludes and frees her from the confines of hegemonic masculinity. Her masculinity is not privileged because it is queer, but rather because queerness gives Brienne the option to perform masculinity more flexibly. Because of the demands of her quests, Brienne comes into contact with the abject, but she is not contaminated by it: she maintains her constitutive borders and her violence is reproduced through alternative kinship. Brienne's knightly violence offers a means of (re)working masculinity as it is figured through violence, so that it is performed along healthier lines.

There is a difference between Butlerian gender performativity and transgender theory when it comes to masculine subjects who are AFAB—being versus performing—that is relevant to understanding Brienne's character in *A Song of Ice and Fire* and *Game of Thrones.* The amalgamation of performativity and physicality makes Brienne a useful character through which to bridge the gap between transgender theories, which are often concerned with recentralising the gendered body, and with challenging Butler's argument that the body comes into being through the repetition of stylised acts. Many transgender scholars remain sceptical about the value of performativity because they associate it with theatricality and playfulness and view it as antithetical to "transsexuals who seek very pointedly to be non-performative, to be constative, quite simply to be" (Prosser 1998, 32; also see Namaste 1996; Rubin 2003). This is not to say that transgender theories reject poststructuralism; the field has been heavily influenced by poststructuralist thought, and scholars including Susan Stryker (1994; 2004; 2008) utilise this critical lens in their scholarship. Brienne's relationship to her sword reveals that performativity is intimately bound with the desire "to be" (Prosser 1998, 32): the sword, as genre convention and performative prosthesis, allows her better to embody masculinity.

In this sense, the sword for Brienne is a phallic prosthesis that allows her to enter the embodied history of knighthood, itself a fantasy convention. Brienne does not appropriate discourses and the types of dominating violence they encourage by ownership of the sword but creates an embodied queer phallic power that troubles the lingering connection between masculinity and violence by showing that masculinity is not contingent upon a male body but can be gifted, bought, and forged. Jeanne Hamming (2001, 331) makes a similar argument about dildos, showing how the phallus can be bought in "basically any size, shape, texture and color they desire. [...] A dildo never suffers from impotence or premature ejaculation and most perform feats men only fantasize about." Queerness can (but does not necessarily) denaturalise normative understandings of the gendered body and open space for a broader range of bodies, desires, and practices. An "aggressive reterritorialization" (Butler 1993, 53)—such as that which occurs when female people buy penises, or when they are given swords—reveals that these objects are culturally linked to male embodied masculinity, but that this link can be contested as different subjects engage in such embodiments. The sword symbolises the masculine (and masculinised) history Brienne is entering: a history of bodies and acts that can be made visible through the knight.

It is important to establish the relationship between transgender and Brienne because the way she remakes domination-centred hegemonic violence through her sword is relevant to my argument about subversion. The sword carries a substantial number of meanings. From a gender perspective, it can be read as a phallus, a normative masculine weapon, and a detachable phallus, and/or a prosthesis for transmasculine subjects; and from a fantasy genre perspective, an individual sword is part of a history of swords used for great deeds, signals heroism, and carries the symbolic weight of its name. Brienne's sword allows audiences to see the ways in which both the fantasy genre and masculinity and maleness are comprised of a multiplicity of enactments. Within the pseudo-medieval fantasy text, the sword may be seen to function in a similar way as hormones and gender affirmation surgery in the real world. Writing about his own experiences in the gender clinic, J.R. Latham (2017, 178) argues that sex is "constantly being made and remade in and through particular situations, contexts, practices and encounters." I contend that

112   REIMAGINING MASCULINITY AND VIOLENCE

in fantasy fiction the sword is one such practice, which, like the clinical experience Latham (178) discusses, can reveal *"how* sex is *enacted multiply* across a range of situations. Theorising the multiplicity of sex in this way lets us see how particular possibilities for 'changing sex' become viable, while other ways of being trans are foreclosed." The sword is one way in which masculinity, maleness, and fantasy are enacted in *A Song of Ice and Fire* and *Game of Thrones* and reveals how the genre opens possibilities for radical gendered embodiment.

Adding to these meanings in the novels is Brienne's understanding of the sword as magic. While resting for the night during her quest, Brienne takes her sword out and admires it: "Gold glimmered yellow in the candlelight and rubies smouldered red. When she slid Oathkeeper from the ornate scabbard, Brienne's breath caught in her throat. Black and red the ripples ran, deep within the steel. *Valyrian steel, spell-forged.* It was a sword fit for a hero" (FfC 78; original emphasis). Phrases such as "gold glimmered" and "rubies smouldered" give the scene a lyrical tone that evokes storytelling, denaturalising the narrative. Brienne's description of Oathkeeper as *"spell-forged"* leaves no doubt that this is a magical weapon, and she repeatedly refers to Oathkeeper as a "magic sword" (FfC 327; 716). The sword's characterisation as magic invites readers to view Brienne as a special hero within the narrative while enhancing its potential for destabilising gendered categories. The latter is still true of the sword in *Game of Thrones*, which does not encourage its viewers to see the sword as magic. The intense polyvalence that surrounds the weapon in both texts is useful from a Butlerian perspective because it reveals the unnaturalness and contingency of the patriarchy and the fantasy genre. When a sword is owned by a character such as Brienne who disrupts gender categories even without this accoutrement, its subversive potential is amplified. For this reason, Brienne and her sword have significant potential for rearticulating citational acts in ways that disrupt both the fantasy genre and patriarchal structures. This potential is oriented around Brienne's caring chivalric violence and the proliferation of her knowledges and practices through her entry into queer kinship systems. The sword's function as a performative act allows Brienne's violence to be intelligible as violence, and it allows her "to be," to appropriate Prosser (1998, 32), in the sense that it gives her an embodied way to enter the category that she desires, a knight. At the same time, the sword destabilises all of these categories because it is so saturated with genre and gender meanings, denaturalising the hegemonic violence with which the sword is commonly associated and allowing it to be remade by Brienne. While the sword is performative, it has embodied, material, and psychological effects on or for Brienne,

VILE, SCHEMING, EVIL BITCHES?   113

and offers a way of connecting performativity theory to transgender theory more broadly. The prosthesis allows Brienne to embody chivalric knightly masculinity more fully: recognition by her peer in the form of a traditionally patriarchal weapon gives her greater access to the phallus, as well as violence, class status, and martial prowess because of the sword's quality.

In *Game of Thrones*, the prosthesis plays a more central role in Brienne's embodiment and heroism as Jaime gives her a tailored suit of armour and a squire as well as Oathkeeper (S4E4 "Oathkeeper"). The prosthetic emphasis is spread among multiple sites because the visual vocabulary in the television series often links swords with phallic violence, such as in the case of the sovereigns and their swords. Brienne's armour is tinged with blue for her native Tarth, and the breastplate is cut and shaped as if the wearer has no breasts. Like the sword, the armour can be viewed as a prosthesis: it is a physical object that allows Brienne to shift her embodied personhood so that it can better achieve knightly masculinity. Jaime comments, "I hope I got your measurements right," as if confirming that she does want to pursue this gender identification— which is implied by her acceptance of the armour. According to John Cameron (2014, 198), "the gift of this sword signifies just how much Jaime [...] has come to respect Brienne." The respect is directed towards Brienne's honour as well as her knightly masculinity.

When Jaime presents Brienne with the sword and armour in the White Tower (the historical home of the Kingsguard), the *mise en scène* foreshadows her future heroism. Brienne walks slowly towards the armour with an open mouth and gently touches the metal, then vows, "I'll find her. For Lady Catelyn. [Pause] And for you" (S4E4). Famous swords don the wall behind Brienne, and candles are visible behind Jaime's head, emphasising the sacred role of weaponry among knights as well as the connection between masculinity, swords, and knighthood. Thanks to Jaime, "Brienne is marked by the iconography of knightly prowess—and the close of the fourth Season sees her wearing armor, with a Valyrian steel sword (that she has named Oathkeeper), and a loyal, if perhaps unskilled, squire, Podrick" (Tasker and Steenberg 2016, 176). Thanks to the prostheses Jaime provides, Brienne is better able to pursue her quest to find and protect the Stark girls. Yet Brienne's characterisation indicates that she would have pursued the quest even without this additional prosthesis, which demonstrates that neither the sword nor the phallic power it offers, nor even the literal penis, is necessary for performing masculinity.

For all that the sword draws attention to Brienne's gendered embodiment in both *A Song of Ice and Fire* and *Game of Thrones*, it

114   REIMAGINING MASCULINITY AND VIOLENCE

also directs the audience's attention to her violence. Brienne receives Oathkeeper from Jaime, who charges her with "find[ing] Sansa first, and get[ing] her somewhere safe. How else are the two of us going to make good our stupid vows to your precious dead Lady Catelyn?" (SoS2 344). In the television series, Jaime is less brash but similarly uses chivalric logic to persuade Brienne: "You swore an oath to return the Stark girls to their mother" (S4E4 "Oathkeeper"). The sword is from the outset tied to notions of "good" and chivalrous "vows," foreshadowing the effects that her violence will have on the world. Brienne's reworking of Westerosi hegemonic masculinity is emphasised when Jaime explains the sword's origins. In *Game of Thrones*, he says, "it was reforged from Ned Stark's sword. You'll use it to defend Ned Stark's daughter." The brief dialogue references an earlier scene that was added to the television series in which Tywin gives Oathkeeper to Jaime in an attempt to bring him back into the patriarchal fold (S4E1 "Two Swords"). "When Ned Stark died, his greatsword was given to the King's Justice. [...] my father [...] had Ice melted down and reforged. There was enough metal for two blades. You're holding one. So you'll be defending Ned Stark's daughter with Ned Stark's own steel, if that makes any difference to you" (SoS2 434–435). *A Song of Ice and Fire* explicitly draws attention to the sword's patriarchal lineage at this moment, highlighting the way in which Brienne intervenes in this process. Ned Stark's name is repeated three times as Jaime gives Oathkeeper to Brienne, citing his flawed sovereign violence as well as his phallic power. Yet the fact that his greatsword is "reforged" speaks not only to remaking the sword, but to the potential for (re)imaging Eddard's violence, the law of the father, and its connections to the phallus.

Brienne cites chivalric masculinity: a collective set of practices associated with medieval knighthood in which courtesy, respect, prowess, and honour are expected of the subject. Through Brienne, chivalry is reinvigorated in *A Song of Ice and Fire* and *Game of Thrones* as a non-binarising and mutually beneficial masculine resource. Brienne has no specific human reference point for her masculinity. She mentions her father Lord Selwyn Tarth, Jaime, and her master-at-arms Ser Goodwin, but she does not hold these men as models for masculine conduct as Cersei does with Tywin and Robert. Brienne's emotional and geographical distance from her biological father and her lack of a husband give her a critical distance from heteronormative patriarchal kinship and this provides her additional room to negotiate her own masculinity. Instead, she cites the concept of the knight: as Tasker and Steenberg (2016, 175) argue, Brienne "embodies many legacies of medievalism that have shaped the fantasy genre and the nostalgic view of the past formed by codes of chivalry and ideals of courtly love and honorable war."

Brienne's character is certainly informed by "codes of chivalry," but because of her category-collapsing gender identity, they can be removed from the nostalgic model, and the patriarchal version of chivalry that is critiqued by feminists who correctly align it with male supremacy and oppressive gender binaries (Hackney 2015). The act of protecting others forces one subject into the discursive position of victim and the other as protector, and Elyce Rae Helford (2000) argues that, even when AFAB characters are protectors, the protector/protected binary demands a victim, and that victim is almost always a woman. Yet even as Brienne repeats the protector/protected binary, her chivalric practices are embedded within an enactment of caring masculinity. Caring is "a complex web of different forms of labour deployed in emotional relationships of varying significance and imbuing a sense of belonging and identity" (Hanlon 2012, 41). Brienne's masculinity can be understood through what Hanlon (2012, 31) defines as "caring for," "the provision of personal care services, nursing care and other work [...] central to the provision of interpersonal needs" and "caring about": "the other-centred disposition or identity that care work engenders." Brienne often enacts masculinity in other-centred ways and uses violence to provide others with bodily protection. Where masculinity scholars such as Hanlon (2012) and Karla Elliott (2015) have theorised caring masculinity in the context of cisgender men and domestic labour tasks such as cleaning and toileting, Brienne's character offers a way of expanding this theory to transgender identities and to unexpected labour tasks like violence. Brienne's violence is always other-centred and she uses it to empower others: she repeats the connection between masculinity and violence as she remakes it. Brienne's chivalry in *A Song of Ice and Fire* and *Game of Thrones* operates in the same way that Butler describes being at once produced by and resistant to dominant gender norms: being "occupied by such terms and yet occupying them oneself risks a complicity, a repetition, a relapse into injury, but it is also the occasion to work the mobilizing power of injury, of an interpellation one never chose" (Butler 1993, 83). Between reproducing women's victimisation and remaking chivalry, Brienne negotiates the association of masculinity and hegemonic violence established by many male-embodied characters into a productive marker of heroism that rejects its heterosexist underpinnings. It is Brienne's chivalric and caring values and practices that make her masculine violence heroic, where Cersei's fails and is made monstrous.

For Brienne, these chivalric codes are the model after which her own masculinity is repeated. She regularly insists that she wants "to

116   REIMAGINING MASCULINITY AND VIOLENCE

be a knight" (FfC 238, 240), and acts accordingly. During her quest to return Jaime to King's Landing, she comes across "a live oak full of dead women," and tells her companions, "I'll leave no innocents to be food for crows" (SoS1 25). Similarly, in *Game of Thrones*, Brienne and Jaime encounter hanged prostitutes, and when Jaime asks why Brienne has stopped, she says that she is "burying them" (S2E10 "Valar Morghulis"). Though Brienne is interrupted before she can bury the women, her readiness to tend their bodies is an act of care. Brienne also criticises the (many) male-bodied knights who fail to act chivalrously: *"Old or young, a true knight is sworn to protect those who are weaker than himself* [sic]*, or die in the attempt"* (FfC 526; original emphasis). In *A Song of Ice and Fire*, Brienne views masculinity as that which is performed through chivalric codes, knighthood, and protecting others, and rejects those who fail to live up to this standard. In *Game of Thrones*, Brienne critiques other lords' lack of chivalry to Podrick on their quest: "All I ever wanted was to fight for a lord I believed in. All the good lords are dead and the rest are monsters" (S5E1 "The Wars to Come"). Brienne has experienced the harsh realities of her world: bullied, harassed, and threatened with sexual violence from a young age, she consciously chooses to stand by her idealised version of knighthood and fight for a worthy liege despite knowing that most of the characters around her do not. The concept of chivalric knighthood is Brienne's point of masculine reference: she does not encounter any "true" knights or living lords who are not "monsters" and it is therefore without a purported "original" that informs her gendered actions. Her lack of a stable citation point is itself a queer position that enables her to rework her own masculinity. Writing on the as yet unfinished novels, Charles Hackney (2015, 139–140) argues that "although [Brienne] is never anointed as a knight due to her sex, in every other sense she lives according to the chivalric code, and is a far better exemplar of honour than most of her male counterparts." Brienne is formally anointed in the final season of *Game of Thrones* (S8E2 "A Knight of the Seven Kingdoms") when her masculinity becomes recognised under the new hegemonic masculinity as fighting skills and protecting others become paramount because of the battle against the white walkers. Brienne chooses to interpret this chivalric code in ways that enable others to break free from patriarchal repetition. Her violence makes the world easier to live in and she is ultimately given the most revered knightly position in Westeros, Captain of the Kingsguard ("S8E6 "The Iron Throne").

While the sword is the central item that cements Brienne's masculinity, it is not the crux, as is demonstrated by the fact that she continues to engage in chivalric violence even when she knows that she lacks sufficient weapons because she enacts her masculinity primarily through chivalry. When Jaime and Brienne fight in the bear pit at Harrenhal, their conversation over the presence/absence of phallic swords highlights the fact that while neither Jaime nor Brienne can perform phallic masculinity—because they are female or disabled, but also because it is an impossible ideal that no one can embody—they choose to use violent care to protect one another. In both the novel and television series, the sword is the central point of measure for each character's capability in the fight. When Jaime jumps into the bear pit in the novel, Brienne resists his help, saying, "You get behind. I have the sword," although Jaime points out that it is "a sword with no point and no edge": "useless" (SoS2 47). Likewise, in *Game of Thrones*, Jaime has confidence in Brienne's ability to protect herself with a phallic weapon— until he realises that her captor "gave her a wooden sword" (S3E7 "The Bear and the Maiden Fair"). Jaime's lack of any kind of weapon reflects the recent loss of his sword hand, the body part which allowed him to access hegemonic violence. Brienne's "wooden sword"/"sword with no point and no edge" speaks to her reliance upon prostheses to perform masculinity: like a practice sword, she appears from a distance to embody phallic masculinity, but upon closer inspection that embodiment is only partial. The same is true of Jaime, meaning that this partiality is not an issue unique to Brienne: the embodiment of the ideal is always incomplete. Brienne's lack of phallic power is presumed to make her vulnerable, an assumption that presents the phallus as the source of all masculine power. However, Brienne's queer relationship to masculinity means that she is not dissuaded when she loses access to her phallic sword; she knows that masculinity is not defined by the presence of a penis or phallic prostheses, nor is masculinity so easily classified as absent or present.

Along with using masculine violence to aid others, Brienne actively challenges the patriarchal systems that dominate the pseudo-medieval world. In both the televisions series and novels, Brienne pauses her quest with Jaime to bury a group of hanged prostitutes, but in *Game of Thrones* she also comes face to face with their murderers (S2E10 "Valar Morghulis"). Sexual violence is woven throughout the scene; before they see the women Jaime implies that Brienne wishes someone were strong enough to overpower and rape her because she wants to know what it "feels like to be a woman," and right afterwards the pair pause as they see the corpses dangling from a tree. The abrupt transition highlights the sharp contrast between Brienne's ability to resist sexual violence through her class and knightly training and the prostitutes' vulnerability as working-class women. Brienne registers her comparative privilege in the pseudo-medieval world and pauses to bury the women, but before she can untie the rope, the three men who killed them return. They laugh when they realise Brienne is a woman and continue to insult her throughout the scene. When she attempts to leave, they ask her what she thinks of "these beauties"—the corpses—and Brienne responds, "I hope you gave them quick deaths." Their leader says, "Two of them we did, yeah." Brienne again attempts to leave, but the men realise that she is transporting the infamous Jaime Lannister and she must fight them. She kills the first two men quickly, but when she approaches their leader, she asks, "two quick deaths?" and draws her sword, which she slowly plunges through the man's torso. Viewers are encouraged to see this violence as masculine because of the prominence of the sword within the shots, Brienne's masculine costume, and Brienne's clear desire to protect the dead women's honour. Brienne's decision to repeat the men's violence and dialogue is subversive in the sense that it reproduces dominating hegemonic violence "in directions that reverse and displace their originating aims" (Butler 1993, 83): to punish rather than to perpetrate sexual violence against women. While Brienne thus reinforces the link between masculinity and violence, she also contests the notion that such violence must be used for domination: instead, she uses violence to care for the women and their honour by treating their corpses with respect.

In *Game of Thrones*, Brienne's resistance to abjection is more ambiguous, especially when she enacts sovereign violence against King Stannis Baratheon. After Brienne finds Stannis wounded in the woods, she accuses him of murdering her former liege Renly Baratheon, and he affirms his guilt. Brienne says, "In the name of Renly of House Baratheon, first of his name, rightful King of the Andals and the first men, Lord of the Seven Kingdoms and Protector of the Realm, I Brienne of Tarth sentence you to die" (S5E10 "Mother's Mercy"). In citing Renly and acting as his vassal, Brienne's murder becomes sovereign violence, a highly masculine act in Westeros. She carries it out almost perfectly: Stannis confesses his violation of the law, and Brienne uses Oathkeeper to restore its borders.

Yet there is some ambiguity around Brienne's sovereign violence. The objectiveness that is promised by sovereign violence is absent. Brienne was in love with Renly, and when she swears herself to Catelyn in season two she implies that she wishes to avenge his death (S2E5 "The Ghost in Harrenhal"), making her sovereign violence an act of revenge. Brienne's phallic desire to dominate Stannis in vengeance is hinted at through the sword's angle to her groin. The music adds another level of complexity. The song, "The Old Gods and the New," plays from the moment Brienne

VILE, SCHEMING, EVIL BITCHES? 119

sentences Stannis, a song that draws attention to Brienne's multiple oaths: to Renly, as well as to Catelyn Stark. The two oaths are brought into conflict in this scene because Brienne must sideline her oath to protect Sansa while she executes Stannis. In season five, Brienne attempts to save Sansa from Ramsay Bolton, and covertly instructs her to light a candle in her window when she wishes to be rescued. Brienne is watching Winterfell when she hears that she may be able to avenge Renly and chooses to leave her post to fulfil this quest. Moments after she turns away, the candle is lit, signalling Sansa's plea for help. The song "The Old God and the New" cites Catelyn because it was most often linked to her earlier in the series, which reminds viewers that Brienne has missed Sansa's call for help in order to avenge the long-deceased Renly. The complexity of Brienne's multiple oaths is highlighted and her sovereign violence becomes ambiguous: she fulfils one by avenging the deceased Renly but fails to protect the living Sansa. Brienne's citation of Renly as she executes Stannis raises questions as to whether a dead sovereign's name can be used to legitimise sovereign violence. Brienne's position as the sovereign's representative is ambivalent, much like Jon's when he murders Daenerys in season eight. No clear answers are provided for either character, and further ambivalence is added when Stannis tells Brienne to "Do your duty." Stannis is portrayed as cold and hyper-conservative throughout the series, so his sanctioning his own execution adds a further layer of uncertainty around whether Brienne's sovereign violence is just.

Further ambiguity enters the scene through a rapid editing transition that stops Brienne from encountering the abject on screen. As Brienne makes the killing blow, the shot is abruptly intercut with a shot of Ramsay Bolton killing a nameless Baratheon soldier. The transition adds a layer of ambivalence: on the one hand, the quick cutaway means that Brienne never comes into contact with the abject (blood, corpse, and so on) nor has her own borders blurred by them—unlike the Stark sovereigns. A similar ambiguity is present when Brienne fights Sandor Clegane in season four: after (seemingly) killing the man, the body falls from a cliff face and so Brienne does not come into close contact with the abject corpse (S4E10 "The Children"). On the other hand, transposing Brienne's violence onto Ramsay's—a monstrous and dishonourable sadist—may speak to a broader critique of all forms of violence. These contradictory meanings in *Game of Thrones* lead to an irresolution over the meaning of the association of violence and masculinity as Brienne enacts both.

Because Brienne uses violence as a means of empowering others, she does not become abject even when she comes into contact with objects

120   REIMAGINING MASCULINITY AND VIOLENCE

and acts that might otherwise undo her subjectivating borders. When she defends a band of orphan children from the Bloody Mummers in *A Song of Ice and Fire*, she defeats several men and is then overpowered by Biter, who begins to attack her face: "When [Biter's teeth] closed on the soft meat of her cheek, she hardly felt it. [...] Biter's mouth tore free, full of blood and flesh. He spat, grinned, and sank his pointed teeth into her flesh again" (FfC 633). The blood, spit, and animalistic "pointed teeth" disrupt the binaries between inside/outside the body and human/animal, and so present the moment as grotesque. The scene becomes even more horrifying when Biter begins to eat Brienne's flesh: "This time he chewed and swallowed. *He is eating me*, she realized [...] *It will be finished soon* [...] *Then it will not matter if he eats me*" (FfC 633; original emphasis).

For Kristeva (1982, 79), cannibalism represents a lack of "respect for the body of the other, my fellow man, my brother." It blurs the boundaries between inside/outside the body, living/dead, and human/animal. We may expect Brienne to become abject when she becomes the subject of cannibalism, but her borders are quickly restored. Her wounds are tended by her rescuers, the Brotherhood Without Banners, who choose to help her specifically because she used caring violence to protect the children: "If not for you, only corpses might have remained at the inn by the time that Lem and his men got back. *That* was why Jeyne dressed your wounds, mayhaps. Whatever else you may have done, you won those wounds honorably, in the best of causes" (FfC 769–770; original emphasis). Because Brienne used other-oriented violence, she is deemed worthy of medical treatment that allows her to resist abjection. Her wounds are quickly "dressed" and linked to knightly masculinity rather than broken borders.

In *Game of Thrones*, Brienne is similarly shown to resist abjection because of her caring masculinity and her connections to others, although in this case it is during the battle against the army of the living dead in "The Long Night" (S8E3). It is Brienne's embrace of the Other that saves her from abjection, as in the novels. Brienne is overwhelmed by white walkers, moments into the battle in "The Long Night," and in a brief medium shot, audiences see Jaime turn backwards to check on her, where he and the audience see white walkers running over her and appearing to envelop her in their abject onslaught. Jaime runs over to Brienne and kills the wights with his sword, freeing her from becoming a living corpse. Though the scene is framed in ways that invite the viewer to identify with Jaime rather than Brienne, and there is an element of Jaime saving Brienne as though she were a damsel in distress, the remainder of the episode presents a more equal relationship.

VILE, SCHEMING, EVIL BITCHES?

Later in the battle, the pair are shown saving one another and fighting in perfect sync in a long shot of one of Winterfell's parapets. Jaime and Brienne care for one another through violence, protecting each other's body from abjection. While Brienne's relationship with Jaime becomes far more ambiguous in the final episodes of *Game of Thrones*, it is her care-oriented violence and willingness to embrace the Other that allows her to maintain her constitutive borders even as they appear to be overwhelmed with abject corpses.

Departing from the domination-based model, Brienne uses violence in ways that not only allow her to escape abjection but enable her acts to proliferate through queer kinship rather than becoming trapped in a destructive loop. In both *A Song of Ice and Fire* and *Game of Thrones*, Brienne has relationships with other knights that reflect such a "reelaboration of kinship" (Butler 1993, 95). As I have shown through Cersei and Gregor's relationship, queer kinship is not necessarily productive or healthy. Yet Brienne uses her queer kinship bonds to empower others: she passes on her chivalric violence outside of heteropatriarchal reproduction and opens up space for its proliferation via a form of queer reproduction that benefits her personally as well as those who learn from her. The knight–squire bond is often presented as a site where "squires are capable of 'inheriting' the characteristics of their lord," "learning [...] the performance of a particular *kind* of heterosexuality," and I would add masculinity (Nel 2015, 212). One such relationship is with Jaime, the ambiguity and reciprocity of which is demonstrated in the bear pit scene in the novels, when he chooses to come to Brienne's aid. The scene is a reflection of Brienne's positive chivalric influence on Jaime. John Cameron (2014, 198) suggests that "like a true knight, Jaime saves Brienne, but, in a true twist on convention, he has learned how to be a knight and a hero from Brienne herself." Brienne's knightly masculine violence is reproduced through her kinship bonds with those around her. While Jaime breaks their bond at the end of season eight and returns to Cersei, the previous seasons demonstrate that Brienne is able to pass on the performative acts that constitute her masculinity, even as those acts can be repeated in ambivalent ways.

Brienne's chivalric violence also proliferates through her relationship with her squire Podrick ("Pod"). Pod and Brienne share a relationship that may be understood as queer kinship because they spend considerable time together as knight and squire and are mutually invested in one another's well-being and growth. Their relationship is non-sexual but it is oriented around queer reproduction. Brienne trains Pod in arms and knightly behaviour after learning that his martial skills are underdeveloped. Teaching becomes an act of care because of an emphasis on

122   REIMAGINING MASCULINITY AND VIOLENCE

growth: Hanlon (2012, 33) argues that "care is nurturing" and "focussed on the well-being of another, and its intention is to produce nurturing outcomes." In *A Song of Ice and Fire* and *Game of Thrones* it becomes possible to see teaching as an Other-centred act of nurturing, further extending Hanlon's original theorisation of caring masculinity. Not only can violence be an act of care but teaching that violence to others can also be a means of nurturing them in a violent world. Brienne is able and willing to share the masculinity she has reforged out of existing structures because she has no affective attachment to heteropatriarchal systems. In the novels, the productive nature of Brienne's violence is implied even from this early stage in Pod's training: when she "cut two wooden swords from fallen branches to get a sense of Podrick's skills" (FfC 225). The decision to use "fallen branches" as "wooden swords" can be illuminated through Butler's (1993, 94) discussion of queer kinship as "a resignification of the very terms which effect our exclusion" that shifts "the terms of domination [...] toward a more enabling future." The phallic sword remains central to knightly masculinity and is one of the ways through which the teaching is coded as masculinity but is reworked as it is used by a female knight to teach a middle-class boy, and the productive potential of this resignification is implied through their training swords, which are now made of wood, an organic material which has a history of growth, rather than the inflexible steel or iron with which swords are commonly made in Westeros.

Pod comes to fully embody and further to proliferate Brienne's chivalric masculinity in season eight of *Game of Thrones* through his own queer kinship networks. In "A Knight of the Seven Kingdoms," Brienne supervises the training yard at Winterfell prior to the battle against the living dead. The camera moves through various battle preparations and ends on a medium shot of Pod and another man practising their swordsmanship. Pod easily defeats his opponent, and as he holds his sword to the man's neck, he tilts his head to the side and grins. The camera moves to a close-up of Brienne smiling, and in the background the sound of Pod giving instruction to his peer is muffled but audible. Jaime joins Brienne and they watch the younger men spar again. Jaime commends Pod's progress and Brienne responds, "He's all right. Still has a lot to learn." To which Jaime says, "I'm sure you'll teach him" (S8E2). Brienne has a history of being a blunt teacher, and seldom praises Pod, so the admission that he is "all right" is for her a warm commendation. Pod has fully embraced Brienne's chivalric violence, which is now complicit with the other-centred hegemonic masculinity needed to defeat the white walkers. Brienne's knowledge and power are democratised and passed to Pod, who in turn passes his skills and

VILE, SCHEMING, EVIL BITCHES?   123

chivalric masculine violence onto others in order to empower them. Pod has begun forming new connections to others and sharing this caring violence through them, as well as practising care himself through teaching violence to others. Brienne's caring masculinity is repeated through Pod, both as he trains his fellow knights and as he becomes a knight and a member of the Kingsguard in the final episode of *Game of Thrones* (S8E6 "The Iron Throne").

Brienne's violence continues to proliferate via queer means as she begins to train Arya Stark in the television series, although in this case the boundary between teacher and student is more fraught. Arya comes across Brienne and Pod training in the yard at Winterfell in season seven. When Brienne offers to fetch the master-at-arms for her, Arya says, "He didn't beat the Hound. You did. I want to train with you. [...] You swore to serve both my mother's daughters, didn't you?" (S7E4 "The Spoils of War"). Brienne acquiesces with a nod, and the two characters spar. The act is presented as masculine through their clothing (both wear breeches and surcoats), short hair, and the visual and dialogic emphasis on their swords, Needle and Oathkeeper. Arya wins the first two fights, but in the third they draw. The latter is emphasised because it is the only one to feature music: a variation of Arya's theme song "Needle" plays, a fast-paced track featuring strings and drums. The music and the fight end in unison, with both Arya and Brienne grinning as they realise that they are evenly matched despite their different fighting styles. The music and the actors' performances position the scene as a mutually beneficial exchange that will aid their survival in the pseudo-medieval world. In this brief kinship bond there is also an element of the "potentially sexually charged social bond" between knight and squire, which "may be a source of homoeroticism" (Nel 2015, 212). While brief, their relationship is loaded with tension that blurs the boundaries between mentor, lover, and parent as well as the tension between winning and losing. All positions are blurred, which demonstrates how "the demand to resignify or repeat the very terms which constitute the 'we' cannot be summarily refused, but neither can they be followed in strict obedience" (Butler 1993, 84). Brienne cannot refuse the connection between masculinity and violence because it is necessary to her intelligibility and power as a knight, but she works the weakness in the norm by using violence to care for others and to repeat that violence in disobedient directions, such as when she shares it with Arya in *Game of Thrones*.

For Butler (1993, 84), "ambivalence," such as that which occurs when violence proliferates queerly in this scene with Brienne and Arya and in those scenes with Brienne and Jaime, "opens up the possibility of a

124   REIMAGINING MASCULINITY AND VIOLENCE

reworking of the very terms by which subjectivation proceeds—and fails to proceed." Jaime's decision to adopt Brienne's chivalric masculinity leads him to abandon her and return to King's Landing at the end of *Game of Thrones*, though it is unclear whether he does this to save Cersei and honour his vows as Lord Commander of the Kingsguard, to kill her to redress his misdeeds, or to save the smallfolk living in the city. Brienne herself positions his reworking of dominating violence as heroic, writing in the Book of White that Jaime "rode south in an attempt to save the capital from destruction" and "died defending his Queen" (S8E6). These descriptions are true, and it is worth noting that Jaime attempts to escape the city without using any violence. The "ambivalent" reworking of hegemonic violence is also visible earlier in the series when Brienne asks Arya "who taught you how to do that?" and Arya responds, "No one" (S7E4 "The Spoils of War"). Arya is referring to the House of Black and White in which she learnt to fight and magically transform her flesh, but "no one" also speaks to her lack of a masculine citation point. She dresses and styles her hair exactly like her father, but Eddard never inducted her into masculine violence: although he arranged for Arya to learn the sword from Syrio Forel in season one, he had no direct hand in her learning, and Arya earlier told Brienne that Eddard "never wanted to [teach her the sword]. Said, fighting was for boys" (S4E10 "The Children"). Arya replicates knightly masculinity in her physical appearance. But she reworks self-oriented hegemonic violence because she uses it to empower others. Indeed, in *Game of Thrones*, one of the fighting moves she uses while sparring with Brienne—flipping her dragonglass dagger from one hand to the other—is used to destroy the Night King and thereby save Westeros from an apocalyptic winter in "The Long Night" (S8E3). The lack of a patriarch as citation point for either character gives them an alternative position to heteropatriarchal reproduction and this alterity gives them space to rework masculinity in a number of ways. Because they choose to use violence to empower the Other, their violence, like the alternative kinship they are building, is turned "toward a more enabling future" (Butler 1993, 95).

Conclusion

Brienne and Cersei represent two ways in which female masculinity can be seen to relate to hegemonic masculine violence, that which is individualistic, phallic, and repeats and legitimises patriarchal structures. In both *A Song of Ice and Fire* and *Game of Thrones*, Cersei cites certain patriarchs (her father Tywin, and in the novel her husband Robert), and Brienne

VILE, SCHEMING, EVIL BITCHES? 125

cites the figure of the knight. These citations disclose the characters' violence as masculine, although they are expressed in medium-specific ways. The novels primarily use interior monologue and memory, and in Brienne's case material objects like the magic sword. *Game of Thrones* encourages its audiences to recognise the citations through costumes and dialogue, as well as more subtle means like intertextual references to previous episodes and music. However, Brienne and Cersei practise masculine violence in different ways. Cersei uses violence to dominate others and maintain her power as queen as well as her attachment to patriarchal systems of reproduction. When she comes into contact with abjection, it spreads to her body and she becomes grotesque. Further monstrosity abounds when Cersei and Gregor enter into a bastardised form of queer kinship in *Game of Thrones*: a pattern of reproduction that is radically removed from the heterosexual biological family. Rather than using this bond to contest the patriarchal power structures that limit her agency, Cersei reproduces domination-based hegemonic violence and for this reason her bond with Gregor is made monstrous: both characters are linked with the queer monstrous feminine and disrupt accepted ideas about identity, bodies, and subjectivity. In the television series, Cersei is trapped under the Red Keep and killed by falling debris, a death that echoes her hegemonic violence and foregrounds her being imprisoned within a never-ending cycle of destruction. By contrast, both the novels and television series show that Brienne embraces the Other and uses violence to empower and protect them, and when she is faced with the abject, it is her connections to others that allow her to maintain her constitutive borders. From this position, Brienne can transfer her caring violence onto others through queer kinship without being trapped inside a ruinous loop. Through her friendships with other knights, she passes her knowledge and identity practices—chivalrous violence—from one subject to another and makes the world a more liveable place. Brienne's relation to the Other is what makes her masculine violence acceptable where Cersei's fails: she is not invested in patriarchal reproduction and so does not use power to dominate the Other but to empower them. Her position as Lord Commander of the Kingsguard in the finale of *Game of Thrones* cements her position as hero, and her final scenes in the series—updating the Book of White and sitting on a Small Council meeting—imply that she will continue to rewrite the relationship between masculinity and violence in Westeros.

Alternative masculinities——those that depart from the white, male, heterosexual, cisgender, able-bodied norm——are not always productive, as I have demonstrated through my discussion of Cersei. But in *A Song of Ice and Fire* and *Game of Thrones*, they inevitably compel a remaking

126   REIMAGINING MASCULINITY AND VIOLENCE

of masculinity because in that pseudo-medieval world non-normative gender presentations are unintelligible without general alignment with either masculinity or femininity. In this remaking, it is possible to find "repetitions of hegemonic forms of power which fail to repeat loyally and, in that failure, open possibilities for resignifying the terms of violation against their violating aims" (Butler 1993, 84). In this way, the repetition and (re)articulation of violence in relation to female masculinities offers a way of imagining how to work the weakness in the norm––as it does for the disabled masculinities I explore in the next chapter.

Chapter 4

Disabled Masculinities and the Potential and Limits of Queered Masculine Violence

> But Jaime's walls were gone. They had taken his hand, they had taken his *sword hand*, and without it he was nothing. [...] It was his right hand that made him a knight; his right arm that made him a man. (SoS 417)

I'll never forget reading this page for the first time. It was 2013 and I had been flirting with the idea of researching *A Song of Ice and Fire*, but it was then that I knew. I didn't know what I knew, only that the novels were playing with masculinity at even the most surface level, and that both texts were gaining cultural momentum as *Game of Thrones* grew in popularity. Since then, the texts and my research have taken many forms, but I have often thought back to that moment of curious joy and clarity that has underscored for me the importance of disability for thinking critically about the (mis)use of bodily autonomy and the potential for change.

Disabled masculinities force the relationship between masculinity and violence to take a different shape to its normative materialisations by breaking the pretence of naturalness and therefore enabling new types of performance. However, in this case, the body's abilities are at the heart of this separation. According to Garland-Thomson (1997, 92), "the disabled body is a body whose variations or transformations have rendered it out of sync with its environment, both the physical and the attitudinal environment." The notion of a body "out of sync" is particularly obvious when cisgender men become disabled, for the two are seen by dominant discourses to cancel one another out (Gerschick and Miller 1995; Ostrander 2008a; 2008b; Shuttleworth 2004; Shuttleworth, Wedgwood, and Wilson 2012). Writing on the relation between gender and disability, Garland-Thomson (2002, 18) argues that while disabled women are often denied femininity and sexuality, "banishment from femininity can be both a liability and a benefit." For Garland-Thomson, disability

128   REIMAGINING MASCULINITY AND VIOLENCE

allows women to escape destructive feminine performative practices and reimagine gender in new and creative ways. Masculinity scholars such as Thomas Gerschick and Adam Miller (1995) and Margaret Torrell (2013) suggest that disabled men may similarly be able to creatively (re)inscribe Western masculinities, and Gerschick (1998), Tom Shakespeare (1999), Russell Shuttleworth (2004), and Brett Smith (2013) reveal that, while disabled men often struggle to perform normative masculinity, "not being able to use their bodies in conventional ways may have given some men impetus to go beyond hegemonic masculinity and to focus on alternatives" (Shuttleworth 2004, 172). Gerschick and Miller (1995, 202–203) claim that "the experiences of men with physical disabilities are important because they illuminate both the insidious power and the limitations of contemporary masculinity" and for this reason "the gender practices of some of these men exemplify alternative visions of masculinity that are obscured, but available to men in our culture." The ambivalent relation between the disabled body and masculinity is reflected in *A Song of Ice and Fire* and *Game of Thrones* through characters' ambiguous relation to hegemonic violence: they reject it, but this rejection stems from an inability to perform violence, and for this reason they enter into an ambivalent space where they sometimes relapse into using these acts when they do become available.

In *A Song of Ice and Fire* and *Game of Thrones*, disabled men who use hegemonic violence become abject, but their non-normative bodies give them the opportunity to use violence in different ways, and with messy and ambiguous results. Disability necessitates a revised relationship between masculinity and violence. There are many complex disability representations in *A Song of Ice and Fire* and *Game of Thrones*, and this chapter will focus upon physical impairment as it is experienced by male characters who are white, high-class, and masculine. Despite these privileged positions, the men are often denied access to normative masculinity and the power its enactment bestows at the same time, as they are thereby freed from its narrow and destructive constraints. Disabled masculine characters in both texts allow their audiences to engage with forms of embodiment that diverge from the repetition of an allegedly original manhood, and instead to conceive of a masculinity that resists patriarchal society. Sometimes these alternatives are strange and frightening; at other times they offer a way of making the world more liveable. In order to tease out these proliferations, I analyse three of the major perspective characters with a disability: the greenseer Brandon Stark, who loses the use of his legs while gaining third sight following an accident; the infamous knight and Kingslayer Jaime Lannister, whose hand is severed halfway through the series; and the witty "Imp," Tyrion

Lannister, who is short-statured. Each character undergoes a messy and partial rejection of hegemonic masculine violence, showing new possibilities for queer kinship, but also its limits.

When disabled characters repeat hegemonic violence in *A Song of Ice and Fire* and *Game of Thrones* they become abject, but when they adopt a new citational point they learn to care for the Other and are able to proliferate their ideas and values through queer kinship. Disabled characters in both the books and television show cite a specific patriarch who shaped their gender performance: Tyrion and Jaime both reference their father Tywin, whereas Bran is attached to a phallic idealisation of the knight. These figures encourage the men to reproduce domination-based violence and come into contact with abjection. This citational structure can be illuminated through Judith Butler's notion of performativity, which is useful for unpacking how the heterosexual matrix produces the able body as well as heterosexuality and gender normativity (Corker 2001; 1999; McRuer 2006; Shildrick and Price 1996). A system of compulsory able-bodiedness has been postulated in order to link disability theory to queer theory and the intersections of multiple matrices of power (McRuer 2006). Butler's arguments about the process of subject formation through citational acts and attempts to banish the Other are highly relevant for analysing disability alongside gender. Following Butler, I understand disability as a discourse that is produced through a complex interaction between bodies, environments, attitudes, and practices (see Davis 1995; Garland-Thomson 1997; McRuer 2006; Mitchell and Snyder 2000). This is not to deny the materiality of the body nor the reality of pain or persecution for disabled individuals, but to recognise both able bodies and disabled ones as neither essential nor monolithic but variable and fluid (see Barnes, Oliver, and Barton 2002; McRuer 2006).

Entry into this borderless space leads the characters in both *A Song of Ice and Fire* and *Game of Thrones* to realise that they must change to survive, and they are symbolically reborn via imagery that connotes the queer monstrous feminine as they alter their masculine performance. As in my application of Kristevian abjection and Barbara Creed's monstrosity theories to female bodies in Chapter 4, I do not assume that the disabled body is automatically horrifying because, by its very definition, it disrupts normative ideas about the mind and body. Rather, I take these differences as my starting point, and any new instances which disrupt the borders we expect to find in the world are understood as abject. In other words, I do not view Bran, Jaime, or Tyrion as abject because of their impairments, but because they are faced with abject signifiers such as the corpse, blood, and further damage to their bodily borders.

130   REIMAGINING MASCULINITY AND VIOLENCE

Contact with the abject necessitates a new masculine role model: Bran learns from the Three-Eyed Crow/Raven, Jaime realises the value of honour thanks to Brienne of Tarth, and Tyrion enters Daenerys Targaryen's service. These other characters enable Bran, Jaime, and Tyrion to escape the destructive cycle of hegemonic violence and develop more connected forms of subjectivity through queer kinship. However, this is not a simple transformation and the rebirths are shown to be partial and complex. Characters relapse into individualistic violence even as they strive to reject it, reflecting difficulties inherent in contesting the law as a subject who is also produced through the law (Butler 1993, 169–185). Nonetheless, the lone, singular model of masculinity is revealed to be flawed, and Bran, Jaime, and Tyrion begin to perform masculinity by rejecting domination and caring for others. In temporarily adopting a caring masculinity, the characters become radically connected to the people, animals, and environment around them.

In exploring how disability changes the dynamic between masculinity and violence, I show that because of this supposed discordance, when disabled men insist upon being intelligible as masculine, and when this insistence takes the form of hegemonic violence, the price of intelligibility is monstrosity. Disabled men who repeat this violence come into contact with abjection, but when they change their masculine performance and learn to enact a caring masculinity, they enter an ambivalent position between monstrosity and passing on their knowledge through queer kinship. Additionally, the characters I examine are enmeshed in a queer adaptation process because their narratives in *Game of Thrones* outpace the events of the most recently published novel at the time of writing, *A Dance with Dragons*, and their expanded narratives often foreclose or enhance this ambivalence around violence. I chart how disabled masculine bodies in *A Song of Ice and Fire* and *Game of Thrones* come to experience abjection and rebirth as they oscillate between the violent domination of others and connection to them.

"A Thousand Eyes, A Hundred Skins"

While all the Stark children have supernatural connections to their direwolves, Bran's is by far the most advanced following the accident that breaks his spine. Bran is a main character throughout the series, in which he becomes disabled and travels beyond the Wall to learn to harness his magical powers. *Game of Thrones* has expanded his narrative. He becomes a magical wise person and aids the battle against the living dead, after which he is named King of the Seven Kingdoms.

DISABLED MASCULINITIES 131

Bran's acquisition of supernatural powers can be seen as a form of the "supercrip" trope, which presents "a character having some compensatory, mystical superpower as a result of his [*sic*] disability" because "being disabled isn't enough [...] the character needs to be somehow otherworldly to be interesting" (Harvey and Nelles 2014). However, Bran's characterisation is more nuanced because he never achieves the "superhero" spectacularity that would make his magical, disabled body problematic. Bran's powers are made explicit through conversations with Jojen Reed, the son of one of the Stark bannermen, who can see the future in "green dreams." In the novels, Jojen explains that when Bran dreams he is his direwolf Summer, he is magically entering the wolf's consciousness: "When I touched Summer, I felt you in him. Just as you are in him now" (CoK 397). Likewise, in *Game of Thrones*, Jojen says, "You can get inside [Summer's] head. See through his eyes" (S3E2 "Dark Wings, Dark Words").

Despite his potential for magical heroism, Bran bases his masculine performance on a phallic idealisation of the knight. Bran has a very simplistic view of knighthood in *A Song of Ice and Fire*: the narrator observes, "Bran was going to be a knight himself someday, one of the Kingsguard. Old Nan said they were the finest swords in all the realm. There were only seven of them, and they wore white armor and had no wives or children, but lived only to serve the king" (GoT 73). The knightly masculinity to which Bran aspires would allow him to gain power by performing complicit and hegemonic acts in service to the king and, by extension, the feudal patriarchy. Bran's attachment to patriarchal knightly masculinity is also evident in *Game of Thrones*. The first scene to feature Bran shows him practising archery with his eldest brothers Robb and Jon as his parents look on. The act of passing violent practices from older brother to younger frames Bran's training around his expected future as a Northern lord and knight. The three boys are shown together in a medium long shot that obscures their individual faces, emphasising their near-identical dark brown costumes and features as a reflection of their place within the patriarchal system of reproduction. The shot is framed by Eddard and Catelyn Stark's shoulders, the presence of Bran's watchful parents further foregrounding the family's desire to reproduce the biological family and the nation, and Bran's place within it as a future knight.

Bran maintains an affective attachment to his imagined phallic version of knighthood even after he loses the use of his legs. In *Game of Thrones*, Bran tells his brother Robb, "I'd rather be dead" than disabled (S1E3), and when the older boy tells him not to say such things, Bran repeats his words. The repeated dialogue and the notion that death

132   REIMAGINING MASCULINITY AND VIOLENCE

is preferable to disablement reflects Bran's attachment to Westerosi hegemonic masculinity, which privileges the repeated performance of compulsory able-bodiedness. Bran's lingering faith in the value of hegemonic masculinity is also reflected in his green dreams throughout the series. In season three, while Bran and his companions are travelling to Castle Black, Bran dreams that he is trying to shoot a three-eyed raven with his bow and arrows. As Bran aims, his brothers Robb and Jon appear, recreating the scene in season one where Bran practises with the bow as his parents look on (S1E1). As in the real version, Bran misses the shot in the dream and his brothers laugh, but now Jojen appears and tells him, "You can't kill it, you know. [...] Because the raven is you" (S3E2). The raven "is" Bran in the sense that Bran will one day become the new magical seer called the Three-Eyed Raven (known in the novels as the Three-Eyed Crow and hereafter called the Three-Eyed Crow/Raven), but the raven here also represents Bran's magical powers, which are intimately bound with his disability. In attempting to shoot the Raven and dreaming himself able, Bran attempts to use phallic violence (bow and arrows) to dominate the part of him that cannot walk. The repeated suicidal ideation and repetition of the earlier Winterfell scene foreground the fact that this desire comes from an attachment to phallic hegemonic masculinity and the patriarchal reproductive logics that it supports, and they bring Bran pain rather than solace. While Bran does not consider suicide again in reality or dreams, he continues to envision himself as able-bodied in green dreams throughout the series, reflecting his lingering desire to embody hegemonic knightly masculinity.

In *A Song of Ice and Fire*, Bran similarly clings to hegemonic masculine ideals after his disablement, seeing knighthood as defined by "bright armor and streaming banners, lance and sword, a warhorse between his legs" (CoK 221). For Bran, the knight is comprised of a cluster of promises: phallic power ("finest swords," "lance and sword," "warhorse between his legs"), prestige ("all the realm"), legal and legitimate violence ("lived to serve the king"), glory ("streaming banners"), and legitimising the existing patriarchal system. In other words, Bran's "knight" allows him to perform hegemonic and complicit masculinity, becoming an exemplar of masculinity in the Westerosi public imaginary, if not in practice. Bran's knightly masculinity is far removed from the more complex version invested in chivalry, protecting others, and virtue; Bran seeks power rather than seeing protecting another life as an act of care. Even when Bran begins his training under a magical elder known as the Three-Eyed Crow/Raven he maintains his attachment to knightly masculinity: "*I was going to be a knight*, Bran remembered. *I used*

DISABLED MASCULINITIES

to run and climb and fight" (DwD 530; original emphasis). The version of knighthood to which Bran aspires in both the novels and television series is informed by a narrow masculine norm that demands and is defined by an able body that can reproduce heteropatriarchal attitudes and the symbolic order. Bran remains attached to this model of masculinity long after he is impaired, an affective investment that can be illuminated by McRuer's claim (2006, 10; adapting Butler 1999, 122) that "able-bodied identity" is "both a compulsory system and an intrinsic comedy." Bran cannot see himself or his life as a masculine subject without an able body, and for this reason he repeats hegemonic violence in ways that inadvertently parody his desire for able-bodiedness.

Bran's dominating hegemonic violence materialises and is critiqued when he learns to magically control other humans, specifically the intellectually impaired half-giant Hodor. Hodor can be seen as a "narrative prosthesis" (Mitchell and Snyder 2000) in both the televisual and textual iterations of Bran's quest because he is the foil against which the boy's lack of physical strength is emphasised and he unwillingly provides his own body as a surrogate for Bran's. Bran enters and controls Hodor's mind using magic, a more complex version of the connection he has with his direwolf. In the novels Bran's magical relationship with Hodor is figured as a form of domination and is critiqued through language that evokes sexual assault, which inscribes Bran as abject and monstrous. By contrast, the Bran of *Game of Thrones* magically dominates Hodor less often, but in the expanded narrative that takes place after the events of *A Dance with Dragons* these brief acts of domination lead directly to Hodor's death and (through temporal travel) his disability.

Bran's magical hegemonic domination over Hodor is initially presented as ambiguous in *A Song of Ice and Fire* because it is intended as an act of other-centred care rather than a self-oriented attempt to gain power. The other-centred nature of Bran's violence is foregrounded when he sees his friend Meera moving to attack an unknown assailant and he thinks, *"I can't let her fight the thing alone.* [...] Summer was far away, but ... he slipped his skin, and reached for Hodor" (SoS2 196). Bran anticipates violence from the unknown stranger because he lives in a violent world and feels compelled to make these tools available to himself for his own and his friends' survival. The violent domination Bran anticipates from the stranger leads him to employ violent domination against Hodor. In this moment, Bran achieves, as Butler says of the film *Paris Is Burning,* "neither an efficacious insurrection nor a painful resubordination, but an unstable coexistence of both" (1993, 95). Bran's violence highlights the ways in which surviving in patriarchal Westeros is contingent upon an able body.

134   REIMAGINING MASCULINITY AND VIOLENCE

Bran's magical domination is critiqued when he persists despite Hodor's clear protestations, marking a shift from other-centred to self-oriented violence that results in abjection. Bran describes his experience with Hodor by using the metaphor of putting on a boot, at the same time emphasising his attempts to see Hodor as less than human: "this was harder [than his direwolf], like trying to pull a left boot on your right foot. It fit all wrong, and the boot was *scared* too, the boot didn't know what was happening, the boot was pushing the foot away" (SoS2 196; original emphasis). Bran mentally transforms Hodor from a thinking and feeling man to an inanimate object, an intellectual manoeuvre that is informed by a hierarchical understanding of masculinity and power and which makes dominating the other man sound moral. However, Bran's attempts to dehumanise and dominate Hodor are immediately critiqued as he comes into intimate contact with the abject.

As soon as Bran begins to enact hegemonic violence by dehumanising and dominating Hodor, "He tasted vomit in the back of *Hodor's* throat, and that was almost enough to make him flee" (SoS2 196; original emphasis). As Bran takes Hodor's mind, he becomes a representation of the abject within, and can be seen as a literal interpretation of Julia Kristeva's claim that "during that course in which 'I' become, I give birth to myself amid the violence of sobs, of vomit" (1982, 3). Hodor attempts to "give birth" to himself by vomiting Bran out mentally and physically, but the boy resists and takes control. For this reason, Bran is confronted with the grotesque experience of "tast[ing] vomit" in "*Hodor's* throat." Bran senses vomit both as himself and as Hodor, making the abject substance both part of himself and part of Hodor at the same time. The reader is also brought into this experience between Bran's and Hodor's vomit, for they are encouraged to identify with Bran because of his status as a perspective character, and to feel what he feels, sense what he senses. The horror of this confused moment is related through the emphasis upon Hodor's name—"*Hodor's* throat"—revealing Bran's disgust and surprise at finding himself someone else. Kristeva (1982, 2–3, 45) claims that vomit is abject because it disturbs the boundary between inside/outside the body. When that border crossing also brings about confusion over whether the vomit/body is mine/not mine, identity and corporeality are disrupted and a feeling of abjection takes hold (4). Bran is almost forced to "flee" to maintain his own borders, yet he chooses to dominate the Other, and the abjection that comes along with it, as the price of able knightly embodiment and gaining Hodor's body as a detachable phallus, much like the relationship between Cersei and Gregor. Bran's increased abjection exposes the fallacy of the able body:

he is not abject because he is disabled but becomes abject because he feels compelled to magically gain an able body. The able body is exposed as an impossible ideal that no one can embody *and* as a compulsory regime. Because the abjection that Bran experiences is so closely tied to his desire for an able body and his own (and by extension the reader's) senses, Bran's hegemonic violence is presented as revolting.

While Bran's violence is magical and psychological, it is increasingly narrated with an emphasis upon embodiment that betrays its likeness to sexual violence and presents Bran's mind as a phallic tool. When Bran seizes Hodor's body, he describes the man "whimper[ing] when he felt him" and being able to "taste the fear at the back of his mouth" (DwD 69–70). The encounters are a psychological violation by Bran, yet they are deeply corporeal for Hodor. The embodied terror is hinted at through Bran's narration: he describes being "inside Hodor's skin" (DwD 69–70). Bran enters Hodor's body forcefully and without his consent, using his mind powers as a phallus, an act that can be understood as psychological or metaphorical rape. The phallic penetration codes Bran's mental domination as masculine and reveals that the phallus is a phantasm that may be discursively produced in a conflation of mind and body, as demonstrated through phrases such as "whimper when he felt him" (DwD 69). The omniscient third-person narrator provides a particularly harrowing insight into Hodor's experience and links it to sexual violence. The narration also reveals the ways in which compulsory able-bodiedness, like gender, is achieved through violent processes. At the same time, the scene can be illuminated through McRuer's claim (2006, 9) that able-bodied identity "is always deferred and thus never really guaranteed." By entering Hodor's mind, Bran feminises the older man and effectively undoes his own attempt to gain a muscular, able body. The attempt to enter able-bodied subjectivity fails—there is no able body, or, rather, the able body is produced by an array of discursive and material practices that also *dis*able Hodor's body. Hodor feels Bran's mental invasions intellectually, but he processes them physically. In this way, Bran's mental abuse is linked with hegemonic violence.

The pervasive desire to be able-bodied twists Bran's magic into an act of hegemonic domination. Bran wants to be intelligible as masculine rather than gain power, but to become intelligible he feels that he must acquire an able body at any cost. Compulsory able-bodiedness causes Bran's initial desire to care for his friends by turning the violent law against itself into a destructive repetition of that same law. While seizing the other man's mind, near the end of the series, Bran says, "*I just want to be strong again*" (DwD 528; original emphasis). Bran's desire for strength is at once literal and symbolic. He wants to be physically

136   REIMAGINING MASCULINITY AND VIOLENCE

capable, but he also wants to return to the high-class, able, youthful complicit masculinity he embodied at the beginning of the series. Bran's domination is partially a product of his hierarchical thinking about masculinity; he describes Hodor as a "child-man" (DwD 528) in a more dramatic attempt to infantilise Hodor and make his resistance seem overdramatic, like a child's tantrum. Bran further dehumanises Hodor by describing him in ways that connote animals. Hodor is likened to a "dog that has had all the fight whipped out of him" (DwD 528) and is seen to "whimper," "thrash his shaggy head" (DwD 69), and "curl up and hide" (DwD 528) whenever Bran enters his mind. Bran describes Hodor as a child "whose flesh he'd taken" (DwD 528). "The choice of the word 'flesh,'" argue Massie and Mayer (2014, 54), "stresses internality and materiality," and the material embodiment that is thus stressed connects Bran's psychological assault with hegemonic sexual violence. Bran's relationship with Hodor can be illuminated through Butler's work on alternative kinship, but, as in the case of Cersei and Gregor, it is not necessarily an improvement on "the terms of domination" (Butler 1993, 95). Bran challenges normative ideas about masculine subjectivity because he embraces the Other while repeating the pattern of domination over the less powerful. By repeating the violent system of power in Westeros Bran becomes abject, and abjection denaturalises his desire for an able body. Readers are encouraged to recognise that hegemonic violence in the name of an attachment to compulsory able-bodiedness threatens Bran's constitutive borders, not his disabled body. Bran reinforces ableist masculine discourses by dominating Hodor so that he may momentarily achieve able knightly embodiment, complicit masculinity, and gain a detachable phallus, but instead he comes into contact with abjection.

In *Game of Thrones*, Bran's queer kinship with Hodor is more ambiguous because there is a tension between the need for audiences to view Bran as a protagonist and the fact that Bran effectively uses his magical powers to murder Hodor. Throughout the series, the Bran of *Game of Thrones* is far more ethical in his mental domination and takes over Hodor's mind only three times: in the season three episode, "The Rains of Castamere," the season four episode, "First of His Name," and the season six episode, "The Door." Unlike the novels, where Bran takes Hodor's mind whenever he feels the desire, the Bran of *Game of Thrones* only controls Hodor's mind when he and his companions' lives are threatened. When Bran and friends are ambushed by white walkers in "The Door," Bran dominates Hodor's mind so that the older man can carry him out of the cave and then hold the door closed so that the monsters are trapped within. As Meera runs away with Bran in a

DISABLED MASCULINITIES

137

sledge, she yells back to Hodor, "Hold the door!", which he does until the white walkers overwhelm him. Viewers are encouraged through non-diegetic music to see this scene as Hodor sacrificing himself to save Bran and Meera because he loves them like family. The song "Goodbye Brother" carries significant affective weight in the narrative: it is part of the House Stark theme and is featured multiple times in the narrative when Stark characters say goodbye to loved ones (S1E2), or after their deaths (S1E9, S5E10). In "The Door," "Goodbye Brother" invites viewers to remember that Hodor has a longstanding attachment to the Stark family and positions his death as a noble and tragic sacrifice for his loved ones. As "Goodbye Brother" is repeated in new scenes, it works as a micro adaptation, carrying the meanings from previous scenes forward as it takes on new meanings in new contexts. The song encourages the audience to gloss over the servant/master nature of Hodor's relationship to the Starks through the invocation of familial love, for which there is no narrative mention besides that which "Goodbye Brother" evokes through its status as adaptation. The song also reorients the scene around Bran and the fact that the boy also experiences death in Hodor's body and as Brandon Stark because in these moments he is also magically becoming the Three-Eyed Raven.

Game of Thrones makes considerable efforts to sanction Bran's mental domination through "Goodbye Brother" and the affective meanings it carries, but in reality, Bran takes control over Hodor's body and then forces him to sacrifice himself so that he and Meera can escape. Throughout the scene, Bran is physically in the present but psychologically in the past, where he is in Winterfell at the time when Hodor was a boy and before he became intellectually impaired. As Meera yells for present-Hodor to "hold the door," Bran hears the echo in past-Winterfell and is seen by past-Hodor. People cannot usually see Bran in his visions, so the gaze suggests that something unusual has occurred. An eerie link is created between past-Hodor and present-Hodor, which causes past-Hodor to have a seizure while present Hodor dies protecting Bran and Meera. Past-Hodor mutters, "hold the door" as his body spasms, which is eventually reduced to "Hodor," with the implication that the seizure has caused Hodor's intellectual disability. Both past-Hodor's seizure and present Hodor's death are presented as tragic, although more affective weight is placed on present-Hodor's death because the most dramatic sections of "Goodbye Brother" play in the narrative present as Hodor holds the door and Meera and Bran escape. In other words, audiences are encouraged to feel grief over Hodor's death as opposed to recognising that Bran forced Hodor to sacrifice himself. The connection to past-Hodor makes little logical sense within the narrative,

138   REIMAGINING MASCULINITY AND VIOLENCE

and I suggest that it functions to displace Bran's horrific violence against present-Hodor. Viewers need to see that Bran's actions have consequences for him, but those consequences in the present are too monstrous to be reconciled with Bran as a protagonist, even in the morally ambiguous world of Westeros. The horror is displaced onto past-Hodor, where it becomes less of an immediate threat but also has far greater effects, as Hodor will be intellectually impaired for the rest of his life. While Bran's violence is rooted in his embrace of interdependence and relationality, he fails to reject domination and this causes him to use hegemonic violence with horrific consequences, even if these consequences are expressed through a prosthesis. The scene highlights the violence of psychological manipulation, especially how it can be a tool for hegemonic domination.

Bran's psychological rapes of Hodor bring about only horror, which reaches its climax in both *Game of Thrones* and *A Song of Ice and Fire* when he enters the Three-Eyed Crow/Raven's cave, a symbolic womb and site of change. In the novel, Bran observes that "the way was cramped and twisty," with "dripping water somewhere to his right" (DwD 204) and "a thick white root growing from the tunnel wall, with tendrils hanging from it and spiderwebs between its fingers" (DwD 204). Similarly, when Bran and his companions enter the cave in "The Children" (S4E10), they follow a Child of the Forest called Leaf through a series of dark, narrow, twisting tunnels brimming with organic matter, which lead to a central chamber in which the Three-Eyed Crow/Raven is ensconced. In both the book and television series, the setting is reminiscent of the "intra-uterine" landscapes that Creed (1993) discusses in relation to the horror film *Alien*: "the interior is dark and slimy" (51), consisting of "dark, narrow, winding passages leading to a central room" (53).

The unsettling tone that the symbolic womb evokes is emphasised by a reference to abjection when Bran is set down before the Three-Eyed Crow/Raven. In *Game of Thrones*, viewers see a brief close-up of a human skull in the foreground as Bran pulls himself across the ground, and in the novel he realises that "the floor of the passage was littered with the bones of birds and beasts" (DwD 205). Both the novel and television series use bones to evoke the corpse and its abjection. The Three-Eyed Crow's/Raven's cavernous home is presented as an abject womb, and it is indeed a place where Bran is going to be reborn. As of the end of *A Dance with Dragons*, Bran is still learning and forming new connections within the cave/womb. *Game of Thrones* takes Bran's narrative and his symbolic rebirth further. During Bran's "mind meld" with the Three-Eyed Crow/Raven and the white walkers' attack, Leaf detonates a bomb and the entire cave is destroyed in a graphic explosion (S6E5 "The Door"). For Creed (1993, 51), explosions can be read as births, "a bursting forth

DISABLED MASCULINITIES

139

from the inside to the outside." In Bran's case, it is a reversal of the usual relations to the symbolic, in which "representations of the birth scenario [...] point to the split between the natural world of the mother and the paternal symbolic which is regulated by a completely different set of rules, rules that reinforce proper civilized codes of behavior and the clean and proper body" (Creed 1993, 49). Bran's rebirth does cite a "split," but it is a split from the paternal symbolic. As Bran is reborn as the Three-Eyed Crow/Raven in *Game of Thrones*, the cave/womb in which he undertook his training explodes in a fiery inferno that symbolises the violence of Bran's rebirth apart from hegemonic violence.

When normative masculine discourses bring Bran nothing but short bursts of power entangled with monstrosity––and with few other options for intelligibility because of his disabled body––he begins to accept that he must rework his gender along new lines. Disability often demands that gender be enacted in new ways, with both enabling and limiting outcomes, as I have noted. In *A Song of Ice and Fire* and *Game of Thrones*, Bran is one such example of a masculine character who adopts an alternative enactment of his gender performance because he shifts his point of reference from the "knight" discourse to the Three-Eyed Crow/Raven.

Bran's repetition of his mentor's masculinity is encouraged in *A Song of Ice and Fire* by the Children of the Forest, who "made Bran a throne of his own, like the one [on which] Lord Brynden [the Three-Eyed Crow/ Raven] sat" (DwD 523). In his final perspective chapter, to date, Bran begins to adopt the Three-Eyed Crow/Raven as a citation point of his own choosing. His mentor tells him that greenseers have "a thousand eyes, a hundred skins, wisdom deep as the roots of ancient trees" (DwD 525–526), and Bran repeats the words three times later in the chapter. He asks himself, "What was he now?": *"A thousand eyes, a hundred skins, wisdom deep as the roots of ancient trees.* That was as good as being a knight. *Almost as good, anyway"* (DwD 530; original emphasis). Bran likewise repeats his mentor's words when he consumes a magical paste that he is told will "help awaken your gifts and wed you to the trees" (DwD 531). Bran is reluctant: he "did not want to be married to a tree ... but who else would wed a broken boy like him? *A thousand eyes, a hundred skins, wisdom deep as the roots of ancient trees. A greenseer"* (DwD 532). Finally, when Bran returns to his bed, he thinks, *"A thousand eyes, a hundred skins, wisdom deep as the roots of ancient trees"* (DwD 534; original emphasis), but this time there is no caveat. Bran's repetition of the greenseer's words can be understood through Butler's (1990, 191) argument that gendered "repetition is at once a reenactment and re-experiencing of a set of meanings already socially established." Bran becomes attached to the idea of performing greenseer masculinity, even if that choice is informed by his own internalised ableism. As Bran gains access to a magical new means of performing masculinity, the very process through which he is indoctrinated is figured as a last resort for entering the patriarchal system of reproduction ("who else would wed a broken boy") as well as a radical and parodic kinship ("Bran did not want to be married to a tree"). From this ambivalent place, Bran begins repeating in earnest the "set of meanings" that his mentor has established—in this case, his words and his radical and powerful caring masculinity.

Bran's interpolation into the Three-Eyed Crow/Raven masculinity in *Game of Thrones* provides an insight into the process of adaptation between texts and the tension and possibilities queer adaptations provoke. The end of "The Door" (S6E5) sees Bran become the new Three-Eyed Crow/Raven, a process whereby he receives the entire history of Westeros and everyone in it at the expense of his own identity, subjectivity, and affective capacity. As the older Three-Eyed Crow/Raven tells him: "It is time for you to become me." Bran becomes abject in the sense that he loses the borders that secure his identity and subjectivity, yet it is a rewarding abjection because he is able to perform a magical caring masculinity that is constituted through shared emotion, hyper-interdependence, and celebrated relationality. Bran adapts the Three-Eyed Crow/Raven's masculinity with absolute fidelity: he does not alter the words and takes them as a mantra. However, the act of adapting allows Bran to repeat in unexpected and potentially subversive directions—to misunderstand his mentor's words because of his youth and to seriously believe that he will enter a (presumed) heterosexual marriage with a tree. There is a tension between Bran's desire to repeat perfectly and the unexpected option to repeat unfaithfully: an adaptation that enables.

Bran's transformation, especially Meera's frustration with his lack of feeling when they part ways, also offer insights into the value of infidelity to both patriarchal reproduction and faithful adaptations. Bran/The Three-Eyed Crow/Raven is a perfect copy of the previous Three-Eyed Crow/Raven: while he maintains an awareness of his subjectivity as Bran Stark, his dialogue, mannerisms, and emotions are an exact replica of his mentor's. The reproduction allows him to embrace subversive connections to the Other and lean into healthier ways of doing masculinity, but the process also makes him uniquely unlikeable as a character, both in the fictional world of Westeros and among fans, and in ways that signal a weakness in patriarchal reproductive logics. Bran embodies "repetition as perfect reproduction," whereby "adaptation works to help reproduce the nation" (Handyside 2012, 54). Bran/The Three-Eyed Crow/Raven embodies the patriarchal desire to reproduce

DISABLED MASCULINITIES

the nation perfectly, both between one text and another and from one patriarch to the next (even as he queers this impulse because the reproduction was through queer kinship rather than hetero-biological means). However, Bran/The Three-Eyed Crow/Raven is rejected by Meera because he stops caring for her as he did when he was Bran Stark. In becoming a magically perfect result of patriarchal reproduction/ adaptation, Bran loses the subjectivity that made him unique and loved by those around him. Indeed, Meera's response foreshadows the way *Game of Thrones* fans received Bran/The Three-Eyed Crow/Raven from this point in the narrative. While it is beyond the scope of this chapter to analyse fan responses in depth, it is worth noting that Bran/The Three-Eyed Crow/Raven received widespread disinterest and/or hatred from fans because of his lack of personality and action after his magical transformation (see, for example, Hansen 2016; Heifetz 2019). Fans' apathetic or vitriolic responses and Meera's rejection point towards the lack of pleasure and/or interest that the flawless patriarchal reproduction/ faithful adaptation can affectively produce. His status as perfect copy does allow him to become King of Westeros, but his rejection by real fans and other characters in the show creates ambivalence around the practice of patriarchal reproduction and faithful adaptation.

The twin desires to achieve fidelity and the impossibility of doing so are highlighted in Bran's transformation and by Butler (1993, 176) in relation to gender: "it is an assignment which never is quite carried out according to expectation, whose addressee never quite inhabits the idea s/he is compelled to approximate." For Butler, this space of failure and parody is one where gender might be denaturalised and the hetero-sexual matrix subverted. Moreover, the act of repetition is "precisely that which *undermines* the conceit of voluntarist mastery designated by the subject in language" (Butler 1993, 176; original emphasis): there is no original actor behind the act. These ideas can be productively applied to adaptation studies, as in the case of Bran in *Game of Thrones*. By focusing on the adapted texts' inevitable failure to achieve fidelity *and* questioning the political structures through which the desire for fidelity is constituted, queer approaches to adaptation illuminate the ways in which adaptations open space for subversion even as their existence is the product of a desire to flawlessly reproduce the patriarchal nation.

Failed and/or ambivalent repetitions such as Bran's in *A Song of Ice and Fire* foreground this ambivalence and highlight its productive potential, as the boy learns to repeat The Three-Eyed Crow/Raven's rejection of domination and his embrace of relationality and interdependence. In addition, the novels draw attention to Bran's failed repetition as one in a series of repetitions rather than a copy of an original. The Three-Eyed

142   REIMAGINING MASCULINITY AND VIOLENCE

Crow/Raven troubles the notion of an original subject because his subjectivity is explicitly assembled out of a constellation of past greenseers who have left their souls in animals and trees. While Bran is still oscillating between the hegemonic knight and the greenseer masculinity at this point in *A Song of Ice and Fire*, he is learning the value of a form of identity/subjectivity that is caring, or that embraces the interconnectedness of all beings and rejects any attempt to privilege some bodies over others.

In both *Game of Thrones* and *A Song of Ice and Fire*, Bran's character and his merging with the Other illuminate one way in which masculinity might be embodied as a site of connection rather than isolation. Discussing psychic powers in fantasy fiction generally, Lenise Prater (2016, 23) argues that they "help to reimagine the boundaries between the self and the other, and this destabilization of the unified masculine subject provides space for an alternative understanding of identity." Bran's potential is also noted by Massie and Mayer (2014, 53), who argue that in *A Song of Ice and Fire* "Bran's paralysis allows him, paradoxically, to move more freely: to cross two borders, the first one, of a shamanistic nature, between humans and animals, the second of a metaphysical nature between mind and body." This movement is not necessarily of the liberating kind usually associated with the crossing of boundaries. Nevertheless, Bran's altered subjectivity has significant implications for his relationship to hegemonic violence and gender norms; his disruption of normative ideas about Cartesian dualism, identity, and subjectivity is demonstrated through his psychic bonds with the natural world, specifically animals and trees.

In *A Song of Ice and Fire*, Bran's magical powers allow him to foster kinship with animals, whereby he shares his consciousness with his direwolf. Early on in their adventures, Jojen tells Bran, "Part of you is Summer, and part of Summer is you" (CoK 398), and he later explains that "as you drift off [to sleep, your third eye] flutters open and your soul seeks out its other half" (CoK 472). Bran's relationship with Summer is defined by interdependence and relationality: phrases such as "part of you" and "other half" speak to the experience as one of mind-sharing rather than mind control. In these relationships, working together makes hegemonic violence unnecessary: there is no need for force or domination when each party recognises the value of intellectual and affective interdependence. Indeed, it is the caring masculinity that is prized here, and gives way to the potential for a non-hierarchical conceptualisation of kinship.

The capacity for proliferating the self through queer reproduction is emphasised through Bran's relationships with ravens. The first bird that Bran's mind magically enters consents to the experience: after a brief stint of mental cohabitation ends, "It flew to him and landed on his arm, and Bran stroked its feathers and slipped inside of it again" (DwD 524). The affectionate exchange between Bran and the bird indicates that the mind meld is consensual and rewarding for both subjects. The fact that the bird "flew to him" emphasises the equal partnership between the bird and the boy, and Bran's willingness to "stroke" the bird shows an awareness of their relationality; giving physical affection to the bird makes it comfortable allowing Bran to enter its mind. These two facets of the interaction indicate that Bran is beginning to adopt caring values and so begin to shift his masculine performance.

The boy finds that the relationship has more to offer than he expected. Soon after Bran re-enters the animal's mind, he "realized he was not alone" and the Three-Eyed Crow/Raven tells him that it is "A woman, of those who sing the song of earth [...] Long dead, yet a part of her remains, just as a part of you would remain in Summer if your boy's flesh were to die upon the morrow. A shadow on the soul" (DwD 524). It is by embracing the Other—the human embracing the animal, and the animal embracing the human—that the self is allowed to live on, to proliferate by entering a larger system of connection, to reproduce queerly. Bran's narrative provides a way of expanding the notion of caring masculinity, especially in relation to its potential for ambiguity, the affective rewards carers experience, and the non-human places where care work takes place, such as with animals and plants. The dynamic differs from the Kristevian model of abjection, whereby the subject pushes away the other (both actual others and parts of the self that one does not want to acknowledge) in order to produce the self. In *A Song of Ice and Fire*, Bran offers a means of breaking free from this cycle of rejection by fully embracing the Other. He shares his subjectivity to varying degrees with animals, trees, and other humans, and it is this caring masculinity and the web of connections it generates that allows him to enter the system of queer reproduction.

In *Game of Thrones*, Bran's alternative kinship and queer reproduction are expressed through his temporality and its effects on the narrative. At the start of season six, Bran and the previous Three-Eyed Crow/ Raven begin to share visions of the past, many of which concern Bran's father Eddard. Bran's insistent return to his father reflects his lingering investment in the patriarchal system of reproduction. He looks to his father for support and affection, as demonstrated by the fact that Bran tries to speak to Eddard, but he is unsuccessful. Some scenes indicate that Eddard hears Bran, but the Three-Eyed Crow/Raven insists that "The past is already written. The ink is dry" (S6E3 "Oathbreaker"). There is no growth to be found in biological and patriarchal family structures: it

144   REIMAGINING MASCULINITY AND VIOLENCE

is to queer kinship that Bran must turn. It is only when Bran embraces the fact that he "can see everything. Everything that's ever happened to everyone. Everything that's happening right now" (S7E3 "The Queen's Justice"), that his character begins to influence narrative events outside of his small group of companions.

Bran's queer kinship and caring masculinity grant him a unique power within *Game of Thrones*, one that leads him to have a significant effect on the narrative and be crowned King of Westeros. Bran (along with Sam Tarly and a wildling woman called Gilly) is responsible for unearthing the truth of Jon Snow's parentage and his status as legitimate heir to the Iron Throne (S7E7 "The Dragon and the Wolf"), and it is Bran who witnesses the white walkers' successful attack on the Wall, one which undoes ancient magic and allows them to enter Westeros proper for the first time (S7E7 "The Dragon and the Wolf"). Bran's queer kinship with ravens allows him to relay these important wartime updates to his family, allowing him to proliferate his knowledge queerly. The proliferation takes on increased importance at the end of season eight when the possibility for a more sustainable model of masculine repetition is highlighted as one of Bran's main credentials when Tyrion proposes that he become King of Westeros in "The Bells." The other nobles are initially dubious; Sansa points out that Bran "can't father children," but Tyrion argues that Bran's inability to reproduce the patriarchal system of reproduction is critical to his sovereignty. He says, "Sons of kings can be cruel and stupid, as you well know. [...] That is the wheel our Queen wanted to break. From now on rulers will not be born. They will be chosen." The reason for Bran's choosing is that his psychic powers allow him to embrace what Karla Elliott (2015, 2) calls "values of care" on a national scale. As the Three-Eyed Crow/Raven, Bran can see how all people are connected and shape one another's lives in the past and the present. Tyrion claims that Bran "is our memory. The keeper of all our stories. The wars, weddings, births, massacres, famines, our triumphs, our defeats, our past. Who better to lead us into the future?" (S8E6). Through his visions, Bran can see "all" of Westerosi history and thus the interdependence and relationality between all people. He is able to perform a caring masculinity on a mass scale, and it is implied that he will use these powers to reject domination because he can see how it has historically been used for monstrous ends. Bran's ascension can be seen as a blow to the system of patriarchal reproduction: its heteronormative logics are troubled as the biological family loses its central connection to power, as reflected by the dissemination of the Stark family across the land in the episode's final scenes. The normative masculine discourses with which

DISABLED MASCULINITIES

heterosexuality is tied are also contested as a disabled man is named king because of—rather than in spite of—his caring masculinity and his radical connection to other lives and stories.

While Bran's narrative ending in *Game of Thrones* appears to offer an intervention into the dominating, patriarchal masculinity that informed the pseudo-medieval feudal system, the reception of Bran's ascension reveals a more complex reality. Fans and critics alike have critiqued Bran's characterisation in the television series since he became the Three-Eyed Crow, primarily for his unhelpfulness and vague, eerie dialogue. His promotion to king inspired further criticism, with some claiming that the choice reinforces toxic curatorial fan culture (Romano 2019) and others highlighting his post-human magical identity as a political blessing and a narrative curse: "After seasons of remarkably inhumane rulers, Bran's true inhumanity is also the thing that makes him the most sensible choice" (VanArendonk 2019, para. 7). Bran being king makes sense, but he is not an exciting or satisfying option when compared to the other major contenders. The general dissatisfaction with Bran's ascension can be partially explained by my argument about masculinity, violence, and queer kinship. As I have shown throughout this book, *Game of Thrones* and *A Song of Ice and Fire* follow an internal narrative logic whereby characters who perform violence to dominate the Other have that violence turned against them with grisly ends, whereas characters who use violence to care for others have their knowledge and values proliferate through queer kinship. In *Game of Thrones*, Bran uses dominating violence in earlier seasons but trades this for care and queer kinship as the Three-Eyed Raven. While Bran can share his knowledge and wisdom with others as King of Westeros, the closing episodes and scenes do not highlight this potential or circularity. Bran is selected explicitly because he cannot sire children, but no form of queer proliferation is offered, as is the case for other characters. Instead, Bran becomes a dead end in a pseudo-medieval world that privileges repetition of families, Houses, bloodlines. Bran's ending, which is tied intimately to the ending of *Game of Thrones*, is unsatisfactory because it fails to follow its own logics around violence, care, circularity, and queer kinship. Bran's narrative reception undermines the subversive potential within the textual depiction of magically queered subjecthood.

Reception notwithstanding, the practice of reproducing queerly by spreading one's consciousness has valuable implications for how audiences are led to understand masculinity. T.A. Leederman (2015, 193) contends that *"A Song of Ice and Fire* suggests that hegemonic knowledge alone cannot solve our problems; we must look back, to earlier eras now wreathed in legend, and sideways, to other species,

146 REIMAGINING MASCULINITY AND VIOLENCE

for new conceptual tools and ways of being in the world." Key among these diverse ways of being is a sense of connection: "Bran is learning to see the world as a plane of immanence, of all people, times and happenings occurring in a web of connections, actions and reactions" (200). The "web of connections" in both the novels and television series facilitates a conception of subjectivity that breaks away from the patriarchal model, whereby the male body is singular, closed, and stable, and acts only in the interests of the self and for the purpose of perfectly reproducing the culture that sustains it. While *A Song of Ice and Fire* is incomplete, Bran's narrative in *Game of Thrones* reveals that hegemonic violence—such as that which underpins the version of knighthood to which he aspires—can only bring about domination and abjection, whereas caring masculinities that thrive on connection and mutual co-operation can provide a means of repeating that is not dependent upon others' destruction. Bran's narrative illuminates new theoretical directions for caring masculinity: the centrality of rejecting domination, the rewards for carers, and the fact that caring masculinities can be a source of power. Rejecting domination and embracing relationality does not mean rejecting an increase of social and political power; rather, it can lead to a type of power that is distinct from patriarchal structures.

"The Things I Do For Love"

"The things I do for love"—uttered as Jaime Lannister unflinchingly attempts to murder Bran to prevent the boy revealing his incestuous relationship with his twin sister Cersei (GoT 81; S1E1 "Winter is Coming")—combines hegemonic violence with supposed romantic devotion and thus captures some of that character's complex relationship to masculinity, disability, violence, and heteronormative kinship. From the first book of *A Song of Fire and Ice* and the first season of *Game of Thrones*, Jaime is constructed so that his appearance and masculine performance align with "the knights in the stories"—with his bright blonde hair, white armour, and renowned skill with a blade (GoT 73; S1E1 "Winter is Coming"). Yet this knight in white shining armour is in a relationship with his sister and secretly fathers her three children. This incestuous state at once bolsters and challenges the patriarchal system of reproduction and becomes a microcosm of Jaime's relation to his body. Jaime begins the series as an able-bodied character in a relationship that supports and contests heteropatriarchal systems of reproduction, and after his hand is severed his relation to Cersei drastically changes in the sense that he enters new queer kinships that allow him to share

DISABLED MASCULINITIES   147

his attitudes and skills in more enabling ways, even as he meets an ambiguous end in *Game of Thrones*.

Jaime cites his father, the patriarch Tywin Lannister, as informing his masculine performance before and after he is disabled in *A Song of Ice and Fire*. The most explicit example occurs after Tywin is murdered. As Jaime watches over his father's corpse, he says: "Father [...] it was you who told me that tears were a mark of weakness in a man, so you cannot expect that I should cry for you" (FfC 133). Jaime explicitly locates his father as the person who taught him how "a man" should behave: without "tears" or emotion. Tywin's model of masculinity rejects emotion in readiness to dominate the Other with violence. In this moment, where Jaime reflects on his father's teaching of masculinity, emotional repression is presented as "the result of social practices which require and produce such desires in order to effect their reproductive ends" (Butler 1990, 123). Tywin did not want Jaime to be marked as weak, for this might impede his public reproductive potential and, by extension, his capacity to carry on the Lannister legacy. Yet, by pointing out that by Tywin's own standards he "cannot expect that [his son] should cry" for his death, Jaime engages in one of the "parodic proliferation[s]" that Butler (188) notes in relation to gender subversion, whereby one "deprives hegemonic culture and its critics of the claim to naturalized or essentialist gender identities." A man crying over the death of his father in private is an affect that would appear natural and would therefore bolster the idea of patriarchal society (and normative masculinity), as such. Jaime reinforces the idea that men must be unemotional while revealing that idea as one that is learned rather than natural. Yet, ten pages later, he instils this same masculine practice in his son, King Tommen: "A man can bear almost anything, if he must [...] You can fight them, or laugh at them, or look without seeing ... go away inside" (FfC 143). In passing the act of emotional repression onto Tommen, Jaime imbues it with the power to connote masculinity while simultaneously disclosing gender as a learned practice.

Jaime's reliance on Tywin as a masculine role model is made more significant when he speaks of his father in ways that can be seen to cite religion, reflecting his constraining and enabling relation to patriarchal masculinity. Jaime says that "The warrior had been [his] god since he was old enough to hold a sword. Other men might be fathers, sons, husbands, but never Jaime Lannister, whose sword was as golden as his hair. He was a warrior, and that was all he would ever be" (FfC 138). Violent hegemonic domination over the Other defines Jaime's masculinity, but it also constrains him in embodied and affective ways: he cannot have a biological heterosexual family or gain feudal power from this structure.

148   REIMAGINING MASCULINITY AND VIOLENCE

Jaime is the father of Cersei's children, but he repeatedly indicates that he does not think of them as his own because his paternity is kept secret and he has no hand in raising them. He thinks, *"Joff was no more to me than a squirt of seed in Cersei's cunt"* (SoS2 435; original emphasis). Instead, he places his masculine intelligibility in the hands of the Warrior, one of seven gods in Westeros, who represents masculine battle prowess and courage (Wittingslow 2015). Jaime's description gives away the Warrior's phallic dimensions: he became attached to the Warrior when he could "hold a sword"—when he became capable of using phallic power—and the phallic power he gains from this citation point become as central to his identity as his Lannister lineage ("sword was as golden as his hair"). For Jaime, the Warrior is conflated with his father, Tywin. Readers see here the power of citation to guide identity, but also to constrict it: to his mind, Jaime would only "ever be" a knight. The conflation of Warrior/Tywin in Jaime's mind is reflected after his father's death, when he thinks: "Unbidden, his thoughts went to Brienne of Tarth. [...] *Father, give her strength.* Almost a prayer ... but was it the god he was invoking, the Father Above whose towering gilded likeness glimmered in the candlelight across the sept? Or was he praying to the corpse that lay before him?" (FfC 138; original emphasis). The play on the double meaning of the word "father" reveals Jaime's previously religious attachment to Tywin's hegemonic model of masculinity. Jaime prayed to the Warrior/Father/father and cited them as the "original" on which his own gender performance was based.

In *Game of Thrones*, Jaime's citation of Tywin is expressed through his clothing. In seasons six and seven, Jaime's costumes are near identical to ones his father wore, reflecting his redoubled commitment to his family after being removed from the Kingsguard. In "No One" (S6E8), "The Dragon and the Wolf" (S7E7), and several other episodes, Jaime wears nearly exactly the same clothing that Tywin wore in season one, including armour with a thick golden breastplate that features a gold lion in the centre and a black leather surcoat with gold clasps. The costumes reflects the masculine ideals that Tywin tried to instil in Jaime: heteronormative reproduction ("family"), hardness, practicality, prestige, and power. In short, it is attire that proclaims the wearer ready to dominate both physically and financially. The uncanny likeness between Tywin's and Jaime's costumes, especially in season seven, reflects Jaime's attachment to his father as his hegemonic model of masculinity.

Jaime's attachment to patriarchal systems and their violence in both *A Song of Ice and Fire* and *Game of Thrones* is demonstrated through his complex relationship to (incestuous) reproduction. In psychoanalytic terms, breaking the incest taboo refers to the prohibited love between

DISABLED MASCULINITIES

the infant and their parent (Butler 1990, 38). However, in Jaime's case, he breaks this taboo by having sex with his twin sister and secretly fathering her children. Jaime and Cersei's incestuous reproduction can be seen as an idyllic repetition of heteronormative kinship, which "implicitly figures culture as a whole, a unity, one that has a stake in reproducing itself and its singular wholeness through the reproduction of the child" (Butler 2002, 31). Because Jaime and Cersei are twins, they can reproduce the desired "singular wholeness" to a greater extent than most heterosexual reproductive couples. Yet their twin status also makes their union illegitimate and unacceptable; incest is prohibited by the symbolic law, and it is one of many non-normative sexual practices that is not acknowledged by the state (Butler 2002). Cersei's insistence upon only bearing her brother's children can be seen as parthenogenetic. The parthenogenetic model is especially visible when Cersei's public persona is taken into consideration: Jaime is not in the (sexual) picture, and the children, purportedly fathered by King Robert Baratheon, only bear a likeness to their mother. In short, Jaime's character is presented as at once deeply invested in, and resistant to, reproducing heteronormative kinship.

Jaime's acceptance of this system is unsurprising given that he receives social and literal rewards for his hegemonic violence as a knight of the Kingsguard, but in *A Storm of Swords* and season three of *Game of Thrones*, the limits of the dominant masculine discourse are made apparent by his contact with abjection when he becomes disabled. While Jaime is travelling to King's Landing as Brienne's prisoner, he escapes his bonds and attacks her in an effort to escape (SoS1 289; S3E2 "Dark Wings, Dark Words"). During the fight, Jaime makes a number of misogynistic and patronising comments about Brienne: in the television series, he calls her "a great beast of a woman," and in the novels he calls her "wench" (SoS1 289, 290), and mocks her by saying, "Come on, come on, my sweetling, the music's still playing. Might I have this dance, my lady?" (SoS1 290). Each comment cites one way in which Brienne fails to live up to Westeros's patriarchal expectations of women: she is physically large, not traditionally attractive, and lacks the feminine grace required by traditional courtship practices. Jaime's attempt to subordinate Brienne proves to be a mistake as the fight is long and loud, drawing the attention of a group of violent bandits. Their leader[1] severs Jaime's hand, and he is forced to wear it around his neck.

---

[1] In *A Song of Ice and Fire*, the leader of the group is Vargo Hoat, and in *Game of Thrones*, this character is merged from several in the novel into one: Locke.

150   REIMAGINING MASCULINITY AND VIOLENCE

While Jaime is tied to Brienne to keep him secure on his horse, "His hand was always between them. Urswyck had hung it about his neck on a cord, so it dangled down against his chest, slapping Brienne's breasts as Jaime slipped in and out of consciousness" (SoS1 415).

The severed limb—as partial corpse—represents the same threat of extreme abjection that I have associated with the corpse in previous chapters and it is especially horrifying in Jaime's case because he is not allowed to reject it after separation: he is forced to keep it "about his neck," a sign of his grotesque incompleteness. The hand's placement also gives it an eerie motion: it dangles and slaps, somewhere between life and death. The binary blurring is brought up repeatedly through the scene in *A Song of Ice and Fire*: Jaime comments that "Blood and pus seeped from his stump, and the missing hand throbbed every time the horse took a step" (SoS1 415). Alongside "blood and pus," Jaime experiences phantom limb syndrome, feeling as if his "missing hand [is] throbb[ing]," at once present and absent in a way that disrupts the binary between life and death. Likewise, in *Game of Thrones*, the hand takes up uncanny positions within the frame. In "And Now His Watch is Ended" (S3E4), Jaime tries to fight Locke and fails, after which he lies on the ground and there is a five-second-long close-up of his head and his hand. The two objects take up almost the same amount of screen space, speaking to the hand's presence as a character in its own right. Indeed, the mud obscures the limb to such an extent that it could well be alive. Jaime is correspondingly diminished as a character, from a whole and complex person to a severed hand. In both the television series and novels, the hand around Jaime's neck signals his descent into abjection, a collapse of his personal boundaries that results directly from his attempt violently to dominate Brienne.

In *Game of Thrones*, Jaime's abjection is coupled with references to his permeable sexual body. The first scene to feature Jaime after his hand is severed in "And Now His Watch Is Ended" (S3E4) begins with a six-second close-up of the dead hand, which pans to Jaime's face. In the same shot, the audience hears a man ask, "How many of those fingers do you reckon we could shove up his arse?" Locke responds, "Depends if he's had any practice. Is that the sort of thing you and your sister go in for, Kingslayer? She loosen you up for us?" Once Jaime's hand is taken, his body's fragility is exposed, and his private sexual exploits are revealed to have been public all along. States of vulnerability such as this are unacceptable for men because the male body is expected to be closed and firm so that it can support the symbolic order. While no man is actually able to embody these ideals, Jaime's amputation stands as an ongoing public reminder that his flesh is fragile and vulnerable,

DISABLED MASCULINITIES   151

and for this reason he becomes an open target for mockery as well as sexual assault. His body is no longer closed and contained but "loose" and vulnerable.

As the fragility of Jaime's male body is exposed, so too his masculine identity is shaken. After his wound is cleaned and he has time to reflect on the experience, it becomes clear that his hand and the acts it allowed him to perform were fundamental to his understanding of his own masculinity. Writing on Jaime's impairment in the novels, Massie and Mayer (2014, 52–53) argue that "his eventual mutilation, the loss of his sword hand, reduces him to the most abject form of dependency, for he had no abilities other than his fighting skills." The authors go on to claim that "disability, for Jaime, is punishment; it is a castration, the loss of his masculinity" (53). I agree that Jaime's masculinity is irrevocably altered, but his amputation is one part of a series of moments in which he is associated with the abject. In *A Storm of Swords*, Jaime thinks, "They had taken his hand, they had taken his *sword hand*, and without it he was nothing. [...] It was his right hand that made him a knight; his right arm that made him a man" (SoS1 417; original emphasis). Jaime's thoughts contain two sets of repeated phrases: "they had taken his hand" and "it was his right hand that made him." The repetition reflects the performativity of gender: Jaime repeatedly enacted masculinity by using his sword hand to perpetrate hegemonic violence, but once he loses the hand these repetitions become unintelligible.

Jaime's borders have been fundamentally disrupted and his sudden openness is interpreted as emasculation, reflected in *Game of Thrones* through other characters' dialogue. In *Game of Thrones*, Jaime laments that he has lost "my sword hand. I was that hand," and Brienne tells him that he "sound[s] like a bloody woman" (S3E4 "And Now His Watch Is Ended"). When Jaime refuses to speak as he leaves Harrenhal for the first time, Locke says, "I don't remember chopping your balls off" (S3E7 "The Bear and the Maiden Fair"), the reference to severed balls speaking to a loss of embodied masculinity. Once Jaime cannot repeat the form of phallic violence that granted him access to patriarchal power, it becomes clear that hegemonic violence has limited generative options. Violence is one of the stylised acts that produces Jaime as a knightly subject, but it also brings him into contact with the abject.

Jaime undergoes a symbolic rebirth after his hand is severed, which reflects his changed relationship to hegemonic violence in both the novels and television show. The rebirth occurs in the baths of Harrenhal, which in *Game of Thrones* is shown on screen as two tubs of steaming hot water in the ground inside a dark, cavernous chamber lit by candles

152   REIMAGINING MASCULINITY AND VIOLENCE

(S3E5 "Kissed by Fire") and is described in the novels as a "dim, steamy, low-ceilinged room filled with great stone tubs" (SoS1 503). Amid the womb-like imagery, Jaime tells Brienne why he murdered King Aerys II, relaying the sovereign's horrifying plan to set King's Landing ablaze with wildfire. When Jaime faints and Brienne calls out for help for "the Kingslayer," Jaime corrects her, saying "Jaime... my name is Jaime" (S3E5/SoS1 508). Jaime's invocation of his birth name as opposed to the nickname Kingslayer can be understood in both texts as an interpellation: just as Butler (1993, 177) argues that when a doctor says, "It's a girl!" they begin a process of "girling," so too does Jaime thrust himself out of the Kingslayer identity. The dark, cavernous space, the water, and the naming, all connote birth, but, as in the case of Bran, it is a reversal of the normative birth paradigm whereby the subject moves from the maternal to the paternal law, rejecting their kinship with the mother. Instead, Jaime is reborn as he rejects the law of the father and begins to untangle his repetition of hegemonic violence.

At the time of writing, *A Song of Ice and Fire* offers a stable and linear progression of Jaime's gender subversion whereby his rejection of patriarchal kinship is tied to his decision to adopt Brienne's caring masculinity and other-centred violence when he gives her the sword Oathkeeper. In the novels, Jaime says, "There was a time that I would have given my right hand to wield a sword like that. Now it appears I have, so the blade is wasted on me. Take it. [...] It would please me if you would call this one Oathkeeper" (SoS2 434). The way Jaime phrases the gift of the sword signals its relationship to his rejection of his Lannister ties and his desire to change his approach to violence through a more caring masculinity. Swords carry considerable phallic meaning in the fantasy genre, and Jaime's decision to name the sword Oathkeeper and to bequeath it to Brienne and her/their quest to save Sansa reflects his developing investment in caring masculinity as opposed to hegemonic masculinity. Audrey Moyce (2018, 66) argues that in *Game of Thrones* Oathkeeper is "an outward symbol of their living life on terms that do not fit with the harshly enforced norms around them [...] his gift of Oathkeeper to her is evidence of his remaking of his self and sense of honour." I agree that Oathkeeper is highly symbolic, and part of Jaime's and Brienne's divergence from the "norms around them" comes from their approach to violence.

Jaime's disability and the transference of the sword to Brienne also provide a moment for the creation of queer kinship structures and a rejection of the heteropatriarchal project. Jaime and Brienne create what Moyce (67) calls a "queer lineage," which is signalled through the sword. Tywin fetishised the Valyrian steel sword as a family heirloom

DISABLED MASCULINITIES

that would reflect the Lannisters' phallic power and be passed on from father to son, an exact copy reflecting the masculinity he also hoped to reproduce. However, in giving the sword to Brienne, Jaime wilfully abandons this heteropatriarchal project and instead privileges queer kinship. Jaime's gift can be seen to reflect the non-normative kinship that Butler (2002, 34) describes: "a kind of doing, one that does not reflect a prior structure but which can only be understood as an enacted practice." Jaime uses the sword and his inherited wealth to honour his oaths, but his growing sense of interconnectedness with others allows him to fulfil these oaths by working collaboratively with Brienne.

As Lord Commander of the Kingsguard, it is Jaime's sacred duty to record the order's history in the Book of White—the record of the Kingsguard's noble exploits—and when he reflects upon his own narrative, his rejection of hegemonic violence is foregrounded. Jaime observes that "more than three-quarters of his page still remained to be filled between the gold lion on the crimson shield on top and the blank white shield at the bottom. [...] the rest Jaime Lannister would need to write for himself. He could write whatever he chose, henceforth. Whatever he chose ..." (SoS2 436). Jaime realises that since he has abandoned patriarchal kinship ties in joining the Kingsguard and breaking from Cersei, he is now free to practise whatever type of heroism he chooses. As his narrative in the Book of White moves away from the Lannister shield to Kingsguard white, so too does Jaime plan to diverge from the heteropatriarchal violence that his father taught him. The repetition in the passage (write/write, chose/chose) reflects his entry into a new order of reproduction, but the openness of this queer kinship is disclosed through the exact words that are repeated: "write" and "chose" evoke a sense of agency that is denied by patriarchal systems. Jaime's family—the Kingsguard—is now chosen and passed on through writing rather than paternity. The scene also offers a metatextual commentary on the power of writing to recreate narratives about the real world. As the ellipsis ends the chapter in an open moment of possibility, so too do fantasy fictions more broadly leave space for unexpected masculine discourses that are separate from hegemonic violence.

After these introspective scenes Jaime transforms his approach to his own violence: he uses violence to care for others and recognises his relationality and interdependence with the Other. Long after Jaime leaves Brienne's company he talks to a man who mocks her appearance, and he responds with violence that defends her honour in her absence: "Jaime's golden hand cracked him across the mouth so hard the other knight went stumbling down the steps. [...] 'You are speaking of a

154 REIMAGINING MASCULINITY AND VIOLENCE

highborn lady, ser. Call her by her name. Call her Brienne'" (FfC 459–460). Jaime uses violence to care for Brienne and her reputation as he interpolates her into personhood: "Call her Brienne." The repetition in these sentences reflects the way in which Jaime's other-centred violence has become part of his performative repertoire, the means through which he enacts masculinity. The lack of abject signifiers in the scene may be seen as inviting readers to accept Jaime's violence, although the phrase "cracked him across the mouth" also foregrounds the embodied immediacy of the violence. Moreover, calling Brienne a "highborn lady" highlights the social class hierarchies that chivalry is associated with, suggesting that her intelligibility as human is dependent upon her (high) class status. Where once Jaime would have joined in the sexist banter, he now defends Brienne even against his own men, but ambivalence remains because Jaime is still enacting domination over the Other. The difference between Jaime's act of violence in this scene and hegemonic violence is power. Jaime does not dominate in order to gain power over the Other but to redress another act of domination, to take power from a subject who is discursively dominating the Other and return it symbolically to that Other. Jaime's act of violence, like the gender performativity Butler discusses in *Bodies That Matter* (1993, 184), is "implicated in that which one opposes, this turning of power against itself to produce alternative modalities of power [...] a difficult labor of forging a future from resources inevitably impure." Jaime's caring masculinity and its violence illuminate the fragility of caring masculinities, especially when care is assembled by turning the tools of a violent society against itself.

In both the novels and television series, Jaime rejects his father in favour of his queer kinship among the Kingsguard. Prior to his impairment, Jaime had little interest in this role: he joined so that he could be near Cersei (SoS1 156), and he infamously murdered the king he swore to protect. Yet after his maiming, Jaime realises that the Kingsguard may offer him an authentic set of connections and a type of power that is more rewarding than hegemonic violence. After Jaime's adventure with Brienne, but prior to Tywin's death, Tywin attempts to force Jaime out of the Kingsguard so that he can be heir to Casterly Rock, as I have noted. In the novels, Jaime vehemently rejects this idea, saying, "*'I don't want her, and I don't want your Rock!'* [...] 'I am a knight of the Kingsguard. The *Lord Commander* of the Kingsguard! And that is *all* I mean to be!'" (SoS2 282). In response, Tywin disowns Jaime: "'You are not my son.' Lord Tywin turned his face away. 'You say you are the Lord Commander of the Kingsguard, and only that. Very well, ser. Go do your duty'" (SoS2 283).

DISABLED MASCULINITIES 155

The text illuminates the intersection of queer and disability studies ideas through Jaime's interior monologue as he becomes Lord Commander in *A Song of Ice and Fire*, embracing a masculine performance, a title, and a body that denaturalise heteropatriarchal structures. Where once Jaime felt that he could only "ever" be a hegemonic warrior, "*all*" he now "mean[s] to be" is Lord Commander of the Kingsguard (SoS2 282; original emphasis)—a position that he means to use to enact violence in service of others. When Jaime first meets with his underlings as Lord Commander, he thinks, "It seemed queer to him to sit in the Lord Commander's seat where Barristan the Bold had sat for so many years. *And even queerer to sit here crippled.* Nonetheless, it was his seat, and this was his Kingsguard now" (SoS2 343; original emphasis). The repetition of the word "queer" highlights Jaime's experience of strangeness, as well as the non-normative system of reproduction into which he is entering. In the next book, Jaime thinks, "*No man can choose his brothers. [...] Give me leave to pick my own men, and the Kingsguard will be great again*" (FfC 255; original emphasis). By "great," Jaime means an order that practises other-centred violence and caring masculinity, which he learned from Brienne. Jaime's queer kinship and reproduction within the Kingsguard is one instance of the "radical social transformation" that is, according to Butler (2002, 40), "at stake when we refuse, for instance, to allow kinship to become reducible to 'family,' or when we refuse to allow the field of sexuality to become gauged against the marriage form."

As Jaime embraces the Kingsguard as a queer kinship structure, he also severs ties with his sister Cersei, a decision that reflects his rejection of the normative kinship bonds that privilege repetition. The breakdown of their relationship begins when Jaime returns to King's Landing after his hand is severed and he has begun to embrace Brienne's caring masculinity. Cersei's attachment to hegemonic masculinity as the ideal and her own emerging complicit masculinity lead her to reject him. Cersei struggles to reconcile Jaime's masculinity with his disability, "verbally attacking his physical appearance by insulting his 'ugly stump' [FfC 335] and criticizing his masculinity. Cersei equates Jaime's amputation with castration and emasculation" (Tarnowski 2019, 94). Jaime and Cersei's relationship breakdown comes to a climax when Jaime ignores Cersei's letter begging for help while she is imprisoned by the Church: "A snowflake landed on the letter. As it melted, the ink began to blur. Jaime rolled the parchment up again, as tight as one hand would allow, and handed it to Peck. 'No,' he said. 'Put this in the fire'" (FfC 761). Jaime chooses to ignore Cersei's "fevered and fervent" words: "*Come at once*, she said. *Help me. Save me. I need you now as I have*

156   REIMAGINING MASCULINITY AND VIOLENCE

never needed you before. I love you. I love you. I love you. Come at once" (FfC 761; original emphasis). Cersei's letter is rife with repetition, a reflection of her fear and urgency but also a symbol of her reliance upon the patriarchal system of reproduction. While *A Song of Ice and Fire* is still incomplete, it appears that in this moment Jaime chooses to break free from these repetitions when he puts her letter "in the fire," seemingly burning his last stake in hegemonic violence and its reproductive logics.

In *Game of Thrones*, Jaime's relationship with Cersei and the patriarchal logics it represents are far more ambivalent and foreground the ways in which reworking the terms of the law is a fragile strategy for subversion that holds the potential for relapse. Jaime returns to King's Landing in both the novels and television series after his sword hand is severed, although the exact timing of his return is different in each text and has a significant effect on his relation to patriarchal reproduction.

Jaime's ambivalent attachment to hegemonic masculine violence and patriarchal reproduction is emphasised in "Breaker of Chains" (S4E3), in which Jaime sexually assaults Cersei in anger over her self-oriented violence and, by extension, his frustration with his family and the patriarchal structures it supports. The rape scene is added to the television series as an expansion of Jaime's homecoming scene in *A Storm of Swords*. In the novel, Jaime returns after Joffrey's death, at the moment Cersei is in the Sept of Baelor. Joffrey's corpse is laid out near the altar to the Stranger (God of death) and the pair have consensual sex on a nearby altar to the Mother. In *Game of Thrones*, Jaime and Cersei's sex scene is changed to rape after Cersei begs Jaime to kill their brother Tyrion, whom Cersei believes is responsible for Joffrey's death. The pair kiss for a few moments, then Jaime says, "You're a hateful woman ... Why would the gods make me love a hateful woman?" (S4E3). Jaime kisses Cersei forcefully for a few moments, after which he pulls her to the ground and rapes her on the floor next to Joffrey's corpse.

The rape is complex and represents Jaime's attempt to turn the patriarchal law against itself while highlighting the fragility of this strategy. Cersei represents the Lannister family and the ableist patriarchal feudal system that sustains it, and this is emphasised throughout the scene. Cersei is shown in medium close-up while she speaks, with Joffrey's corpse in the foreground and his sword visible at his mother's chest. The viewer's eye is drawn from Joffrey's crowned head to the sword to Cersei's face, the vector highlighting Joffrey's status as patriarch and his repetition of hegemonic masculine violence, continued now through his mother as she attempts violently to dominate Tyrion through Jaime. In addition, the presence of Joffrey's corpse specifically cites heterosexual reproduction (he is Jaime and Cersei's son), though

DISABLED MASCULINITIES

it is the failure of this type of reproduction that is emphasised because Joffrey personifies both perfect heteropatriarchal reproduction as the son of two twins and failed heteropatriarchal reproduction because he performed a monstrous masculinity in life and died before he could continue his line by producing an heir. Jaime's decision to have sex right next to his son's corpse and within a holy site further speaks to a radical lack of attachment to patriarchal reproduction and the structures (here, the Church) that upload it. Jaime's decision sexually to assault Cersei comes from a desire to reject hegemonic masculine violence and the Lannister family (as a symbol of heteropatriarchal reproduction), although at this point in the narrative hegemonic masculine violence is also one of the only tools available to him. Jaime was raised to use self-oriented violence to perform masculinity and solve problems, and he has few options but to turn this strategy against the patriarchal system when his disablement and queer kinship with Brienne of Tarth allow him to reject this structure.

Turning the law against itself is a fragile strategy, as Butler (1993, 181) argues, and this tenuousness is foregrounded as Jaime's act of hegemonic masculine violence is shown to be a repetition that viewers are invited to critique through abjection. Regardless of Jaime's motives, he uses violence to dominate a woman, and the act of rape specifically highlights his sexual power and greater physical strength, and naturalises the idea that women are inferior to men. The violence is also self-oriented: Jaime rapes Cersei because he is angry with her for asking him to murder their brother Tyrion and because he is frustrated with her and their family's violent quest for power. His act of violence is hegemonic and self-oriented, like the sovereign and monstrous men I have analysed, and similarly leads to an encounter with the abject. The presence of Joffrey's corpse gives the scene an unsettling tone, especially because the stones that are used to cover corpses' eyes in Westeros are painted with pupils and irises and give an uncanny illusion of wakefulness. The blurring of life and death is most pronounced when the corpse's arm moves twice in the background because it is bumped as Jaime pushes Cersei up against the bier. Jaime's act of hegemonic masculine violence leads to a physical encounter with the abject corpse and an increase in the corpse's own abjection as it is momentarily reanimated. In addition to the moving arm, there is also a momentary threat that the corpse will fall from the bier and onto Jaime and Cersei because Cersei clutches the blanket under the corpse as Jaime is raping her. The scene ends with Cersei repeating the words, "It's not right," to which Jaime counters the words, "I don't care" three times as Cersei grasps the blanket. The repeated dialogue can be seen to foreground

158   REIMAGINING MASCULINITY AND VIOLENCE

Jaime's decision to uphold patriarchal systems of reproduction that privilege perfect repetitions, a decision which is critiqued because it leads to a moment where the corpse threatens intense abjection, namely, falling on Jaime and Cersei mid-coitus. Jaime's violence tenuously balances between repeating hegemonic masculine violence and the ensuing abjection critique and turning that violence against itself in order to resist patriarchal structures and rework his masculinity as a disabled man. Jaime's act of rape is similar to the way Butler (1993, 88) describes the film *Paris Is Burning*: it "remains caught in an irresolvable tension" wherein "a fatally unsubversive appropriation takes place." Jaime's act of hegemonic masculine violence is complex and multifaceted, but it is ultimately a "fatally unsubversive appropriation" because it repeats the heteropatriarchal reproductive logics he aims to resist.

Jaime is positioned as more successfully reworking his masculine performance and rejecting hegemonic masculine violence in the next episode, "Oathkeeper," when he begins to embrace a caring masculinity by aiding Brienne of Tarth on her quest. In both *A Song of Ice and Fire* and *Game of Thrones*, Jaime gives Brienne the Valyrian steel sword, which she names Oathkeeper, and in *Game of Thrones* the gift is expanded to include armour and a squire called Podrick. In the previous chapter, I noted that this gift affirms Brienne's queer gender identity and represents a desire to rework the sovereign and hegemonic masculine performances of Eddard Stark and Tywin Lannister. Now I wish to consider how the act can be viewed as one of care from Jaime to Brienne and a rejection of patriarchal systems of reproduction that, as with the rape, does repeat these structures but more successfully reforges them. This is largely achieved through the additional scene where Tywin gives the sword to Jaime (S4E1 "Two Swords"), making the connection between the phallic sword, Tywin's masculine performance, and hegemonic violence apparent. The added scene encourages audiences to see Jaime's transferral of Oathkeeper to Brienne as an act in which he is attempting to perform caring masculinity by rejecting patriarchal domination, embracing his affective attachment to Brienne and his own honour, and recognising their interconnectedness as Brienne fulfils an oath that Jaime swore to Catelyn Stark. Jaime is using the tools of hegemonic masculine violence, namely, the Valyrian steel sword, armour, and a squire, but he successfully reroutes their original aims by removing them from their patriarchal lineage (Eddard to Tywin to Jaime) and intended use as a phallic symbol of patriarchal reproduction (biological father to son). Instead, Jaime uses these objects to perform a caring masculinity that actively disrupts heteronormative phallic power and

DISABLED MASCULINITIES   159

patriarchal reproduction, turning these tools against the law by giving phallic power to a queer character through a queer kinship bond that supplants Westerosi patriarchal reproductive logics. Jaime's masculine performance continues to shift fluidly between hegemonic and caring in the season that follows, and his relationship to violence becomes even more ambiguous.

Jaime's caring masculinity, especially his embrace of relationality and interconnectedness, causes him temporarily to reject Cersei at the end of season seven after he learns that she has no intention of fulfilling her pledge to fight the white walkers. When Cersei reveals her true intentions to Jaime, he says, "I pledged to ride north. I intend to honour that pledge" (S7E7 "The Dragon and the Wolf"). Jaime's decision to fulfil his pledge reflects his embrace of "values of care" (Elliott 2015, 2) in this moment, as he recognises that all Westerosi people are connected in this battle and the outcome. Cersei tells him that he is committing treason and she stands on the verge of violence. It is here that Jaime brings up their complex investment in traditional heterosexual kinship. He tells Cersei, "I'm the only one you have left. Our children are gone. Our father is gone. It's just me and you now." Yet Cersei still has faith in their House, telling Jaime, "There's one more left to come," and placing her hand on her stomach. Gregor pulls out his sword, and Jaime walks away. In the beginning of season eight, viewers learn that Jaime has travelled to Winterfell to honour his oath to fight the white walkers rather than remain with Cersei and support her plans to dominate Westeros. His attachment to caring masculinity leads him to embrace the fact that the peoples of Westeros are interrelated and interconnected: if the living armies that oppose the Lannisters are defeated at Winterfell, then the nation is doomed to an endless Long Night. Jaime's decision to abandon Cersei is thus a means of using violence to care for the nation.

Jaime reworks his masculine performance by embracing and reorienting the acts of violence that his society encourages, and viewers are encouraged to recognise the fragility of this strategy through his narrative arc in season eight. In the episode "A Knight of the Seven Kingdoms," Jaime arrives in Winterfell and Daenerys, Jon, and Sansa decide whether to accept his offer to fight the living dead. Daenerys asks why he has "abandoned [his] house and family," and Jaime says that the battle "goes beyond loyalty. This is about survival" (S8E2). Jaime's caring masculinity allows him to recognise the interdependence and relationality of all humans, although the rulers are dubious until Brienne vouches for his honour. She says, "I know Ser Jaime. He is a man of honour. [...] Ser Jaime defended me and lost his hand because of it.

160   REIMAGINING MASCULINITY AND VIOLENCE

Without him, my lady, you would not be alive. He armed me, armoured me, and sent me to find you and bring you home because he'd sworn an oath to your mother." Jaime's acts of care are linked to honour by Brienne, who is in turn in a position to defend Jaime because of their queer kinship bond. Jaime repeats Brienne's caring masculinity and is accepted into Winterfell because of it, although he still chooses to use violence as a tool for survival. Jaime's attempts to use violence as a form of care can be illuminated by Butler's arguments about subversion: "occupied by such terms and yet occupying them oneself risks a complicity, a repetition, a relapse into injury, but it is also the occasion to work the mobilizing power of injury, of an interpellation one never chose" (1993, 83). Jaime actively attempts to constitute his masculinity through violence and care, and in the first half of season eight audiences are invited to view this strategy as a success as Jaime is accepted into Winterfell, survives the Long Night, and begins an emotional and sexual relationship with Brienne. Jaime attempts to "rework the mobilizing power of injury" that the hegemonic masculine model has caused him, but his continued citation of these norms is precarious and makes him susceptible to relapse.

Jaime's caring masculinity is centrally constituted through reworking masculine violence, and the ambivalent potential for this strategy is highlighted when he learns of Cersei's impending death and chooses to return to King's Landing. The decision itself appears to be motivated by concern for Cersei; immediately after Jaime learns that Cersei will probably be executed soon, the scene changes to a shot of Jaime later in the evening. The scene begins with a close-up of Jaime sitting on a chair in front of Brienne's bed wearing his dark red leather coat, his shoulder and torso taking up three-quarters of the frame. The tone is pensive, and the low lighting and sombre string music indicate that Jaime is experiencing an emotional struggle. His arms are folded and his prosthetic and non-prosthetic hand are emphasised because they are the lightest colours (gold and flesh) in the frame. The visual focus on Jaime's red coat and golden hand indicate that his familial ties are weighing upon him, and this is confirmed through dialogue after he leaves and Brienne confronts him. She says, "You're not like your sister. You're not. You're better than she is. You're a good man and you can't save her. You don't need to die with her. Stay here. [pause] Stay with me. Please. Stay." Jaime responds, "You think I'm a good man? I pushed a boy out a tower window, crippled him for life. For Cersei. I strangled my cousin with my own hands, just to get back to Cersei. I would have murdered every man, woman, and child in Riverrun for Cersei. She's hateful. And so am I." There is considerable disjuncture

DISABLED MASCULINITIES 161

between Brienne's dialogue and Jaime's, as well as conflicting meanings coming from each character. Brienne frames his decision through the caring masculinity he has recently adopted, assuming that Jaime wishes to save Cersei's life. At this point in the narrative Brienne's view makes the most sense, given that all that has changed is Cersei's impending execution. Instead, Jaime explains his decision by citing his past acts of hegemonic violence: two murders (one attempted and one successful) and one threat of mass murder and infanticide. The acts Jaime mentions occurred earlier in the series (seasons one, two, and six, respectively) and prior to his break with Cersei at the end of season seven, so it is unclear why he feels they are relevant to his decision.

When Jaime does return to King's Landing in "The Bells" he makes no attempt to aid Cersei's military operations but instead focuses exclusively on finding a way for her to escape the capital. There is a tension between Jaime's insistence that he is a "hateful" man and his attempt to care for Cersei as she loses the war. Indeed, Jaime's final moments in the series are spent caring for Cersei: searching for an escape route, holding her in his arms, and soothing her when she realises they are about to die. His final words exemplify this tension: he says, "Look at me. Look at me! Nothing else matters. Nothing else matters. Only us" (S8E5). The repetition within the dialogue reflects Jaime's ambivalent ties to patriarchal systems of reproduction. Not only does Jaime repeat half of his lines ("look at me" and "nothing else matters"), he is also repeating his own dialogue from "The Red Woman" (S6E1): "Fuck prophecy, fuck fate, fuck everyone who isn't us. We're the only ones who matter. The only ones in this world." In season six, Jaime, like Cersei, is attached to violent and self-centred heteropatriarchal systems, and the echo of this self-oriented dialogue during his death scene suggests a circularity between his previous acts of hegemonic violence and his death, as in the case of the sovereign and monstrous characters in the series. However, there is a tension between Jaime's return to an individualistic hegemonic/complicit masculinity and the acts that constitute those masculine performances. Jaime returns to King's Landing to save Cersei's life and care for her in their final moments, neither of which is a self-centred action. Jaime embraces the relationality and interdependence between Cersei and himself and acts out of love—though it is unclear whether that love is brotherly or romantic. The conflicts and tensions surrounding Jaime's narrative ending in *Game of Thrones* reflect what Butler (1993, 185) calls "the ambivalent condition of the power that binds," and exemplifies Jaime's tenuous struggle and failure to rework the tools of his violent society in order to make the world a more liveable place.

162   REIMAGINING MASCULINITY AND VIOLENCE

"I Drink and I Know Things"

Hegemonic violence is remade in different ways through Jaime's brother Tyrion, whose disability is congenital; he has achondroplasia and scoliosis, leading him to be referred to as a "dwarf" or "imp." Tyrion is arguably the central protagonist in both the novels and television series: he has the most perspective chapters in the novels and in *Game of Thrones* he is features in fifty-four episodes and has 697 minutes of on screen time, the most of any character (Payne 2017; Snowarkgaryan 2019). He is venerated among fan blogs and discussion boards (Moglia 2014; Sparky 2012; Winteriscoming 2013), and a collection of his witticisms has been published as a companion text (Martin 2013). Tyrion has several official appointments in service to the Crown but is unjustly tried and convicted of murdering his nephew Joffrey. On the eve of his execution, Tyrion escapes thanks to his brother Jaime, and after murdering his father he travels to Essos where he allies himself with Daenerys. In the novels, Tyrion has yet to meet Daenerys, but travels to her with a group of companions only to be kidnapped by Daenerys's former confidant Jorah Mormont, who intends to win back his former queen's favour. *Game of Thrones* has expanded Tyrion's narrative, in which he officially joins with Daenerys and is appointed Hand of the Queen and acts in this role as they return to Westeros. After seeing the devastation Daenerys causes in King's Landing, Tyrion breaks from Daenerys and is sentenced to die, but persuades Jon to murder Daenerys before she does so and later becomes Bran's Hand of the King.

Tyrion's character in *Game of Thrones* is informed by the history of dwarfism in the West rather than by discourses of disability (Backstrom 2012), and like dwarves in freak shows, one of Tyrion's main functions within the narrative is to entertain readers with humour. While this historical background may reinforce the idea that small-statured people are servants whose function is to entertain their masters, Tyrion implicitly critiques ableist discourses on numerous occasions rather than his own non-normative body (Harrison 2019). Having been born with his disabilities, Tyrion has a different relationship to masculinity than the other two men I have analysed: Jaime pushes Bran from a window and the boy becomes paraplegic; and Jaime's hand is severed and he becomes disabled. By contrast, Tyrion's impairment is always part of his life in both *A Song of Ice and Fire* and *Game of Thrones*. He is hyper aware of the ways in which he must negotiate his masculinity—through intellect and sexuality—so that he remains intelligible.

Tyrion, like his older brother Jaime, cites his father Tywin. Tyrion says that "all his authority derived from his father" (GoT 61), a statement that speaks to Tyrion's literal, gendered, and symbolic reliance upon the Lord of Casterly Rock. Even Tyrion's name is embedded in a patriarchal system of reproduction; the "Ty" prefix is passed on from Tywin, who was named by his father Tytos. The Lannister name—"My name," as Tywin says (SoS1 65)—and Tyrion's male body spares him from being killed as an infant, as most short-statured people in Westeros are, and gives him power and wealth. Tyrion's masculinity is also "derived from his father": he expects to be like Tywin and this expectation is what leads him to repeat his father's masculinity in some ways. On a deeper level, all of Tyrion's authority is derived from the Law of the Father, the symbolic order that ensures the repetition of hegemonic violence. Tyrion relies upon Tywin as a representation of the paternal law through which he is produced as an intelligible subject.

In *A Song of Ice and Fire*, Tyrion's multiple dependencies on his father are revealed when he talks about adopting Tywin's masculine performance to bolster his political power. While negotiating with Cersei, Tyrion thinks, "He loved his brother's reckless wrath, but it was their lord father he must try and emulate. *Stone, I must be stone, I must be Casterly Rock, hard and unmovable*" (CoK 703; original emphasis). The word "emulate" explicitly discloses Tyrion's repetition of his father's masculinity, which he associates with "stone," being "hard" and "unmovable." Moreover, the repetitiveness of Tyrion's phrasing—"*I must be stone, I must be Casterly Rock*"—reflects the repetitive nature of gender performance, while the words themselves suggest phallic power, emotional repression, and physical strength, thus highlighting the hegemonic aspirations that inform Tywin's masculinity. The narrator claims that Tyrion has successfully repeated his father's masculine performance during his conversation with Cersei: "he'd reached for his father's voice, and found it" (CoK 704). In this instance, the "father's voice" is one that speaks in hegemonic violence; Tyrion pretends that he would be repeating self-oriented violence to subordinate the Other. Tyrion says, "Whatever happens to [Tyrion's friend Alayaya] happens to Tommen as well, and that includes the beatings and rapes" (CoK 704). Tywin's/Tyrion's "voice" emotionlessly threatens to perpetrate violence against his young nephew to gain power over Cersei, even though he has no intention of actually doing so. While Tyrion's compassion stops him from repeating Tywin's masculinity more faithfully, he claims that he is Tywin "writ small" (SoS2 498–499), signalling the central role that his father plays in shaping his masculinity.

In *Game of Thrones*, these repetitions are expressed through Tyrion's dialogue and costumes. Tyrion regularly uses his father's wrath as an indirect threat or promise of reward: he tells Cersei that "father would

164   REIMAGINING MASCULINITY AND VIOLENCE

be furious" (S2E1 "The North Remembers"), and he uses his family name and informal motto—"a Lannister always pays his debts"—to create the illusion of power. Likewise, Tyrion's costumes reflect his citation of his father when he is acting as Hand of the King in season two. Tyrion wears a black leather surcoat with gold clasps, exactly what Tywin wears in the same season (S2E8 "The Prince of Winterfell"). Tyrion's gender proves to be, as Butler (1990, 34) argues, a compulsory performance that grants gendered coherence and intelligibility.

This all changes when Tyrion is unjustly accused of Joffrey's murder and he undergoes a symbolic rebirth as he violently abandons Tywin's masculine ethos. As Tyrion escapes his jail cell, the spymaster Varys leads him through a series of dark, damp tunnels that evoke a womb. In the novel, Tyrion describes "the dark of a twisting turnpike stair," a "place of cold stone and echoing darkness" (SoS2 492), "traps for the unwary," "a damp bone-chilling cold" (SoS2 493) within "the blackness of the tunnel," and describes himself as *scuttling through the dark, holding hands with a spider*" (SoS2 494; original emphasis). In *Game of Thrones*, the viewer sees a sequence of shots totalling fifteen seconds in which Jaime and Tyrion run through a series of tunnels. The scene is made unsettling in two ways: Jaime holds a flickering torch that gives the tunnels an eerie atmosphere, and the music is fast paced and punctuated with low drum beats that imply looming danger. In the same way that tunnels function in horror films, this journey can be illuminated by Creed's (1993, 53) argument that dark tunnels and enclosed spaces reflect patriarchal society's fear of the female reproductive system. Tyrion's journey through the black cells is a kind of transformation, marking the gestation period in which he moves through hegemonic violence to a different citation point. When Tyrion emerges from the tunnels, he is faced with abjection.

In *Game of Thrones*, Tyrion discovers and kills his former lover/ prostitute Shae in his father's bed and a considerable amount of screen time is spent on her corpse, emphasising Tyrion's abjection in the moment of his rebirth (S4E10 "The Children"). Tyrion's discovery of Shae is horrifying because Tyrion thought that she had fully accepted his masculine performance and reciprocated with heterosexual love, despite her testifying against Tyrion when he is on trial for Joffrey's murder. Shae's seeming betrayal is coded as one born out of heartbreak because the song "I Am Hers, She Is Mine" plays when Tyrion breaks up with Shae (S4E2 "The Lion and the Rose") and when she enters the court room to testify (S4E6 "The Laws of Gods and Men"). Shae's presence in Tywin's bed reveals that she takes the opportunity to gain favour from a more powerful patriarch. In response, Tyrion fully embraces hegemonic violence in the sense that he violently dominates a woman because she made choices about her own bodily autonomy, but this decision is met with extreme abjection. Right after Tyrion strangles Shae to death, there is a forty-four-second close-up of his face, which tracks right to include Shae's. The extreme length of the shot forces the audience to witness Tyrion come undone in two ways: through his contact with the corpse and through his emotions. Tyrion does not "thrust [the corpse] aside in order to live," as Kristeva (1982, 3) posits, but sits with the corpse and we see his realisation that he never enacted the masculine performance he sought because Shae never loved him. Her open eyes and mouth add an additional layer of horror as the line between life and death is blurred. The framing suggests an unsettling duality between them: Tyrion and Shae both take up a third of the frame on either side of the screen, with another third between them. It is fitting that Tyrion's unemotional masculinity also falters here even as the emotion makes Tyrion's violence more acceptable for a fantasy genre where violence is expected to be met with negative feelings: during the close-up, his emotions are on display because his facial expressions are highlighted: fear, anger, sadness, and regret. Tears glisten on the skin around his eyes and he continues to hold the chain he used to strangle Shae while he cries. His hands shake, and he says, "I'm sorry," twice. After the first time, the camera shifts to a long shot of the silent bedroom where Tyrion appears small and alone. Tyrion repeats his apology, and the audience sees that this is where the repetition of hegemonic masculine violence has brought him: nothing but death, abjection, and isolation.

In the novels, Tyrion is faced with the abject not when he kills Shae, but when he murders his father and the man defecates, taking the rebirth metaphor through additional moments of abjection and ambiguity. As he shoots his father, Tyrion observes, "the bolt slammed into [Tywin] above the groin and he sat back down with a grunt [...] blood seeped out around the shaft, dripping down into his pubic hair and over his bare thighs." As Tywin dies, Tyrion smells "the sudden stench, as his bowels loosened in the moment of death. [...] Lord Tywin Lannister did not, in the end, shit gold" (SoS2 498–499). The conflation of corpse, blood, and faeces works alongside the tunnels Tyrion travelled through: as Creed (1993, 49) argues in relation to the horror film, "blood, afterbirth, faeces" are the signs of the womb's inherent "contamination" because it "represents the utmost in abjection [...] it contains a new life form which will pass from inside to outside."

On a symbolic level, Tyrion rejects phallic hegemonic violence in the novel through echoes of his actual birth and references to his father's penis. The idea that Tyrion is (re)born as he kills his father shares a parallel with his literal birth, after which his mother died. Tywin claims that Tyrion "killed your mother to come into the world" (SoS1 65), an assertion that reflects his patriarchal assumptions, namely, that men murder women in order to gain power. Tyrion dismisses Tywin's masculine practices, a change that is made clear when he reflects, *"If only I was better with a crossbow, I would have put [the bolt] through that cock you made me with"* (DwD 16; original emphasis). Tyrion recognises that his father *"made me"*—it was Tywin who sired him, and it was Tywin's phallic masculine performance that allowed Tyrion to become intelligible—but he severs his repetition of this hegemonic gender model and its violence by diminishing his father's phallic power to a fleshy and vulnerable penis, and then expressing a desire to destroy it (and the phallic legacy that lingers). Tyrion's murder is highly symbolic: he destroys his father, the Westerosi patriarch who represents the Law of the Father/symbolic order, as he also resists this system of violence. At the same time, he uses violence to satisfy his personal desire for revenge and in that way reproduces hegemonic violence. Tyrion's escape to Essos on a boat can be seen as a metaphor for the liminal and ambivalent masculine space he enters, without a firm point of reference for his life or his gender.

When Tyrion lands on Essos in *A Song of Ice and Fire* he gives his gendered and political allegiance to his imagined version of Daenerys and her quest to reclaim the Iron Throne. More specifically, Tyrion shifts the object or intention of his performance of masculinity: where once he attempted to reproduce his father's hegemonic masculinity, he now emphasises his role as political negotiator. In the novels, Tyrion has only just entered Daenerys's life, but his intentions are made clear. He tells his fellow Daenerys supporter, Illyrio Mopatis, "Knights know only one way to solve a problem. They couch their lances and charge. A dwarf has a different way of looking at the world" (DwD 87). The "different way" is elucidated later in the novel: Tyrion explains that "I can tell Her Grace how my sweet sister thinks, if you call it thinking. I can tell her captains the best way to defeat my brother, Jaime, in battle. I know which lords are brave and which are craven, which are loyal and which are venal. I can deliver allies to her. And I know much and more of dragons" (DwD 139). Political knowledge, persuasion, and negotiation are now Tyrion's gendered currency, and he intends to use them to make himself intelligible as valuable to the queen. It is significant that Tyrion is working against the members of his biological family by claiming queer kinship with Daenerys, both literally in the way he describes his skills to Illyrio and symbolically as Daenerys intends to destroy the system from which the Lannisters gain their power. The transition from

DISABLED MASCULINITIES

Tywin to Daenerys is made explicit in Tyrion's internal monologue. He thinks: *"Are you down there in some hell, Father? A nice cold hell where you can look up and see me help restore Mad Aerys's daughter to the Iron Throne?"* (DwD 88; original emphasis). Tyrion uses an imagined version of Daenerys to legitimise and makes intelligible a masculinity that privileges intelligence, negotiation, and knowledge, and their application to the task of restoring Daenerys to the Iron Throne so that she may give Tyrion his birthright—Casterly Rock—and destroy Cersei.

In *A Song of Ice and Fire*, Tyrion's reworked masculine performance appears to be a healthier alternative, though he does still work towards violent domination of the Other and rejects his own emotions. He reverses these hegemonically masculine tools, though as in Jaime's case this strategy is tenuous and prone to relapse. For Tyrion, these regressions take the form of sexual violence. Tyrion rapes two prostitutes on two separate occasions (DwD 27; 338–339), and these acts are linked to hegemonic masculinity through references to Tywin. In Volantis, Tyrion purchases the woman's services and then sees "revulsion in her eyes" (DwD 337). Tyrion cites his father Tywin in response, asking: "Do I offend you, sweetling? I am an offensive creature, as my father would be glad to tell you if he were not dead and rotting" (DwD 337). After the rape, "He rolled off feeling more ashamed than sated. *This was a mistake. What a wretched creature I've become.* [...] *This girl is as good as dead. I have just fucked a corpse.* Even her eyes looked dead. *She does not even have the strength to loathe me*" (DwD 338). The abjection in this instance is far more pronounced. Two corpses are evoked, and rather than banish the corpse-prostitute Tyrion embraces her abjection and *"fucked a corpse."* The resonances between the two rape scenes are striking: Tyrion feels disempowered by a woman's disgust, cites Tywin, performs hegemonic masculine violence in order to subordinate the Other, and is met with abjection. It is easy for Tyrion to slip back into heteropatri-archal reproductive logics because his reworked masculine performance as Daenerys's future advisor is based upon a fragile appropriation of domination, where he uses his intelligence and knowledge to help her conquer the Other. Even though he appears to leave his hegemonic masculine models behind, he is prone to relapse and rupture: he seeks to help make the world a more livable place by helping Daenerys, but he also claims that the only reward he seeks for his service is to "rape and kill my sister" (DwD 430). Reversing the terms of domination proves a tenuous strategy, and in the novels it leads Tyrion to be haunted by a desire to dominate and the danger of abjection.

Tyrion begins to resist hegemonic masculine violence by entering a form of queer reproduction through his relationship with another

168   REIMAGINING MASCULINITY AND VIOLENCE

short-statured character, although his attempts to embrace caring values are fragile and ambiguous. Tyrion creates new kinship ties by acting as a brother- and mother-figure to the character Penny while they are enslaved in Essos. He reflects that, "Sometimes he wanted to slap her, shake her, scream at her, anything to wake her from her dreams. [...] Instead of giving her a good hard crack across that ugly face of hers to knock the blinders from her eyes, he would find himself squeezing her shoulder or giving her a hug" (DwD 888; original emphasis). Tyrion desires violently to dominate Penny and force her to recognise the ableism in her world and that which she has internalised. He wants to empower her by "knock[ing] the blinders from her eyes," but the masculine tools he wishes to repeat are those of violence: to "slap," "shake," "scream," give "her a good hard crack" across the face. And yet, Tyrion chooses not to repeat and instead offers Penny physical affection. He cares for Penny despite his frustration, embracing their interdependence and relationality even as he struggles internally with a desire to relapse into hegemonic acts of violence.

Tyrion's attempts to embrace caring values while maintaining a partial attachment to hegemonic masculinity is further highlighted as he attempts to interpret Penny's melancholy. Tyrion observes, "Penny had been searching for a new master since the day her brother Groat had lost his head. *She wants someone to take care of her, someone to tell her what to do*" (DwD 1014; original emphasis). Tyrion's interpretation of Penny's desire is highly ambivalent. His assumption that she wants "a new master" is inflected with a hegemonically masculine assumption that all relationships are unequal and that being "*take[n] care of*" is a subordinate position, synonymous with being told "*what to do.*" He does not treat Penny as an equal and ask her what she wants; he actively refuses her romantic overtures on several occasions and refuses to believe that she may want a romantic partnership with him. Yet Tyrion does attempt to care for Penny based on his flawed interpretation of her wishes. Tyrion believes that Penny derives a sense of security and love from being consensually dominated—what we might call caring domination. Her desire illuminates a new aspect of caring masculinity, namely, that domination can be an act of care when it is mutually agreed upon and comes from a place of emotional openness and a recognition of interdependence and relationality, such as in the case of bondage and discipline, domination and submission, sadism and masochism (BDSM) (see, for example, Smith Rainey 2018). Tyrion recognises that he does not have the capacity to provide this type of connection but Penny needs hope in order to survive, so he lies to her "to stop her mooning" and offers to "find [her] a kind master when this war is done" (DwD 1014).

DISABLED MASCULINITIES

Tyrion's relationship with Penny demonstrates his new capacity to enter into the system of queer kinship, which Butler (1993, 94) describes as "a set of kinship relations that manage and sustain [...] in the face of dislocation, poverty, homelessness." Now that Tyrion has severed ties with his biological family and the system of patriarchal reproduction and violence that it represents, he can build these queer kinship relationships in which he embraces the Other.

Tyrion's changing relationship to hegemonic masculine violence and patriarchal systems of reproduction is likewise partial in *Game of Thrones*, in which his costumes correspond with a change in his masculine performance and where he begins to perform caring masculinity as he adopts Daenerys as his masculine citation point. Tyrion references Daenerys's gender performance in seasons six and seven to validate his own masculinity, demonstrating his connection to a powerful figure and her family's symbolism, and the change is expressed through the similarities between their clothing. While Daenerys's masculine performance becomes monstrous in the final season as her violence becomes self-oriented, in previous seasons she performs a caring masculinity whereby she uses violence to care for the Other. During this time, Tyrion's costumes mimic Daenerys's in colour, light/dark ratio, texture, or pattern. In "Battle of the Bastards" (S6E9), Tyrion and Daenerys wear brown tunics with an intricate pattern, a lighter trouser, a belt, and near-identical brown boots. The similarities between their costumes are emphasised because of the vastly different costumes of the other characters: the Unsullied soldiers wear dark grey leather, Missandei wears a blue dress, and the Great Masters wear loose white robes decorated with intricate knots in colourful fabrics. Similar examples abound. In "The Winds of Winter" (S6E10), Tyrion and Daenerys wear the same shade of dark grey and when Daenerys lands on Dragonstone in season seven, she, Tyrion, Varys, and Missandei wear near-identical costumes but Daenerys stands and the others sit. The height difference implies that Daenerys is the most powerful person on the boat and that her costume is the one which the others have copied. Importantly, this is not to suggest that Tyrion's gender performance is derivative where other characters' performances are not; Tyrion's costumes have previously been used to signal his masculine point of reference, as I have demonstrated with the similarities between his and Tywin's costumes in earlier seasons. Rather, Tyrion's change in costume reflects his attempts to cite Daenerys as his model of caring masculinity.

The end of season eight of *Game of Thrones* sees him further embrace queer kinship and champion the disassembling of patriarchal systems of reproduction. Tyrion has an increasingly tenuous relationship with

Daenerys throughout season eight as she sheds her caring masculine performance and increasingly adopts self-oriented violence, culminating in her violent dragon-fire attack on King's Landing. After the massacre, Tyrion accuses Daenerys of having "slaughtered a city," removes his Hand of the King pin, and throws it away: a symbolic rejection of both Daenerys and her hegemonic violence (S8E6). When the nobles debate who will rule after Daenerys is murdered, Tyrion advocates for disassembling the system of patriarchal reproduction by moving to elect leaders rather than allow them to be dictated by familial lines. "This is the wheel our Queen wanted to break," Tyrion says, gesturing towards the hegemonic feudal system that supports and is supported by a cycle of destructive hegemonic masculine violence. Tyrion's suggestion that Westeros move from a patrilineal to a pseudo-democratic system challenges his society's focus on patriarchal reproduction, for under this new framework reproduction does not guarantee power. In its place, Tyrion elects Bran as a non-reproductive monarch in part because of his caring values, and Tyrion is in turn appointed as Hand of the King. Tyrion leads a small council comprised of Brienne of Tarth (Lord Commander of the Kingsguard), Davos Seaworth (Master of Ships), Bronn of the Blackwater (Master of Coin), and Sam Tarly (Arch-Maester). The council itself becomes a space for queer kinship; the final moments of their first meeting see the characters fall into a tongue-in-cheek conversation where they refer to themselves in the third person, denaturalising the council positions and associated feudal power. For example, Bronn says, "The Master of Coin looks forward to helping the Master of Ships, but first he has to ensure we aren't wasting coin, or there won't be no more coin" (S8E6). The combination of high-class titles ("Master of Coin ... Master of Ships") and smallfolk phrasing ("won't be no more") highlights the performativity of class and gender within the patriarchal feudal system, as well as the possibilities for destabilising them through comedy. The camp humour is in some ways similar to the kinship systems that Butler discusses in *Bodies That Matter*. In *Game of Thrones*, Tyrion becomes part of such a community in which the terms of domination—here "Master of Ships" and so on—are parodied and their artifice is revealed and turned into comedy. The narrative ends before audiences can glean whether this camp kinship–leadership will change the patriarchal feudal system from within, or whether turning the terms of domination against the system will lead to further relapse and repetition for both Tyrion and Westeros.

Conclusion

Tyrion, Jaime, and Bran undergo symbolic rebirths that signal their decision to relinquish their attachment to hegemonic violence and the power structures that uphold it. Not only are these births messy, as might be expected, they are also partial in the sense that the men who undergo them do not suddenly and permanently reject acts of violence that subjugate others and/or reproduce patriarchal norms. In *Game of Thrones*, Jaime returns to Cersei and dies with her, though his reasons for doing so are ambiguous. In *A Song of Ice and Fire*, Tyrion breaks free from the patriarchal system of reproduction and shifts his allegiance to Daenerys's caring masculinity, although he occasionally relapses into hegemonic sexual violence. When Bran has visions as the Three-Eyed Crow/Raven in the television series, his dream-self is able-bodied and he is obsessed with his long-dead father. Moving away from patriarchal and ableist structures proves to be rife with regression and ambivalence.

These partial rebirths reflect Butler's argument about the challenges of gender subversion: that *"working the weakness in the norm* [...] becomes a matter of inhabiting the practices of its rearticulation [...] [exposing] the failure of heterosexual regimes ever to fully legislate or contain their own ideals" (Butler 1993, 181; original emphasis). The subject can never be free of the law because they are produced by it; rather, one must find the weaknesses in that production and twist them into something more empowering. Bran, Jaime, and Tyrion must work within the "ambivalent condition of the power that binds" (185) to maintain their subjectivity and power, and to work against it by enacting a caring masculinity that makes the world a more livable place.

Tyrion's tangled relation with, and relapses into, hegemonic masculine violence are perhaps the most significant of those I have discussed. It is impossible to say what has struck the twenty-first-century audience about Tyrion's character, but my analysis of his relation to hegemonic violence indicates that he may well reveal to audiences the possibilities for reworking destructive norms without destroying them entirely, capturing the complexity of any attempt to negotiate masculinity.

Chapter 5

Queer Magical Violence and Gender Fluidity

This book follows violent bodies through their various incarnations in *A Song of Ice and Fire* and *Game of Thrones* as they enact two types of violence. I have showcased how queerness and femininity haunt cisgender men in both texts, as well as the ways that disabled subjects and those who were AFAB find new and old ways of using violence to perform masculinity, with ambivalent results. But there are countless other gendered embodiments where masculinity, violence, and abjection are negotiated, and in this chapter I read three characters from a gender fluid lens to examine how they use magic to restage hegemonic and caring violence. The term "gender fluid" seeks to articulate a gender identity that is untethered to the supposed opposites of masculinity and femininity and may shift between and into the spaces between them. While the characters analysed in this chapter are not explicitly queer in the texts, a gender fluid reading privileges and lingers upon moments where characters embody a disruption to the gender binary, especially through magic. Gender fluidity and magic can both be seen to offer an expansive world of possibility. To some they may seem impossible and impractical, but they invite us to imagine a different version of the world. The fantasy genre and the genre convention magic signify departures from gender norms, such as when the female body is linked to phallic symbols such as the magic sword, but it also affirms those norms by presenting the masculine as more valuable than the feminine. Fantasy texts do not always subvert dominant gender discourses, but they have a unique capacity to play with gender possibilities through magic.

I examine three characters who use magic to perform violence: the experienced warg Varamyr Sixskins, the feisty tomboy Arya Stark, and the dispossessed heir to the Iron Throne and Mother of Dragons, Daenerys Targaryen. I have chosen these characters because they are resistant to normative gendering, explicitly engage with magic, and use it to enact violence. In reading them from a gender fluid perspective, I

173

174   REIMAGINING MASCULINITY AND VIOLENCE

do not mean to imply that they would identify as such nor that they have been received this way by fans. Rather, I want to highlight an additional subject position from which masculinity and violence are negotiated in this popular television series and its source novels, one where characters are queerly gendered and so are less concerned with how violence affects their intelligibility as masculine. These are not the only characters in *A Song of Ice and Fire* or *Game of Thrones* who occupy a queer gender identity that intersects with their violence; Varys and Greyworm, for example, likewise perform acts of violence that encourage audiences to reconsider the centrality of cisgender male genitalia and/or testosterone. However, Daenerys, Arya, and Varamyr are three characters in the series who carry out their violence through magic. In addition, each character's violence reflects a queer process of adaptation, which for Mansbridge (2017, 81) means that it "displace[s] a linear understanding of production and reception" and instead becomes "an unpredictable process involving multiple repetitions, recognitions, and revisions." For the genderqueer characters I analyse, there is a tangled and multidirectional relationship between their acts of violence in *A Song of Ice and Fire*, *Game of Thrones*, advance chapters, and audience responses. Varamyr's character is only given a perspective chapter once in *A Song of Ice and Fire* and is cut from the television series; Arya's most violent scenes in *Game of Thrones* have overtaken her narrative in *A Song of Ice and Fire* but are loosely adapted from an advance sample chapter from *The Winds of Winter* that has since been retracted; and Daenerys's violence is also added after the television series outpaced the novels but has been widely rejected by fans. As these characters denaturalise the myth of linear adaptation, they also disrupt the notion of an "original" act of violence because the violence they perform is very similar to the characters I analyse in the previous chapters: Varamyr echoes Ramsay Bolton and Gregor Clegane, Daenerys reworks Eddard's sovereign violence but later repeats it in monstrous ways, and both Daenerys and Arya share parallels with Cersei. In addition to these repetitions, the characters also engage in various processes of queer adaptation whereby their violence remakes other characters' (often hegemonic) violence in an attempt to disrupt the law from within its own terms. Varamyr adapts his mentor's social position as shaman; Arya adapts the Westerosi fable of the Rat Cook as well as the Red Wedding; and Daenerys adapts the Great Masters' violence and her deceased husband Drogo's. Each adaptation is an instance of the character turning the law against itself, although this strategy proves ambivalent at best. When these queer characters use violence for their own personal gain—as is particularly the case with Varamyr and his attempts magically to dominate a human woman's body—they are presented as monstrous. But when they use violence because they care about others—as does Arya when she uses magic to violently destroy patriarchal men, families, and institutions—her actions are presented as both acceptable and ambivalent. The presence of magic, in its association with sexuality and gender, suggests that the fantasy genre and its conventions, especially as they are deployed in these queer adaptations in *A Song of Ice and Fire* and *Game of Thrones*, make it a unique site where caring for others is privileged, as opposed to dominant masculine discourses that promote singularity and impenetrability.

The Way of the Warg

The prologue of *A Dance with Dragons* features the only chapter narrated from the perspective of the warg Varamyr, a minor character in the novels who does not feature in the television series. I read Varamyr as a queer character because he is known in *A Song of Ice and Fire* for spreading his subjectivity across multiple sites ("Sixskins" refers to his six animal companions). In this dispersal Varamyr feels little inhibition about changing sex: his human body is male and he appears to identify as a man, but he takes the skin of multiple male animals as well as a female wolf (DwD 11), a female bear (DwD 9), and attempts to do the same with a human woman (DwD 14). Humans with magical connections to animals/creatures are a common fantasy convention, and Lenise Prater (2016, 27) argues that these bonds are often used as a metaphor for (hetero)sexual relationships, observing "parallels between the [magical] Witted relationship between a human and an animal and marriage, emphasising how the establishment of ethical and unethical uses of magic form a metaphor for ethical and unethical sexual relationships." If magical human–animal pairings in the fantasy genre are coded as a metaphor for human relationships, these are largely heterosexual and monogamous. Most pairings reinforce the stability of (cis)gender identity, such as the Stark children having direwolves of the same gender as themselves, and most of these connections are monogamous pairs. The connections Varamyr shares with multiple animals of multiple genders may be read as a pansexual, polyamorous relationship with others that is distinct from the monogamous, same-sex pairings like those among the Stark children. Because of his magical connections, Varamyr lacks the stable, firm, and enclosed borders that are expected of the male body. Yet, rather than embracing interconnectedness with others, he perpetuates hegemonic domination and violence. Varamyr uses

176 REIMAGINING MASCULINITY AND VIOLENCE

aggression to dominate women, but has this violence turned against him in death. Varamyr's chapter at the start of *A Dance with Dragons* echoes Bran's in *A Game of Thrones*, in the sense that both reveal an ongoing pattern of older men teaching younger men how to be masculine in a particular milieu. In each case, the repetition of hegemonic violence leads the characters who pass on their violence, and those to whom it is passed, to lose their bodily boundaries and become abject.

Varamyr cites his mentor Haggon as the alleged original for his warg masculinity. Varamyr was sent to Haggon after his wildling parents learned that he was a warg, and in his perspective chapter he reflects on how much of his identity stems from the older man: *"Haggon taught me much and more. He taught me how to hunt and fish, how to butcher a carcass and bone a fish, how to find my way through the woods. And he taught me the way of the warg and the secrets of the skinchanger, though my gift was stronger than his own"* (DwD 7). Haggon taught Varamyr, and Varamyr takes Haggon's place, literally and symbolically, as an adult: "He lived alone in a hall of moss and mud and hewn logs that had once been Haggon's, attended by his beasts. A dozen villages did him homage in bread and salt and cider, offering him fruit from their orchards and vegetables from their gardens" (DwD 8). Repetition is central to both of these memories. The repeated phrases (*"taught me"* and *"how to"*) and Varamyr's uptake of Haggon's cultural and spatial position suggests the repetitive and citational practices outlined in Butler's theory of gender performativity. It is a specifically masculine form of performativity through which Varamyr becomes intelligible, in the sense that his masculine subject position is centred on acting against supposedly passive others. He describes learning to *"hunt and fish,"* *"butcher,"* and *"bone,"* all of which are active verbs that describe doing something to someone or something else, and specifically to their bodies. Likewise, he is "attended" by animals and "villages did him homage": like Ramsay and his hounds, Varamyr actively dominates the less powerful subjects around him. He is marginalised by wildling society, but he frequently performs hegemonic acts of domination over the Other. His masculinity is based on controlling others for his own personal gain.

Explicitly sexual domination is tied to Varamyr's masculinity and his magic powers. While thinking of his adult life, Varamyr recalls, "Whenever he desired a woman he sent his shadowcat to stalk her, and whatever girl he'd cast his eye upon would follow meekly to his bed. Some came weeping, aye, but still they came. Varamyr gave them his seed, took a hank of their hair to remember them by, and sent them back" (DwD 8). Varamyr constructs an active position for himself and relegates the women to passivity through his language. He "cast[s] his eye upon" women, "g[ives] them his seed," and "sen[ds] them back," leaving no room for them to have agency besides crying, which is, in any case, presented as a passive and helpless response. Varamyr's domination and objectification of the women is exaggerated through the grisly trophies he keeps, "hanks of hair" (DwD 5). Varamyr keeps a physical part of the survivors' bodies, signifying his view of women as objects. His act of violence is hegemonic, though these grotesque trophies invite readers to subordinate his violence. Hair carries significant cultural and personal meanings (Freedman 1994; Hansen 2007; Reed and Blunk 1990; Synnott 1987), and in reducing the women to their hair, and stealing it against their will, Varamyr demonstrates his patriarchal views of women. Varamyr uses his warg abilities to perform sexual violence, repeating the same practices that are perpetrated with more mundane means by Gregor and Ramsay.

Varamyr's objectification of women is critiqued when he is faced with death and he attempts to save himself by magically possessing a human woman's body, a hegemonic act of violence that is linked to the abject. Varamyr "leapt out of his own skin, and forced himself inside her. Thistle arched her back and screamed" (DwD 14). The phrase "forced himself inside her" reflects the deeply corporeal experience of having one's mind taken over. The language connotes rape because psychological domination is experienced as a forced entry into the mind. The act is rendered monstrous through the abject, specifically a loss of borders, blood, auto-cannibalism, and castration: "The spearwife twisted violently, shrieking." And "[w]hen he tried to scream, she spat their tongue out" (DwD 14), not simply projecting it from her mouth but biting it off from her body and spitting it away. The corporeality of the act and its likeness to sexual violence are emphasised through phrases such as "twisted violently," which are coupled with abjection by the biting off and spitting out of "their tongue." The shift from "he" to "she" to "their" presents a sudden and significant change in subjectivity: in one moment Varamyr is a singular man ("he), then he is Thistle ("she"), and the next she and Varamyr combine as an ambiguously gendered "they." The gender binary, here enacted through gendered pronouns, cannot stand the strain of magical mind–body swapping, although the temporary breakdown is presented as grotesque.

The self-mutilation evokes blood, self-cannibalism, and severed limbs, all of which threaten Thistle/Varamyr's remaining borders. It is significant that it is Thistle's tongue—a phallic body part (Butler 1993, 55)—which is subject to this amputation. When spat out, this can be seen as a symbol of castration—a fitting metaphor considering that Varamyr is symbolically relinquishing his phallic power and his penis

178   REIMAGINING MASCULINITY AND VIOLENCE

by abandoning his human male body. Thistle's seeming control over the act of spitting the shared tongue can be viewed as an attempt to abject Varamyr from her mind and reinstate her own borders; Kristeva (1982, 3) claims that "I expel myself, I spit myself out, I abject myself within the same motion through which 'I' claim to establish myself." The tongue-spitting is at once literal abjection, symbolic castration, and grotesque image, all of which work together to associate Varamyr's psychological domination with feelings of disgust.

Varamyr's anticipated and actual death are narrated in ways that suggest a circularity between the hegemonic sexual violence he used in life and his murder. Midway through his chapter, Varamyr thinks about his death and says of his wolves, *"When I die they will feast upon my flesh and leave only bones to greet the thaw come spring"* (DwD 9). The alliteration in *"feast upon my flesh"* makes the sentence feel poetic, yet the choice of the word feast also highlights the reversal because it is being used to describe animals eating a human, rather than the normal use of the term to describe humans eating animals. Varamyr sees a "queerly comforting" circularity in this death, as "His wolves had often foraged for him as they roamed; it seemed only fitting that he should feed them in the end" (DwD 9). Varamyr foresees himself as part of the cycle of life and death. However, where Ramsay Bolton denies the possibility of his wolves turning on him and is horrified when they do, Varamyr's queer perspective on the world makes him open to the revelation and the idea that he will be inhabiting one of the wolves' bodies while they eat him: "He might well begin his second life tearing at the warm dead flesh of his own corpse" (DwD 9). Varamyr poses this fate as an interesting and poetic end as opposed to a horrifying moment of abjection, and his failure to react to the abject possibility of self-cannibalism—the fact that he finds it "queerly comforting"—makes him seem more and less than human. The border between human and animal, inside and outside the body, has collapsed long ago. Varamyr's total embrace of the Other suspends the scene's abjection.

The warg's actual death is more circular than he anticipates; he is murdered by Thistle, the woman whose body he attempted to seize, when she becomes a white walker. Varamyr dies as a human while he is fighting Thistle for control over her body, probably bleeding to death from an existing wound as Thistle attacks him bodily while he attacks her mentally. As Varamyr's man-body dies, he narrates an experience in which his soul flies into the air and settles within the body of his wolf One Eye. His reprieve is short, as it is implied that he dies a "true death" when he is murdered by the Thistle-wight. From inside One Eye's skin he observes the white walkers and identifies Thistle: "Pale pink icicles

QUEER MAGICAL VIOLENCE AND GENDER FLUIDITY   179

hung from her fingertips, ten long knives of frozen blood. […] *She sees me*" (DwD 15). The white walkers are living corpses that create terror by troubling countless boundaries. The description of frozen blood as icicles and knives weaponises this abject fluid. It is frozen as it flows from Thistle's hands, permanently reflecting the uncanny blurring of inside and outside the body. While Varamyr observes the Thistle-wight from One Eye's body, he claims *"She sees me,"* and the chapter ends. Varamyr receives no more perspective chapters in *A Song of Ice and Fire* to date, an absence that implies that he is murdered by the woman he tried to use violence to dominate and joins the army of the dead. The feminine figure that he sought to conquer in life returns with a vengeance, and Varamyr loses his bodily autonomy as an undead soldier.

"Tell them Winter Came for House Frey"

Where Varamyr learns magically to enter the bodies of other characters, Arya Stark learns to use magic to change her appearance and enact violent vengeance upon patriarchal figures. Arya is the daughter of Eddard Stark and sister to Jon, Robb, Bran, and Sansa. She reflects the fantasy tomboy convention because she can be read as a masculine girl, a non-normative gender identification that lays the foundations for her queer gender. At the beginning of both *A Song of Ice and Fire* and *Game of Thrones*, Arya is given a sword called "Needle" by Jon, and she learns to fight throughout the series, first in Westeros and later in Essos. After witnessing her father's treatment and execution in Westeros, as well as the torture practices of Gregor Clegane and his men, she creates a hit list of people she plans to enact violent revenge upon. *Game of Thrones* has expanded her narrative past this point, and the latter half of the show sees Arya return to Westeros.

I explore her violence as a queer restaging of Cersei's torture scenes. While both women use violence for revenge, Cersei acts out of a selfish desire to gain power and enjoys the act, whereas Arya is motivated by her connection to her family and its honour. The end of *A Dance with Dragons* sees her training among the Faceless Men in Essos, a group of magical assassins, although *Game of Thrones* has expanded her narrative. In the television series Arya choses to return to Westeros, where she is reunited with her family, defeats the Night King in single combat, takes part in the siege of King's Landing, and later leaves Westeros to explore the seas. She masters the art of magically wearing other people's faces and uses this skill to disguise herself as she empowers her family.

180   REIMAGINING MASCULINITY AND VIOLENCE

The narrative journey that Arya undertakes in *Game of Thrones* is a queer adaptation because of the way that it denaturalises the process of adaptation from novel to television series and the novels themselves. The television series overtook the novels on which it was originally based, although Arya's violence in *Game of Thrones* is in dialogue with an advance chapter from *The Winds of Winter*. The chapter, entitled "Mercy," was published on Martin's website in January 2013. The story follows Arya as she adopts the identity of a mummer (actress) called Mercy in Braavos, presumably as part of her work or training as a faceless man—a person who can magically alter their appearance. Over the course of the chapter, Mercy/Arya goes about her normal tasks at the theatre and then learns that one of the men on her hit list, Raff the Sweetling, is in Braavos. Mercy/Arya seduces the man and lures him back to her bedroom, where she murders him by cutting his femoral artery and then his throat. The shape of the plot—Arya taking another identity, seeing someone she views as immoral, and murdering them—is similar to one other published chapter in *A Song of Ice and Fire*, "Cat of the Canals," in *A Feast for Crows* in 2005 (569). "Cat of the Canals" sees Arya living as an oyster merchant as part of her training at the House of Black and White. But when she sees a brother of the Night's Watch called Daeron, who has deserted and fled to Braavos, she murders him. "Cat of the Canals" does not show the murder but Cat states that the murderer was "Arya of House Stark" (585). "Mercy" is far more detailed and graphic in its depiction of Arya's violence. In a sense, "Mercy" is an adaptation of "Cat of the Canals," the author expanding or growing previous events to advance Arya's story arc.

The relationship between "Mercy," *The Winds of Winter*, and *Game of Thrones* is complicated by the fact that the chapter has since been deleted from Martin's website and the only way to access it at the time of writing is through the "wayback machine" at the Internet Archive (https://archive.org/web/). Martin has not commented publicly on his reasons for removing the chapter, though he appears to delete a chapter whenever he posts a new one, so that only one chapter is available at a time. However, "Mercy" is unique in that Martin has commented upon its tenuous placement in the novel; on his blog, he states that the chapter was written for a planned (but later removed) five-year time jump within *A Song of Ice and Fire*. In a July 2013 interview with *Observation Deck*, Martin noted that as he was writing *A Song of Ice and Fire*, "Time is not passing here as I want it to pass, so I will jump forward five years in time." He planned to "come back to these characters when they're a little more grown up." The gap "would have come after *A Storm of Swords* [book 3] and before *Feast for Crows* [book 4]" (Anders 2013). The material

QUEER MAGICAL VIOLENCE AND GENDER FLUIDITY 181

Martin intended to place after the gap appears in books four and five: "Some of it is in there. Some of it I've reworked. A version of it is in there, but not the same version is in there. Some of it is just out. It just didn't work" (Anders 2013). "Mercy" may appear in future novels, but Martin stresses: "I would not say it is the final draft [...] the chapter's placement in the novel often requires tweaks, and I do have a long history of moving chapters around and rearranging the chronology until I hit on the best possible sequence" (Martin 2014). Mercy's ephemeral placement in the narrative to date has implications for critical discussions around both gender and adaptation. Disrupting the allegedly linear and stable movement from complete book series to complete television series shares parallels with Butler's (1990, 200) writings on gender: "Just as bodily surfaces are enacted *as* the natural, so these surfaces can become the site of a dissonant and denaturalized performance that reveals the performative status of the natural itself." The "performative status" of the "natural" book to television adaptation is shown to have been a copy of a copy all along because "Mercy" repeats and expands "Cat of the Canals" and is later repeated and expanded in *Game of Thrones*, even though the deletion of "Mercy" from Martin's own website highlights the instability of the alleged original. The fraught repetitions disrupt the notion of "repetition as a perfect reproduction and in which adaptation works to help reproduce the nation" (Handyside 2012, 54). Arya's acts of violence disclose this repetitive chain because the violence highlights the instability and repetitive impulse in the source text and the *Game of Thrones* adaptation.

In *Game of Thrones*, Arya murders one of the men on her hit list, Ser Meryn Trant, and the act is presented as acceptable, if disturbing, because he is characterised as a sadistic paedophile who endangers young girls. Ser Meryn's misogyny has been well established—for example, he beat Sansa on Joffrey's orders—and in Essos his violence takes an even darker turn when his paedophilia is revealed for the first time in "The Dance of Dragons" (S5E9). Arya sees Ser Meryn when he arrives in Essos accompanying Lord Tyrell and follows him and his fellow soldiers to a brothel. Arya watches from behind a door as the Madam brings in young women, and Ser Meryn rejects them by saying they are "too old" (S5E9). Throughout the selection process, Ser Meryn's companions and the Madam show uncomfortable facial expressions as the girls become younger and younger, and the scene takes on an unsettling tone through the low lighting and increasingly sinister string music ("Mother's Mercy" S5E10). A considerable amount of screen time is spent highlighting Ser Meryn's paedophilia—almost two and a half minutes—and when he finally settles on a girl, he tells the Madam, "You'll have a fresh one for me tomorrow" (S5E9). The term "fresh one" indicates that Ser Meryn views the girls as objects to be used for his own sexual pleasure and then discarded: he is an active threat to others. Arya's violence is thus positioned as an act of justice and protection in the next episode, "Mother's Mercy" (S5E10), when she uses her magical powers to kill him. Ser Meryn visits the same brothel and demands a selection of young girls to be brought for him, a repetition of the scene where he chose a girl in the previous episode ("The Dance of Dragons" S5E9). It is implied that one of the girls is Arya wearing a different face. Ser Meryn takes a turn at whipping each of the three pre-pubescent blonde girls on offer, but the third girl/Arya does not respond. Ser Meryn orders the other girls to leave and punches the quiet girl/Arya in the stomach, knocking her to the ground. She begins to rise, but as she does so her body moves unnaturally. The camera lingers on her hunched body in a medium shot for six seconds, moves back to Ser Meryn, and then back to the girl/Arya for four seconds. The lengths of the shots are made uncanny when paired with the high-pitched, eerie music that becomes louder as the shot goes on.

Arya's violent attack on Ser Meryn is coded as masculine and phallic as she magically transforms from the girl/Arya to Arya. The ability to change her face with a magical flesh mask disturbs identity and bodily borders in a way Kristeva would link to the abject. The transition also highlights Arya's violence as masculine because of the dramatic change in her gender presentation. The quiet girl/Arya has long blonde hair and delicate features, whereas Arya has shoulder-length brown hair styled in exactly the same way as her father, and large, thick eyebrows. I do not mean to suggest that she shifts fluidly from feminine to masculine, but that the magical change emphasises the masculine aspects of her appearance. As Arya becomes more masculine, her phallic knife also becomes visible: after the reveal, the audience sees a medium shot that shows Arya's face, and then a knife in her hand as she lunges at Ser Meryn and knocks him to the floor, stabbing first his left eye and then his right as he screams.

The loss of one's eyes is linked to castration in psychoanalytic theory (Freud 1919), making Arya's violence visible as an attack on Ser Meryn's masculinity, both the one complicit with dominating hegemonic masculinity that he displays in public and the sexually deviant one he has revealed in private. By graphically slaughtering powerful, misogynistic white men through her magical powers, *Game of Thrones* invites viewers to condone Arya's act of masculine violence because she challenges patriarchal power structures and saves the other young girls. Right before Arya slits Ser Meryn's throat, she tells him: "You were the first person on my list, you know. For killing Syrio Forrell. [...] You know who I am. I'm Arya Stark" (S5E10). In the moments before Arya cuts Ser Meryn's throat, her theme song "Needle" plays, adding a sense of momentum and heroism to the murder. *Game of Thrones* goes to great lengths to show Arya and her violence in this way, emphasising Ser Meryn as an active threat to young girls in both "The Dance of Dragons" and "Mother's Mercy," on top of his violence in earlier seasons. Arya's act of violence is motivated by an affective desire for revenge, but that affect stems from care for her family and other girls in Essos. The "Mother's Mercy" version of the adaptation presents Arya as a hero, whereas in *A Feast for Crows* Arya murders Daeron because he offends Arya's moral standards and in "Mercy" Arya murders Raff the Sweetling because he has a violent history, but he is not endangering anyone in the narrative present. In *A Song of Ice and Fire*, Arya's violence does not lead her constitutive borders to come undone, but nor is it celebrated: the novels leave considerable room for moral ambiguity. By contrast, the *Game of Thrones* version of the narrative actively distinguishes acts of acceptable and unacceptable masculine violence based on whether they are other-centred. Arya's act of violence in "Mother's Mercy" is positioned as moral, if not heroic, because she acts in the interests of others, and considerable narrative work is performed to highlight this motivation. Arya can be seen to restage hegemonic masculine violence, especially when compared with other masculine women characters in the series such as Cersei Lannister. Where Cersei enacts violence to further her own ends, like the pleasure and power she feels when she tortures less powerful characters such as Septa Unella (S6E10 "The Winds of Winter") and the Dornish women called the Sandsnakes (S7E3 "The Queen's Justice"), Arya uses violence to protect other girls from Ser Meryn, subverting Westerosi power structures that would expect her to be a victim. Arya breaks free from the destructive cycle of hegemonic violence even as she relies on violence to do so, whereas Cersei repeats it by making her own victims.

In terms of both gender and adaptation, the versions of Arya's masculine violence in Essos illuminate the centrality of repetition and the potential for those repetitions to disrupt the binary between original and copy and to rework the original in directions that may make the world more welcoming. Arya repeats and remakes hegemonic masculine violence to serve her own ends, and viewers are invited to view her re-figured violence as acceptable or ambivalent based on whether her violence is other-centred. Adaptation (in this case, from book to television) opens space for this reworking as a site of repetition where, especially in the case of Arya's violence in Essos, the linear and

184   REIMAGINING MASCULINITY AND VIOLENCE

unidirectional adaptation process is denaturalised. The impulse to repeat the original text faithfully, itself a refraction of the desire to repeat the law of the father in order to reproduce the patriarchal nation, is shown to be impossible because the original text is itself a copy. Arya's violence and the adaptation of that act are queer, and that queerness has the potential for subversive change because it challenges the need for fidelity to an original text or hegemonic masculine violence. In the *Game of Thrones* seasons that have overtaken the published and advance material from *A Song of Ice and Fire*, Arya's violence continues to follow these queer patterns of repetition in which they denaturalise both the process of adaptation and the repetition of hegemonic violence.

Arya's violence against Ser Meryn and its tangled status as adaptation are further repeated in later seasons of *Game of Thrones* when she murders Walder Frey and later destroys his House, both of which echo the "Mercy" chapter and the "Mother's Mercy" episode and are positioned as triumphant if frightening attacks on the Westerosi patriarchy. As in her murder of Ser Meryn, the principal way in which Arya's aggression differs from similar scene of hegemonic masculine violence is because she intends to protect and care for the Other, in this case her family and its honour, rather than a desire for personal power. The contrast is highlighted in the season six finale, "The Winds of Winter" (S6E10), which begins with Cersei blowing up the Sept of Baelor and torturing Septa Unella and later shows Arya murdering Walder. Both women cite previous enactments of hegemonic violence as they repeat it in new ways, although Cersei's is presented as monstrous because she repeats the violence faithfully by diminishing the Other in order to empower herself. Arya's violence may be viewed as a queer restaging of Cersei's: she cites past acts of violence, but rather than naturalising and repeating them faithfully and turning them against Walder (as Cersei does with Septa Unella), she uses repetition and adaptation in ways that call attention to the destructive cycle that produces self-oriented violence as she seeks to undo it.

Arya's act of violence against Walder denaturalises and remakes hegemonic masculine violence because it adapts her own past violence in *Game of Thrones*, "Cat of the Canals," and "Mercy," as well as Walder's violence against the Starks at the Red Wedding and the Westerosi fairy tale of the Rat Cook. In "The Winds of Winter" (S6E10), Arya wears the face of a serving girl who brings Walder a pie that (unbeknown to him) is made from the flesh of his heirs, Black Walder and Lothor. Arya draws inspiration for this act from the story of the Rat Cook, a cook at the Nightfort who murdered a king's sons, cooked them in a pie, and was punished by being turned into a rat who is "always hungry" and

QUEER MAGICAL VIOLENCE AND GENDER FLUIDITY   185

could only ever "devour his own babies" (S3E10). The Rat Cook is not punished for murder or forced cannibalism, but for violating guest right, the sacred hospitality law in Westeros whereby any guests in a person's home are guaranteed safety after they have shared a meal with the host. Arya's adaptation of the Rat Cook story as she murders Walder draws attention to his violation of guest right at the Red Wedding, where he murdered several members of her family and friends. The Rat Cook story specifically also carries with it a sense of repetition, for the Rat Cook is permanently trapped within a cycle in which he continually eats his own offspring. The notion of a man–rat eating his children is harrowing for patriarchal society, in which culture and power are expected to be seamlessly reproduced from father to son, and from original text to flawless adaptation. The fear of interrupting the patriarchal line of succession and the fidelity of adaptation is emphasised at the start of the scene when, after the serving woman/Arya sets the pie down, Walder tells her that she is pretty and pinches her backside, then demands to know where his heirs are. Walder is obsessed with reproducing his line and has scores of descendants (S1E9 "Baelor"). In response to his question, the serving woman/Arya repeatedly tells him, "They're here, my lord." Viewers already know Walder to be misogynistic and venal from his interactions with Robb and Catelyn Stark in season one, and his treatment of the serving woman/Arya—objectification, sexual assault, and rudeness—cements his characterisation as a villain and patriarch. Walder almost ingests his sons, a subversive reversal of his status as a patriarch and the patriarchal logic whereby culture is perfectly reproduced through the heteronormative family and the faithful adaptation.

Despite the insistent gestures towards cannibalism, there is very little abjection in this scene. The many references to the cause of Arya's ire—the Red Wedding where her mother and brother were killed—situates Walder's violence within a cycle of hegemonic masculine violence and position Arya's violence as morally ambivalent and emotionally satisfying because it is intended to protect and empower her family and their legacy. After Arya indicates to Walder that the pie is made from his heirs by telling him that his heirs are "here" in the pie, she peels off her serving woman face and says, "My name is Arya Stark. I want you to know that. The last thing you're ever going to see is a Stark smiling down at you as you die" (S6E10). The dialogue, specifically the repeated use of Arya's family name, is intended to remind audiences about the violence that Walder inflicted upon the Stark family, that is, to justify her violence and emphasise the fact that it is motivated by revenge for her family rather than empowering herself personally.

186   REIMAGINING MASCULINITY AND VIOLENCE

By citing the Red Wedding, viewers are encouraged to see how Arya is repeating this pattern by using violence to solve problems, as well the ways in which the Red Wedding cites other acts of hegemonic masculine violence and is part of a larger destructive cycle. In both the novel and television episode, the song "The Rains of Castamere" is used as a signal to attack the Starks. "The Rains of Castamere" mythologises Tywin Lannister's destruction of House Reyne, who rebelled against the Lannister family. The Reyne family was murdered and their corpses displayed to the public at Casterly Rock. In repeating and adapting Tywin's violence within the context of the Red Wedding, Walder positions his violence as part of the patriarchal system of reproduction whereby violence is used to disempower the Other and empower the self. As Stanton argues, "Walder Frey seeks a thymotic afterlife for himself and a new aura of power for his family and, in this, 'The Rains of Castamere' offers not only a mocking prop but a possible template" (Stanton 2015, 58). As Arya turns this violence against Walder in "The Winds of Winter," she adapts her own pattern of violence and his violence, which itself adapts Tywin's violence. The cycle of repetition denaturalises these acts and discloses them as copies of an original that does not exist. From this perspective, the similarities between Arya's, Walder's, and Tywin's violence are foregrounded: all of the characters aim to avenge a wrong against their family through violence. All of the characters use violence in a way that is both public and highly theatrical, orchestrated so that it makes for a lasting legacy.

Arya's vengeance on Walder Frey's House is even more theatrical, building on existing Westerosi tales and leaving not one but two memorable last lines. Arya dons Walder Frey's face after his death and poisons his heirs with wine. After watching the men choke to death, Arya removes Frey's face, turns to his wife, and says, "When people ask you what happened here, tell them the North remembers. Tell them [pause] that Winter came for House Frey" (S7E1). Arya interpolates her mass murder into public discourse and directs the narrative, making it an act of just vengeance that empowers her family rather than a young girl's revenge on the man who killed her mother. However, in so doing, Arya's violence becomes temporarily coded as self-oriented and part of the destructive cycle of hegemonic masculine violence. Both the repetition of gendered acts and the adaptation of those acts within *Game of Thrones* denaturalises the relationship between masculinity and violence and places Arya's violence against the Frey family within a pattern of repetitions that are critiqued through the abject. When Arya's violence is positioned as part of the same cycle as Tywin and Walder Frey, audiences are temporarily encouraged to see the act as morally unacceptable.

QUEER MAGICAL VIOLENCE AND GENDER FLUIDITY   187

In both the murder and the mass murder, Arya's violence is ameliorated because she is not a patriarch but appropriates patriarchal tactics and empowers the Starks rather than herself, and these differences result in a key distinction between Tywin's and Walder's violence in that she has an ambivalent encounter with abject signifiers such as blood and corpses. When Arya murders Walder there is blood in the scene: Arya slits his throat and blood flows visibly from the gash in his neck for a total of twelve seconds. Yet his death takes up a total of thirty-one seconds, making the twelve seconds of blood roughly a third of the death scene, a very brief moment of abjection. During the remaining nineteen seconds, his neck wound is either hidden from view by his own arm or is shot from a high angle that imitates Arya's point of view—the Stark "smiling down." In this time, Walder's neck is not visible and the blood is hidden against his black clothing. Not even his corpse is shown on screen; just as his hand slips away from his neck, the camera moves to a close-up of Arya and the music changes from high-pitched and eerie to also feature the low, triumphant-sounding drum beats of her theme song "Needle." Both instrumental pieces are audible from the moment Arya moves to smile down at Walder as he dies, and they take up equal prominence in the shots of Walder dying. When the camera moves to a close-up of Arya's face, "Needle" becomes the dominant score and evokes a triumphant mood, although the eerie music is still audible and so encourages the audience to experience a shadow of unease. "Needle" is used to rehabilitate Arya's violence from grotesque to heroic, although the musical tension invites a level of ambiguity. Unlike "Mother's Mercy," where "Needle" plays as a means of presenting Arya's violence as a heroic act that protects others, "The Winds of Winter" invites viewers to see the murder as part of a patriarchal system of reproduction as well as a challenge to that system that is achieved by turning its logics against itself. There is disjuncture between Arya's act of violence and hegemonic violence in terms of affect. Arya does not actually smile; if anything, her facial expression is expectant, but it is a far cry from Cersei's smiles as she performs torture and terrorism earlier in the same episode. Arya's lack of emotion, the music within the scene, and the references to the Red Wedding do considerable work in making clear that her violence is not patriarchal because it is not motivated by a desire to empower herself. Arya restages Cersei's failed hegemonic violence, making it ideologically ambivalent because she uses violence to care for others even if she also uses tools that bolster the patriarchal system.

When Arya extends her vengeance against Walder to all of House Frey in season seven, the violence again heavily cites the Red Wedding and is presented as morally ambiguous. Walder's patriarchal attitudes in

188   REIMAGINING MASCULINITY AND VIOLENCE

life are turned against him and his family when Walder/Arya encourages the men to raise a toast and s/he stops Walder's wife from drinking the wine, saying, "Not you. I'm not wasting good wine on a damn woman" (S7E1). Walder/Arya reverses Walder's characterisation as a misogynist by using it to save Walder's wife from being unjustly poisoned. Similarly, s/he uses Walder's slaughter of the Starks at the Red Wedding against the Frey family in a deadly toast: s/he says that s/he is proud of the "brave men" in the room, who "helped me slaughter the Starks at the Red Wedding. [...] Butchered a woman pregnant with her baby. Cut the throat of a mother of five. Slaughtered your guests after inviting them into your home" (S7E1). Arya raises the spectre of the Red Wedding and cites the crimes that the Freys committed as she kills them, just as she did when she murdered Walder in "The Dance of Dragons." She uses dramatic visual language to position the Red Wedding as horrifying: the words "slaughter" and "butchered" are commonly used to describe animals being killed, and so suggest that the Freys treated the Starks with unnecessary brutality.

The timing of Arya's dialogue is pivotal to presenting her violence as somewhat successful: she speaks right before the Freys begin to choke, gesturing towards a connection between her love for her (mostly slaughtered) family rather than an individualistic desire for power. Arya's explicit reference to her family begins to separate her violence from Cersei's: the latter regularly claims to use violence to protect her children, but they are rarely cited alongside her violence. When she destroys the Sept of Baelor, she watches alone in her bedroom and her son commits suicide because of her actions (S6E10 "The Winds of Winter"). Even when Cersei's violence is explicitly linked to her children, such as later in the season when she tortures and kills the Sandsnakes in revenge for her daughter Myrcella's death (S7E3 "The Queen's Justice"), she is acting on her own desire for revenge. Cersei's revenge is more self-oriented than Arya's because there are no Others for her to empower with her violence. All of her children are dead and she has no living family besides Jaime, and the act is committed in secret and so cannot even bolster the Lannister legacy. Likewise, Arya's violence is clearly vengeance and is therefore self-oriented, but it sits alongside an embrace of the Other (in this case, her family) and is emphasised in the moment of violence. Arya says, "You didn't slaughter every one of the Starks" (S7E1), and around her the Frey men begin to clutch their necks and chests, cough, spit up blood, and die. Arya's violence becomes ambiguous because her dialogue explicitly links her self-oriented desire for revenge to her family. As in the season six finale, there is very little abjection, and what is present is downplayed through the repetition of the song "Needle," which I have shown to be linked to heroism and triumph. Aside from the blood that the men cough up, there is no visible damage to their bodies.

Alongside the lack of abject signifiers, music is used to ameliorate Arya's vengeance by placing it in dialogue with her previous and more clearly heroic violence. After Arya/Walder takes off Walder's face, she walks out of the hall, right through the middle of the tables where the men were sitting. The corpses are barely visible; most fell to the floor while choking, or else lie slumped on the tables, hardly recognisable. The only moment when Arya comes into contact with the abject is when the camera moves to a high angle shot of the entire hall, showing the dead men and the horrified serving women. Yet even this room full of corpses is made palatable through music that changes the tone. Arya's theme "Needle" becomes louder as she walks through the room, reaching its climax at the moments when the corpses are visible, right before she walks off screen. The music and its placement right after Arya walks through the corpse-filled hall adapts the violence by inviting the audience to remember that the mass murder is an adaptation of Arya's previous (and, as I have argued, more morally acceptable) murders of Ser Meryn and Walder. The music places Arya's mass murder in a pattern of adaptations, rendering this revenge into one of many other-oriented heroic triumphs and transforming the abject corpses into the site of ambivalent vengeance on behalf of her family. Using violence to care for the Other proves to be the defining difference between Arya's heroic vengeance and Cersei's monstrous torture scenes, between dominating and non-dominating violence, and between failure and success.

The ambivalence circling Arya's masculine violence continue into season eight when she saves Westeros by murdering the Night King during the battle against the white walkers. As in the scenes with Walder Frey and Ser Meryn, this act of violence is a queer expansion of the *A Song of Ice and Fire* novels, although unlike these scenes she does not adapt her own ambivalent violence but rather a specific fighting technique she learns through queer kinship and adapts to save the world. Arya's violence is presented as heroic because she is acting to protect her brother Bran/the Three-Eyed Raven as well as her family and the living Others she is allied with. Her violence is other-centred, making it more (but not entirely) moral in the *Game of Thrones* universe. The morality is tied to Arya's self-sacrifice, which is highlighted through the fast-paced music, the previous scene where Theon sacrifices himself defending Bran, and the intercut scenes of Jon fighting an undead dragon. Despite the emphasis on biological familial ties, there is also a strong sense that Arya's ability to undertake this

190   REIMAGINING MASCULINITY AND VIOLENCE

heroic violence stems from queer kinship. Arya made the choice to go to the Godswood and fight the Night King because she is reminded of her first swordsmanship instructor, Syrio Forell. The value of these bonds with the Other is further emphasised through the fighting form she uses to stab the Night King. As the terrifying corpse moves to grab his sword and kill Bran, Arya appears behind him, aiming her dagger at his head. The Night King turns and grabs her by the throat with one hand and the wrist in the other. They struggle for a moment before the camera moves to a worm's-eye view whereby the audience sees Arya drop the dagger from her left (dominant) hand, only to grab it with her right and stab the Night King in the torso. Arya developed the knife-flipping tactic during a sparring session with Brienne of Tarth in season seven, in which Brienne and Arya shared their knowledge of sword-fighting in a temporary kinship bond. Arya has multiple connections to multiple Others, and they in turn teach her to adapt in two senses: to repeat the patterns she learns in queer kinship that are not aimed at empowering the self at the Other's expense and to adapt to changing circumstances by being open to fluidity rather than fidelity. Arya can be seen to "repeat in order to remake" (Butler 1993, 95) her own patterns of violent adaptation and the connection between masculinity and violence by informing and repeating her own acts of violence through alternative kinship with the Other.

Ambivalence also traces the implications of this scene for the series' depiction of violence. Masculinity remains attached to violence, even as that masculinity materialises through a female bodied character. There is a strong sense that warfare can only ever bring about destruction—as when the Night King brings all of the fresh corpses back to life to increase his army. However, violence is also figured as the solution to the world's problems: Arya stabs the Night King and this act of interpersonal violence destroys the creature and his armies. Arya performs this violence with the Valyrian steel dagger that Bran gave her rather than her trademark sword, Needle. The dagger was originally intended to be used to murder Bran in season one, an event that partially sparked the War of the Five Kings, which fuelled the game of thrones. The dagger begins and ends two of the major conflicts in the entire series, but it is also a weapon with a patriarchal history. The dagger is passed from one man to another until Bran gives it to Arya because he believes that his disability makes him unable to repeat the pattern. At the same time, Arya breaks free from her own pattern of increasingly ambiguous violence through queer kinship bonds. Her connections to others, especially Brienne of Tarth, enable her to disrupt her fidelity to the patriarchal cycle of hegemonic masculine violence and provide her with a new pattern which is fluid and other-centred. The ambivalent representation of violence, gender, and adaptation raises questions about repetition and the possibility of change. Audiences are encouraged to question the value of fidelity to an alleged original, whether that original is a source text or an act of hegemonic violent revenge. Whether an adaptation takes place between texts or through the repetition of gendered acts, the process of remaking is a space for proliferation, change, and/or subversion. Through Arya's narrative and its tangled adaptations, characters AFAB are shown to be capable actors on multiple battlefields, and a willingness to disrupt restricting gender norms is celebrated as heroic. At the same time, masculinity is privileged over femininity and violence is presented as both a problem and a solution.

Breaking the Wheel?

Where Arya moves fluidly between identities with her magical powers, Daenerys Targaryen, the now infamous Mother of Dragons and Breaker of Chains, encompasses multiple identities at once as "woman, man, and beast [...] a queer figure that defies category" (Gresham 2015, 157). She embraces the Other from an early point in the series and is undone—she sets herself alight on her husband's funeral pyre—only to be reborn stronger than ever as her three dragons hatch in the flames. At the time of writing, Daenerys rules the Essos city of Meereen in *A Dance with Dragons*. *Game of Thrones* has expanded her narrative to show her travel to Westeros where she embraces sovereign violence and reclaims the Iron Throne through patriarchal patterns of domination, although this ending has been widely criticised by audiences.

While the reception of Daenerys's final episodes hangs heavy over her story arc, her narrative remains an important case study in the potential of queer masculinities to restage and in some cases rework the domination of the Other that propels sovereign violence. Daenerys's story is worth examining as a whole because she attempts to challenge hegemonic masculine violence and the power structures it supports for most of the series, then suddenly begins to repeat the same dominating practices she fought against and becomes monstrous. Examining Daenerys's entire narrative with attention to her violence provides the opportunity to critically engage with her attempts to subvert the dominant gendered systems and the fragility of such tactics. Daenerys's story can give us tools for rethinking masculinity that do not obscure the challenges of remaking a system through which we ourselves are made intelligible. The cultural interest in Daenerys's narrative may

192   REIMAGINING MASCULINITY AND VIOLENCE

have waned with her fictional downfall, yet it has ongoing value as part of a queer archive of alternative masculinities and imagined violence.

In the final season, Daenerys repeats hegemonic masculine violence, although in earlier seasons of the television series and in all of the novels to date Daenerys eschews this kind of fidelity to gendered or ethnic norms: her queerness comes from her adaptability, her willingness to embrace a range of ethnic traditions in Essos and straddle masculinity and femininity simultaneously, and her dragons. Catherine Pugh (2018, 81) argues that "Daenerys has a habit of combining masculine and feminine traits as a leader (being both the merciful 'Mother' and the brutal authoritarian who burns people alive), utilizing both 'feminine' cooperation and 'masculine' domination to successfully achieve power." Daenerys's gender fluidity stems from her embrace of the grotesque, claims Gresham (2015), who uses Bakhtin (1984) and his concept of carnival to explain Daenerys's ongoing association with bodily filth as Martin's way of positioning her as a forerunner for the Iron Throne in *A Song of Ice and Fire*. I agree that grotesque bodies serve a narrative and political purpose in Martin's novels and, I would add, *Game of Thrones*, but the disgusting imagery that surrounds Daenerys is sometimes aligned with her "'masculine' domination," her "burn[ing] people alive" with her dragons, as a queer restaging of hegemonic masculine violence, such as Cersei's attack on the Sept of Baelor and Eddard Stark's sovereign violence. Daenerys's violence is made morally ambiguous because she *"work[s] the weakness in the norm,"* as Butler (1993, 181) says of gender subversion, by using violence to enable her community and thereby make her violence non-patriarchal, even as she later comes to dominate the Other. As in Arya's case, Daenerys's sovereign violence flirts with acceptability and monstrosity for the majority of the series.

Daenerys murders scores of men in *A Storm of Swords* in vengeance for their killing the same number of slave children, and this complex violence is critiqued in the television series and denaturalised in the novels. Daenerys does not enjoy satisfying her individualistic desire for vengeance, and consequently her contact with the abject is brief and the act is presented as ideologically ambivalent. When Daenerys travels from Yunkai to Meereen, she learns that the Meereen nobles "had nailed a slave child up on every milepost along the coast road from Yunkai, nailed them up still living with their entrails hanging out and one arm always outstretched to point the way to Meereen" (SoS2 204). Daenerys is disgusted and enraged but insists upon looking at each one of their faces and counting the corpses, where they total "one hundred and sixty-three" (SoS1 205). She affirms her vow to take the city, and after doing so later in the novel she orders the citizens to bring her "one

QUEER MAGICAL VIOLENCE AND GENDER FLUIDITY 193

hundred and sixty-three" of their leaders, and "had them nailed to the wooden posts around the plaza, each man pointing at the next" (SoS2 406). Daenerys murders one Master for each slave child, using violence to satisfy her desire to avenge the bodies of the children, whom she views as her own queer kin.

Daenerys's mass murder is positioned as a circular reversal of the Masters' cruelty, a citation of her own past acts of violence, and an adaptation of previous chapters in the series, and this emphasis on repetition denaturalises the violence. The way in which Daenerys carries out the violence, with "each man pointing at the next" (SoS2 406) is highly theatrical and foregrounds and critiques the ways in which the Masters reproduced a violent hegemonic masculine norm. By adapting the Masters' violence and drawing attention to its citationality, Daenerys attempts a "turning of power against itself to produce alternative modalities of power" (Butler 1993, 184). Daenerys redresses the Masters' cruelty, but the "alternative modalities of power" she produces are positioned as flawed because they are, as Butler (1993, 184) writes of gender subversion, "forging a future from resources inevitably impure." Daenerys's recourse to ambivalent violence can be viewed as one such "impure" resource, and she locates her act of violence against the Meereenese Masters as part of a pattern of masculine violence.

Readers are invited to view Daenerys's violence as interfering in the destructive pattern of hegemonic violence, although her interior monologue adds a level of ambiguity by suggesting that she is replacing one violent cycle with another. Daenerys cites her own violence in Astapor after she arranges for the Masters' corpses to be disposed of: "Dany remembered the horror she had felt when she had seen the Plaza of Punishment in Astapor. *I made a horror just as great, but surely they deserved it. Harsh justice is still justice*" (SoS2 407). The interior monologue connects Daenerys's violence in Meereen to her violence in Astapor, foregrounding her violence in the narrative present as an adaptation of her own violence. The scene that Daenerys references also cites other masculine characters' violence. Daenerys recalls her brother Rhaegar and his battle against Robert Baratheon just before she orders the attack on the Masters of Astapor, thinking, "*It is time to cross the Trident*" (SoS1 379). The citation situates Daenerys's mass murder in Astapor within a broader narrative of heroic Targaryen justice, one which is in turn folded into her violence in Meereen. Further ambivalence is added through the specific citation of Rhaegar's violence at the Trident, which was heroic but led to his death. The reference to Rhaegar also genders the act, making it specifically masculine violence. However, the citations within citations also draw attention to Daenerys's violence as a gendered repetition and

194   REIMAGINING MASCULINITY AND VIOLENCE

raise the question of whether any kind of violence can make life more livable or simply reproduce new violence against new bodies.

Daenerys's circular vengeance is presented as acceptable, if morally ambiguous, because readers are encouraged to see her as actively interfering in the destructive cycle of hegemonic masculine violence, despite the fact that her violence was initially motivated by her own rage. Thinking about the mass murder after the fact, Daenerys questions whether her actions were just: "the anger was fierce and hot inside her when she gave the command; it made her feel like an avenging dragon. But later, when she passed the men dying on the posts, when she heard their moans and smelled their bowels and blood ..." (SoS2 406). Daenerys combines normatively feminine maternal concern for her "children" with normatively masculine rage, becoming a genderqueer "avenging dragon." The rage brings Daenerys into contact with "bowels and blood," which are abject fluids, but the past tense reduces their unsettling effect. Daenerys's self-reflections, namely, her awareness that she acted in "anger" only to find that this leads to a wordless sense of horror ("...") also shifts her masculine violence into moral ambiguity. Her internal monologue and her persistent justification are perhaps the most visible critique of her actions. She says: "*It was just. It was. I did it for the children*" (SoS2 406), "*I made a horror just as great, but surely they deserved it. Harsh justice is still justice*" (SoS2 407), and "*Whatever I do, all I make is death and horror*" (SoS2 409).

The lingering self-critique performs a double function. On the one hand, Daenerys's reference to "the children" justifies her actions by suggesting that she is acting to empower her community, even though she has a highly subjective view of who constitutes her community; she chooses to kill the Masters because of their social class rather than the individuals responsible. On the other hand, Daenerys demonstrates an evolving awareness that her violence was too brutal—from "*It was just. It was*" to "*All I make is death and horror*"—which shows a willingness to admit that she was wrong and to intervene in the repetitions of patriarchal violence and produce something different. It is Daenerys's openness to adaptation, deeper awareness of the consequences of her violence for her community, and recognition that she has become part of a new but equally destructive cycle that tips her violence into ambivalence rather than monstrosity. Unlike Cersei, who acts purely in her own interests, Daenerys finds the brief indulgence of her own violent desires distasteful. In this case, Daenerys's individualistic revenge happens to be targeted at those who would otherwise harm her kin, much like Arya, but because she has conquered Meereen the Masters no longer pose an active threat to them. For this reason, Daenerys's violence is less successful, as demonstrated by her self-critique. While her quest is long and fraught, readers are constantly invited to ask whether violence is just, and whom justice serves. Daenerys turns the law against itself in her attempts to rework the hegemonic masculine violence that harms her queer kin, though this practice is shown to offer fragile possibilities for change. She does not use this tactic again in the novels (to date), appearing to recognise after her theatrical display with the Masters that reversing "resources inevitably impure" (Butler 1993, 184) means remaking the impurity alongside the change. It remains to be seen how Daenerys's narrative will end in Martin's novels, although it is clear that Daenerys's violence resists both the naturalisation of violence and the binaries in which women are always and inevitably the subjects, rather than the perpetrators, of violence.

As Daenerys's violence against the Masters is adapted into *Game of Thrones*, the impetus shifts from denaturalising and disrupting the destructive cycle of hegemonic masculine violence to an ambivalent critique as she attempts to reshape the world through reworking dominating violence. The television series expands the events of *A Storm of Swords*, emphasising Daenerys's victory over the city and her growing community of queer kin, as well as foregrounding her decision to use violence as one that is partially born out of an emotional desire for revenge. After commanding the Masters to be impaled on posts as a reversal of their violence against slave children, Daenerys's sworn sword Ser Barristan asks to speak to her privately and questions her choice. He says, "Your Grace [...] the city is yours. All these people are your subjects now. Sometimes it is better to answer injustice with mercy" ("Oathkeeper" S4E4). Ser Barristan explicitly reminds both Daenerys and viewers that by conquering Meereen and disbanding slavery there is no longer a simple moral binary between innocent slaves and guilty masters. The crowd before Daenerys is blended into an amorphous "all these people," who are under her care because they are "[her] subjects now." Despite Ser Barristan's gentle reminder, Daenerys is unwilling to accept the Masters as her queer kin because of her own feelings of anger over their treatment of slave children. Daenerys says, "I will answer injustice with justice" and the scene transitions from a close-up of Daenerys's face to an extreme close-up of a bleeding hand having a stake driven into it as a man screams. Non-diegetic sound is heard in the background, specifically the menacing percussion and string section of the song "Dracarys." The music rapidly changes the scene's tone from celebratory and heroic to ominous, where Daenerys's emotional decision to violently dominate the Other is presented as the cause. "Dracarys" continues to play as the camera moves between close-ups, medium shots,

196 REIMAGINING MASCULINITY AND VIOLENCE

and long shots of Meereen that show Masters being impaled on posts in the same physical position they placed the slave children. The men's faces are bloody and evoke the abject, and their screaming invites the viewer to feel uncomfortable. The screams are still audible when the camera moves to a shot of Daenerys overlooking the city, a dark storm in the background next to the Targaryen flag.

By expanding the scene in the adaptation process, "Oathkeeper" creates an additional layer of nuance around how Daenerys reworks hegemonic masculine violence in her quest to disrupt oppressive systems, turning the law against itself to protect herself and her queer kin. In *A Song of Ice and Fire* these acts are denaturalised and shown to be part of a destructive cycle through interior monologue in which Daenerys admits that she was motivated by anger and cites past acts of violence, although she recognises this cycle and places her energies in negotiation and compromise as she stays to rule Meereen in *A Dance with Dragons*. In the expanded narrative in "Oathkeeper," it is instead Daenerys's decision to practise self-oriented violence in the form of revenge against the Masters that is critiqued. "Oathkeeper" invites viewers to question whether turning the law against itself can interrupt the repetition of harmful gendered acts, or whether it simply reproduces the same encounters with abjection.

Daenerys continues her attempt to successfully rework hegemonic masculine violence in later seasons of *Game of Thrones*, and her attack on the Dothraki Khals (male tribe leaders) shares parallels with Cersei's attack on the Sept of Baelor later in the season with crucial differences that speak to a possibility of successfully refiguring dominating violence. "Book of the Stranger" sees Daenerys imprisoned by the Dothraki Khals after they find her alone in the middle of the Dothraki Sea, a grassy inland region in Essos. Daenerys knows Dothraki customs because she was married to Khal Drogo at the beginning of the series, making her a *khaleesi* (wife of the tribe leader). She uses her knowledge of Dothraki cultural practices to save herself from being raped and enslaved on sight, reminding the men that she is a *khaleesi*. According to Dothraki custom, *khaleesi* become *dosh khaleen* after their Khals die, where they live in Vaes Dothrak, the Dothraki holy city, and are guaranteed safety for life even as they are segregated from the community. Daenerys escapes this fate in *A Game of Thrones* and season one of the television show after Khal Drogo dies, but now that she has been found the Khals meet to decide her future. The theme of men seeking control over women's futures is highlighted as the scene begins with Daenerys talking with the *dosh khaleen*. One of the women comments that she was twelve years old when she was stolen, married, and raped, and was beaten when she bore a daughter rather than a son. A similar fate is presented to Daenerys when she meets with the Khals, who discuss whether she will be gang-raped by men and horses for her insolence, sold into slavery, or a combination of these. Both scenes highlight the hegemonic Dothraki masculinity that views women's bodies as public property, eliding the racial power dynamics at play while inviting the audience to see Daenerys as morally superior. The situation shares many resonances with Cersei's planned trial in season six, where her future is similarly to be judged by a patriarchal institution. Yet both women refuse to be judged. Daenerys interrupts the men, recounting the last time she was in Vaes Dothrak. She says that her husband "promised to kill the men in their iron suits and tear down their stone houses," a vision of dominating violence that repeats exactly the same language Drogo used in season one ("You Win or You Die" S1E7). The repetition of Drogo's words echoes Daenerys's repetition of the Masters' violence in Meereen: she still aims to empower those she views as queer kin (Dothraki women), but she violently rejects the Other (Dothraki Khals). Daenerys reverses the positions so that the Othered group are now kin and those who were previously kin are now the Other, repeating hegemonic masculine violence in an attempt to remake it. She says, "You're not going to serve. You're going to die," and pushes over the torches that light the room, trapping them in an inferno as the song "Dracarys" plays.

The destruction in Vaes Dothrak is highly symbolic. Lindsey Mantoan (2018, 90) argues that Daenerys "sets the temple on fire, burning not only the specific men who threatened her, but also the structures and symbols of male dominance and patriarchal rule that had governed the Dothraki." The same is true of Cersei's terrorism in King's Landing, later in the same season: she murders the people who condemned her as well as the structure—the church—that legitimised them. Repeating violence in this way is tenuous; as Butler (1993, 83) writes of gender subversion, "occupied by such terms and yet occupying them oneself risks a complicity, a repetition, a relapse into injury, but it is also the occasion to work the mobilizing power of injury, of an interpellation one never chose." The key difference to whether the women are able to "work the mobilizing power" of hegemonic masculine violence is whether they act on behalf of their community or for their own ends. Cersei is explicitly shown to smile as she watches the city fall, suggesting that the violence is fulfilling her own personal desire for revenge. This individualistic motivation is emphasised in shots showing innocent bystanders being killed by falling rubble, showing that Cersei did not think of anyone but her own safety and that of her immediate family when planning the attack (S6E10). By contrast, Daenerys is motivated

198   REIMAGINING MASCULINITY AND VIOLENCE

by a desire to save herself and liberate the Dothraki women from the violent social system in which they are subject to dehumanising abuse. In other words, her violence repeats hegemonic patterns but it also intervenes in them by using the tools of domination to enable her community. Daenerys believes that the patriarchal culture is not serving the Dothraki because it does not allow them to adapt to change (which conveniently means aiding her as she travels to Westeros). As in Arya's destruction of House Frey, and unlike Daenerys's murder of the Masters, her violence is ambiguous because it is used to aid her kin, even if it also means violently rejecting a new Other. This difference is what separates Daenerys's violence from Cersei's, showing how the latter must be (re) imagined for it to become acceptable in *Game of Thrones*.

After the fire starts, every *khalasar*, or Dothraki tribe, comes to see the building, and soon thereafter Daenerys emerges from the temple naked, with the inferno behind her. Daenerys's magically fire-resistant body is the only moment that disrupts order in the scene: there is almost no abject imagery to speak of, even though Daenerys's mass murder is incredibly violent. It bears mentioning that the violence is perpetrated in a dark, cavernous room—as in Arya's case—that may evoke the monstrous womb, but this suggestion is fleeting. No blood is present and no corpses or burning bodies are shown on screen. It is the maintenance of Daenerys's bodily borders under incredible duress that is unsettling—not a typical moment of abjection. The image has significant narrative weight because it can be viewed as an adaptation of the season one finale when Daenerys was reborn from her husband's funeral pyre with her three dragons (S1E10 "Fire and Blood"). Daenerys's miraculous survival and entry into queer motherhood signalled a significant shift in her narrative, and this transformational mood—as opposed to abjection—is evoked in "Book of the Stranger" through the textual adaptation. The Dothraki bow in awe, signalling their acknowledgement of her power. She has succeeded in using violence to unite them for the first time, making them an incredibly powerful group in Essos as well as a stronger weapon for her to use in her quest to reclaim the Iron Throne. The white saviour narrative in this scene is also evident in previous episodes, such as the season three finale (S3E10 "Mhysa"). Writing on the episode, Mantoan (2018) points out that "Dany has been worshipped, literally, by the brown slaves she has emancipated, and their deification of this white saviour figure has seeped into the fandom." The same racial dynamic takes place in "Book of the Stranger": Daenerys uses violence to overthrow patriarchal structures and to empower the Dothraki by uniting them, but in doing so she reinforces the existing racial hierarchy. In addition, she imposes a patriarchal Westerosi power

QUEER MAGICAL VIOLENCE AND GENDER FLUIDITY 199

system onto the Dothraki, where a single monarch rules all others rather than the decentralised nomadic culture. Daenerys may act on behalf of her community, but she effectively colonises the Dothraki by assuming that she knows what is best for them. Audiences are encouraged to focus on the former rather than the latter, and the violence becomes heroic rather than horrifying, even as ambiguity remains.

While Daenerys's violence in Essos pushes hegemonic masculine violence in ambivalent new directions, when she returns to Westeros and her violence becomes intelligible as sovereign violence, it can be viewed as a queer restaging of Eddard's actions at the start of the series. As I note in Chapter 2, Eddard's power as a sovereign is related to the phallus: his sovereign violence is positioned as a means of reasserting his phallic power because his sword is emphasised as a phallic symbol. The sword is described at length by Bran in the novel, and in *Game of Thrones* the pommel is visible in multiple shots of Eddard, where its angle is suggestive of an erect penis. Daenerys repeats and remakes the connection between the phallus and sovereign violence through her dragon. Speaking to the captives she has taken after the battle at Casterly Rock, Daenerys steps up onto a boulder to be seen above the crowd of men, and as she does so, Drogon is visible in the background. The pair take up almost the entire bottom half of the frame, and the colour of Daenerys's coat almost perfectly matches the colour of Drogon's wing, making the two characters appear as one. Daenerys's phallic power and her desire to maintain that power through sovereign violence are highlighted through these shots of Drogon, much like the shots of the sovereigns and their swords. Similarly, Daenerys is marked as masculine through her clothing and costume: she wears a dark brown coat with accentuated fabric on the shoulders that makes her appear broader, she wears breeches, and her long silver hair is pulled back into a braid. Combined, these performative acts code Daenerys's sovereign violence as queer and masculine, a duality that is likewise reflected in the ambivalent depiction of her violence. Daenerys tells the soldiers that they must "bend the knee and join me" or "refuse, and die" (S7E5 "Eastwatch"). After Daenerys finishes speaking, some men kneel, but when Drogon roars behind her, the vast majority also submit to her phallic prowess. Several men remain steadfast, including two named characters—the highborn patriarch Randyll Tarly and his heir Dickon. Daenerys speaks to Randyll and afterwards she gestures to her blood riders, who seize him. Daenerys's Hand of the Queen, Tyrion, intercedes and suggests that Randyll be imprisoned or sent to the Night's Watch. When Daenerys refuses, Tyrion says, "Your Grace … if you start beheading entire families—" to which Daenerys replies, "I'm not beheading anyone" and Drogon roars (S7E5 "Eastwatch").

Tyrion's mention of "beheading" makes the act intelligible as hegemonic sovereign violence, discussed in Chapter 2 as a cluster of promises relating to language, bodies, and power that serve to legitimise violence in relation to patriarchal law and the law of the land. Daenerys can be seen to make these promises materialise as she says, "Lord Randyll Tarly. Dickon Tarly. I, Daenerys of House Targaryen, First of my Name, Breaker of Chains and Mother of Dragons, sentence you to die" (S7E5). Sovereign sentencing materialises in the same way that Butler (1993, 177) argues that gender does: Daenerys is "compelled to 'cite' the norm in order to qualify and remain a viable subject [...] thus not the product of a choice, but the forcible citation of a norm." Daenerys cites previous acts of sovereign violence by phrasing her sentence in this way. The textual repetition opens up a space for adaptation, in which Daenerys may either reproduce the patriarchal nation by repeating with fidelity to Westerosi sovereign violence or embrace the moment of adaptation as a means of reworking these norms. Where Eddard follows the former path and his sovereign violence becomes grotesque as his bodily borders are disrupted, Daenerys attempts to turn the law against itself and is positioned as ambiguous because there is almost no abjection: no blood or viscera are shown, and there are no corpses left behind.

Daenerys's hegemonic sovereign violence does not lead her to bodily abjection, but the act is critiqued and denaturalised instead through music. The scene is made unsettling through the ominous instrumental song "Dracarys," which features heavy drumbeats and eerie string music. As in the scenes in "Oathkeeper" and "Book of the Stranger," "Dracarys" plays when Daenerys uses dragonfire as a weapon, leaving her violence ambivalent and suggesting a change in the pattern of her violent acts. The only moment when the borders between life and death are disrupted is a medium shot of Randyll and Dickon burning in the flames, but they are barely distinguishable as human and the shot is only three seconds long. Daenerys's sovereign violence is almost completely void of abjection despite the way her phallic dragon is emphasised, a significant contrast when compared with the other sovereigns I have examined, who are overwhelmed by the blurred boundaries between themselves, the criminals they execute, and the presence of blood and corpses. Daenerys's ambiguous restaging of sovereign violence indicates that patterns of violence that are based on domination can be reworked, but that this reworking is tenuous because it necessarily involves repeating these patterns in order to remake them. There is considerable emphasis in the series on unsuccessful repetitions of sovereign violence, and Daenerys's ambivalent enactment demonstrates that this practice is not inherently destructive; rather, patriarchal structures beget warped repetitions. Patriarchal masculine discourses actively discourage connection to others, so patriarchal violence is likely to fail in fantasy fictions like *Game of Thrones*, where caring for the community is one way of making violence more successful.

Daenerys manipulates the weakness in the act of sovereign violence because she does not use a sword but a dragon; after she passes the sentence, she pauses and then says simply, *"Dracarys,"* the High Valyrian word for fire (S7E5). Daenerys uses Drogon to execute the men, an act that effectively obliterates the patriarchal House Tarly. There are strong resonances between this scene and Cersei's destruction of the Sept of Baelor, as well as the scenes where Daenerys kills the Khals and the Great Masters of Meereen and Astapor and Arya destroys House Frey. Each act of violence is a queer adaptation in the sense that it takes place as an expansion of *A Song of Ice and Fire*, even as it echoes scenes from the published (or unpublished) novels. In each adaptation, the characters also repeat hegemonic violence queerly, denaturalising the correlation between masculinity and violence and highlighting the productive but fragile possibilities for reworking oppressive acts and turning them against their original aims. What makes Daenerys's violence ambivalent is that she has chosen to rework Westerosi sovereign violence, a technology of power that is designed to be used against the Other. Daenerys wields the power of the phallus, and like Eddard and the Stark sovereigns, she uses it to further her own ends.

Daenerys attempts to empower her community by restoring order in Westeros through dominating sovereign violence, another aspect of the act that is promised but rarely fulfilled. Indeed, Eddard and his sons cause more damage to the kingdom through their sovereign violence, losing political information and allies because of their inflexible morals. Similarly, Daenerys's sovereign violence leads her power to come undone. When she meets Randyll's son Sam Tarly in "Winterfell" (S8E1), she tells him that she executed his father and brother and he is distraught. In response to Daenerys's unjust execution, Sam asks Jon whether he would have done the same and it is in this conversation that Sam reveals Jon's status as heir to the Iron Throne. The revelation undermines Daenerys's power and confidence, leading her to make impulsive and self-oriented decisions that culminate in the wholesale repetition of self-serving violence. In other words, murdering Tarly and Dickon damages Daenerys's kingdom because the act of sovereign violence forces her to dominate the Other rather than show mercy by embracing the Other.

Throughout *Game of Thrones*, Daenerys straddles a tension between repeating hegemonic violence and turning that violence against itself in order to remake its dominating logics. The way that tension is resolved in the final season provokes new repetitions that exceed the text and trouble the binary between text and audience. As I have shown, Daenerys has a history of ambivalent violence, one that becomes increasingly apparent as she adopts Westerosi acts of domination. The fragile process is ultimately unsuccessful, and Daenerys's narrative concludes in season eight with her conquering Westeros by destroying King's Landing with dragonfire, only to be murdered by her lover and nephew Jon Snow. Viewers are invited to critique Daenerys's violence through extensive shots of bloody, burning bodies which evoke the abject ("The Bells" S8E5). This pattern of hegemonic violence being critiqued through abjection is consistent across both texts and for characters in a variety of relationships to masculinity. However, the type of masculine violence and accompanying critique do not fit into either Daenerys's narrative of the fantasy genre, where protagonists generally triumph and seldom abandon their morals.

Daenerys's pyrotechnics in King's Landing have arguably come to symbolise everything "wrong" with the final season of *Game of Thrones*, and I suggest that this unsatisfactory ending stems from a break in the series' own logics regarding violence and masculinity. In attempting to mobilise hegemonic masculine violence against its dominating aims, it seemed as if Daenerys offered a way through the question Butler (1993, 185) asks of gender subversion: "How will we know the difference between the power we promote and the power we oppose? [...] For one is, as it were, in power even as one opposes it, formed by it as one reworks it." In *Game of Thrones*, Daenerys is increasingly forced to use "the power [she] oppose[s]"—sovereign violence—in order to promote her radical embrace of the Other. Her decision to attack King's Landing in "The Bells" because of her anger and grief provides a resolution to the tension in her narrative throughout the series. Yet the resolution is unsatisfying and unconvincing because it does not follow the series' logics.

Daenerys, like Cersei and Eddard, attempts to improve her world but ends up repeating a cycle of destructive violence, which is indicated in "The Bells" through the multiple repetitions in the scene with regards to dialogue, costumes, and cinematography. Daenerys's costume, a black leather surcoat with red cloak, recalls the Targaryen colours and motto "fire and blood," although the almost entirely black leather costume also evokes the costumes previously worn by antagonists Tywin and Cersei Lannister. Few other characters in *Game of Thrones* wear costumes of this material and colouring, and the repetition of this combination in "The Bells" invites viewers to recognise the growing similarities between the Lannisters and Daenerys.

QUEER MAGICAL VIOLENCE AND GENDER FLUIDITY   203

Where Daenerys's costume locates her violence within the patriarchal system of Westerosi masculine power, her hairstyle and the cinematography in "The Bells" and "The Iron Throne" are used to further underscore and critique this repeated violence as it is implied that Daenerys and Drogon have merged into one furious subject. Daenerys's hairstyle makes her appear inhuman because the braids at the back of her head make her skull appear reptilian, much like her dragon. Cinematographic choices reinforce this merging, most notably when Drogon delivers Daenerys to the castle for her victory speech. As she walks forward, Drogon opens his wings behind her to create the momentary illusion that she has dragon wings. Unlike previous scenes in Essos, this merging is presented as sinister, recalling the scene when Daenerys used sovereign violence against Randyll and Dickon Tarly. In both scenes, Daenerys momentarily loses her borders, but this instance is presented as unsettling through cinematography. In the scene at King's Landing, eerie music, a bleak colour palette, stormy skies, and dim lighting encourage the audience to feel uncomfortable with the bonding. Daenerys becomes one with her detachable phallus, though in this instance the merging marks a loss of humanity as well as a queer kinship bond in which her subjectivity is radically altered.

Finally, Daenerys's victory speech highlights her newfound reliance upon sovereign violence through repetition in her dialogue. Adapting too faithfully gives away Daenerys's desire for "perfect reproduction" of her conqueror masculinity, in which "adaptation works to help reproduce the nation" (Handyside 2012, 54). The patriarchal desire for fidelity is highlighted during Daenerys's victory speech. She repeats the words that her deceased husband Drogo said to her when he promised to take Westeros in their unborn son's name: "I will kill the men in iron suits and tear down their stone houses" ("You Win or You Die" S1E7). Drogo's position as Khal is not analogous with Westerosi sovereignty, but his approach to leadership through violence is taken up by Daenerys. In her victory speech to the Dothraki, she says: "You killed my enemies in their iron suits. You tore down their stone houses. You gave me the Seven Kingdoms!" (S8E6). Daenerys repeats Drogo's words, which themselves describe violent domination in the name of empowering the self, signalled in the dialogue through the repetition of the words "me" and "you" as opposed to a more collective "we." Daenerys does not copy Drogo's masculinity, but rather the moment of adaptation invites viewers to recognise how Daenerys's dialogue, leadership style, and violence have become part of the destructive cycle of dominating violence that she sought to oppose. Daenerys's challenges to hegemonic masculine violence and the patriarchal order were based on a tenuous reversal of the terms of domination, as demonstrated by the way she cited other patriarchs as she turned their violence against them. However, when she sets King's Landing ablaze because of her anger towards Cersei and her grief over her recently deceased advisor Missandei and dragon Rhaegal, her adaptation of hegemonic masculine violence is too faithful and audiences are invited to view her as another monstrous masculine figure.

Daenerys's fidelity to sovereign violence may be part of the reason that her narrative ending, and that of *Game of Thrones*, has failed to provide a satisfying ending to audiences. In contrast to Daenerys, previous character arcs in the series are fulfilling because they redeploy and rework the characters' actions and become either circular (where dominating violence begets monstrosity) or tied to queer kinship (where caring violence leads to proliferation). Characters can and do change the violence they perform, largely though adopting new modes of repetition. Daenerys's violence and her narrative do not follow this pattern in the final episodes. The norms through which her masculinity becomes intelligible is subject to rapid change: from her brother Rhaegar to the Westerosi patriarchy (symbolised by the Lannisters) and her deceased husband Drogo. Characters in *Game of Thrones* often change their masculine citation point/s, but it is a tenuous process of practised repetition, not a sudden switch. In addition to the change in Daenerys's masculinity, her death itself breaks the series' existing pattern because it is not marked as circular through the mode of death nor filmic devices. Characters who repeat hegemonic masculine violence can escape a circular death, but only through enacting caring masculinity and queer kinship—which Daenerys sheds throughout the final season, ending the series with only her dragon and her army. In season eight, both Daenerys and *Game of Thrones* succeed in "breaking the wheel," but this breakage propels them into cultural abjection. As Butler (1993, 117) writes, "this citation of the gender norm is necessary in order to qualify as a "one," to become viable as a "one," where subject-formation is dependent on the prior operation of legitimating gender norms." Butler's description of gender norms can also be productively applied to the norms of text and genre, here *Game of Thrones'* existing patterns around masculinity and violence and the fantasy genre's norms around protagonists remaining morally consistent and ultimately triumphant. In failing sufficiently to cite the narrative norms that audiences expect, both Daenerys and *Game of Thrones* became textually unviable and illegitimate and were subsequently abjected from the cultural landscape. While the break in *Game of Thrones'* pattern of circular masculine violence is not the only reason for its widespread criticism, Daenerys's previous popularity and the specific fan vitriol regarding her ending suggest that these scenes sparked a particularly powerful negative response.

This necessarily brief exploration of violence, magic, queer subjectivities, and kinship has shown that, even when violence is restaged from a queer angle, its patriarchal forms lead to horror, whereas "*working the weakness in the norm*" (Butler 1993, 181; original emphasis) by using violence to care for the community enables successful enactments that make the world more livable. Like the sovereigns and disabled men in *A Song of Ice and Fire* and *Game of Thrones*, Varamyr insists upon repeating the patriarchal domination he learned from his mentor. He is faced with an onslaught of circular abjection, revealing him to be a part of the cycle of hegemonic masculine violence regardless of his ability to magically spread his subjectivity. Like Ramsay and Gregor, Varamyr uses violence to dominate women and animals, but these are exactly the same figures that later kill him. Arya's violence reimagines Cersei's torture scenes and her destruction of the Sept of Baelor, showing that caring for others is key to making violence tolerable. Arya's gender shifts as she learns to embrace the Other in a new way, magically donning the faces and bodies of other people and using these guises to destroy patriarchs, including Ser Meryn Trant, Walder Frey, and the Night King. And Daenerys is from the outset queer: a mother of dragons who uses this kinship with magical creatures in her efforts to "break the wheel" (S6E10 "The Winds of Winter"), which we may read as the pseudo-medieval patriarchy, killing patriarchs who refuse to change their ways so that she can forge a more enabling future for her community. When she travels to Westeros and adopts sovereign violence, she begins to repeat the patterns of domination embedded within them. She ends the series restaging and embracing the violence she opposed, although her death breaks from existing logics in the show and is consequently abjected from popular interest. Despite this infamous ending, Daenerys's relationship to the phallus is integral to all of my discussions of sovereign violence, to my discussion of female masculinity and prosthetic swords/monsters, and to her sovereign violence against Randyll and Dickon. In most of the executions in *A Song of Ice and Fire* and *Game of Thrones*, including the one Daenerys performs and which echoes Eddard's, the act is carried out by the sword, whether wielded by the monarch or their representative, the sword being a symbol and expression of their phallic power. Daenerys maintains the presence of the phallic weapon, whiteness, masculinity, and the family lineage that comes with it by using her dragon to set the men alight, even as she challenges the need for maleness and the exclusion of femininity. Drogon can be read as Daenerys's detachable phallus, the phallic weapon through which she

206   REIMAGINING MASCULINITY AND VIOLENCE

enacts sovereign violence. Not only does Daenerys share a deep emotional connection with Drogon as his "mother" and the only human allowed to ride him, but she links herself to him biologically by continually referring to herself as "blood of the dragon."[1] This is made explicit in the television series as Daenerys's costumes slowly incorporate more charcoal, which is the colour of Drogon's scales as well as that of House Targaryen's banners. Daenerys contests the idea that subjectivity is stable and singular because her identity resides in multiple locations and is not corporeally bound. It is her embrace of the Other that allows her to gain access to the phallus and use it to perform sovereign violence, to use the norm's fragility against its originating aims. The subversive reversal is also fragile because it necessitates a repetition of the norm that is always in danger of falling back into patriarchal patterns, which is exactly what happens when Daenerys embraces Westerosi sovereign violence. Her violence is ambivalent at first because it confirms her phallic power while also challenging patriarchal structures that inform sovereign violence because, as a woman, Daenerys is more successful than any other sovereign in fulfilling the act's promises. Such success stems from the fact that Daenerys is acting for the good of her community, and as soon as this other-centred approach is lost, in "The Bells," her violence becomes monstrous. Even when masculinity is pushed to its limits of intelligibility, *Game of Thrones* presents its relationship with violence as moral or immoral based on the way it bolsters or challenges existing power structures, which demonstrates that the fantasy genre's conventions are uniquely suited to a critical engagement with normative masculine discourses.

Daenerys's narrative in particular raises questions about the promises that texts and genres make, and the complex affective work that they perform. It is well beyond the scope of this chapter to examine these questions, though I am reminded of Butler's claim about Willa Cather's fiction: "And though it appears that the normativizing law prevails [...] the text exceeds the text, the life of the law exceeds the teleology of the law, enabling an erotic contestation and disruptive repetition of its own terms" (Butler 1993, 97). The sovereign violence that Daenerys performs in "The Bells" exceeds *Game of Thrones*, publicly troubling the binary between audience and maker through fans' rejection of the series. Daenerys's characterisation and her violence are fundamentally

---

[1] In the novels, their connection is also expressed through interior monologue. When Drogon is attacked in the fighting pits of Meereen in *A Dance with Dragons*, "Dany and Drogo screamed as one" (DwD 812) and she realises that Drogon "*is fire made flesh* [...] *and so am I*" (DwD 814; original emphasis).

disrupted, unintentionally resulting in *Game of Thrones*' abjection from the popular culture imaginary—at least for now.

While it is impossible to foresee whether and how Daenerys's violence will be repeated and/or adapted in cultural texts or the real world, her controversial violence in "The Bells" highlights the fact that in *Game of Thrones* and *A Song of Ice and Fire* violence can be put to radically different uses with diffuse consequences. Daenerys's violence in earlier seasons, and *Game of Thrones*' violence more generally, has already been taken up in ambivalent ways in other arenas. Donald Trump (2018), then-President of the United States of America, tweeted a photo of himself overlaid with the phrase "Sanctions Are Coming" in the *Game of Thrones* title typeface, to announce the reimposition of sanctions on Iran, a clear imitation of the phrase "Winter Is Coming," the House Stark words. Later, he issued a similar graphic with "The Wall Is Coming" to promote the wall he planned to build at the border between the United States and Mexico (Trump 2019). Trump instrumentalised *Game of Thrones* to highlight his violent rejection of the Other, though his substitution of sanctions or a wall in place of winter inadvertently suggests that rejecting the Other is a destructive force. The statement from Trump draws on a prominent cultural association of masculinity and violence with white, male, able, cisgender bodies to threaten Iran or subaltern subjects seeking asylum.

But this co-option of *Game of Thrones* does not exhaust the potential meanings of violence and masculinity for this series. Hence, the series is cited by Shangela, a drag queen in *RuPaul's Drag Race: All Stars*, to highlight the necessity of working with others: "Baby, if Daenerys is gunna conquer the seven kingdoms, she's going to need allies. Me and my dragons can't do it alone" (S3E2 "Divas Live"). The quote from Shangela, in referencing women characters who take on leadership roles and, in *Game of Thrones*, thus engage in violent acts, challenges this association in linking violent "conquer[ing]" with other bodies: non-white, queer, feminine. While Daenerys has since come to represent such a conquering, here she also stands in for the personal and political value of unity. The political concerns echo Shangela's personal concerns in the drag competition: in relation to the other contestants, Shangela's individual embodiment and kinship connections with other people and ideas are privileged.

Both Shangela's and Trump's references to *Game of Thrones* are examples of the series' significance and the radically different ways it is being adapted by its audiences. Shangela and Trump see the series' violence as simple, but, as I have demonstrated, it is complex in its relation to gender and power. Monstrosity, masculinity, and violence are not inherently negative in and of themselves. Despite the crisis rhetoric that circulates around contemporary manhood, masculinity itself is not a problem: rather, it is the ways in which it interacts with violence, power, affect, and kinship that directs its popular cultural representations, which are themselves adapted in ways that cannot be predicted in advance. The technology of the fantasy genre, especially magic, provides a unique space for reimaging alternative masculinities and queer kinships that negotiate, refuse, or work the weaknesses in patriarchal logics of reproduction and repetition and that maintain a lack of opportunity for certain subjects unable to access these privileged power dynamics.

Because the fantasy genre's conventions often work in ways that encourage a divergence from hegemonic manhood, it is an ideal place for creating and interrogating alternative versions of masculinity. As the global imagination becomes increasingly occupied by concerns about the future in the face of climate change, nuclear warfare, and rapid technological advances, it is useful to find other models of non-normative masculinity that can contribute to a more equitable world. Fantasy fiction offers a textual site where the patriarchal law comes into conflict with genre, with the result that violence, emotion, bodies, and kinship are often reworked. The ambivalence at the heart of fantasy is useful for thinking differently about masculinity. Just as Daenerys walks into the flames of her husband's funeral pyre and is reborn with three dragons, fantasy texts like *A Song of Ice and Fire* and *Game of Thrones* invite their audiences into a critique of masculinity that is not destructive but transformative, hatching a broader cultural understanding of what it means to be masculine—and what it could mean.

Bibliography

Anders, Charlie Jane. 2013. "George R.R. Martin: The Complete Unedited Interview." *Observation Deck*, 23 July. https://web.archive.org/web/20130726155202/https://observationdeck.io9.com/george-r-r-martin-the-complete-unedited-interview-886117845.

Anglberger, Albert, and Alexander Hieke. 2012. "Lord Eddard Stark, Queen Cersei Lannister: Moral Judgments from Different Perspectives." In Game of Thrones *and Philosophy*: *Logic Cuts Deeper than Swords*, edited by Henry Jacoby, 87–98. Hoboken, N.J.: Wiley.

Arellano, Lisa. 2012. *Vigilantes and Lynch Mobs: Narratives of Community and Nation*. Philadelphia, Pa.: Temple University Press.

—. 2015. "The Heroic Monster: *Dexter*, Masculinity, and Violence." *Television & New Media* 16 (2): 131–147. https://doi.org/10.1177/1527476412450192.

Askey, Brooke. 2018. "'I'd rather have no brains and two balls': Eunuchs, Masculinity, and Power in *Game of Thrones*." *Journal of Popular Culture* 51 (1): 1–18. https://onlinelibrary.wiley.com/doi/abs/10.1111/jpcu.12647.

Attali, Maureen. 2017. "Religious Violence in *Game of Thrones*." In Game of Thrones *versus History: Written in Blood*, edited by Brian A. Pavlac, 185–194. Hoboken, N.J.: Wiley.

Backstrom, Laura. 2012. "From the Freak Show to the Living Room: Cultural Representations of Dwarfism and Obesity." *Sociological Forum* 27 (3): 682–707. https://doi.org/10.1111/j.1573-7861.2012.01341.x.

Baker, Dallas J. 2010. "Monstrous Fairytales: Towards an Écriture Queer." *Colloquy: Text, Theory, Critique* 20: 79–103. http://hdl.handle.net/10072/36548.

Bakhtin, Mikhail Mikhaĭlovich. 1984. *Rabelais and his World*. Bloomington: Indiana University Press.

Balay, Anne. 2010. "'They're closin' up girl land': Female Masculinities in Children's Fantasy." *Femspec* 10 (2): 5–23. https://scholarship.haverford.edu/anthropology_facpubs/286/.

Barker, Martin, and Julian Petley, eds. 2001. *Ill Effects: The Media Violence Debate*. 2nd ed. London: Routledge.

Barnes, Colin, Michael Oliver, and Len Barton. 2002. *Disability Studies Today*. Cambridge: Polity Press.

Battis, Jes. 2006. "Transgendered Magic: The Radical Performance of the Young Wizard in YA Literature." *Looking Glass: New Perspectives on Children's Literature* 10 (1). https://ojs.latrobe.edu.au/ojs/index.php/tlg/article/view/93.

Beaton, Elizabeth. 2016. "Female Machiavellians in Westeros." In *Women of Ice and Fire: Gender,* Game of Thrones *and Multiple Media Engagements,* edited by Anne Gjelsvik and Rikke Schubart, 193–218. London: Bloomsbury.

Berlant, Lauren. 1997. *The Queen of America goes to Washington City: Essays on Sex and Citizenship.* Durham, N.C.: Duke University Press.

—. 2008. *The Female Complaint: The Unfinished Business of Sentimentality in American Culture.* Durham, N.C.: Duke University Press.

Berlant, Lauren, and Michael Warner. 1995. "Guest Column: What Does Queer Theory Teach Us about X?" *PMLA* 110 (3): 343–349. www.jstor.org/stable/462930.

—. 1998. "Sex in Public." *Critical Inquiry* 24 (2): 547–566. www.journals.uchicago.edu/doi/10.1086/448884.

Bersani, Leo. 1987. "Is the Rectum a Grave?" *October* 43: 197–222. www.jstor.org/stable/3397574.

Binnie, Jon. 1997. "Coming out of Geography: Towards a Queer Epistemology?" *Environment and Planning D: Society and Space* 15 (2): 223–237. https://doi.org/10.1068/d150223.

Brodie, Meghan. 2014. "Casting as Queer Dramaturgy: A Case Study of Sarah Ruhl's Adaptation of Virginia Woolf's *Orlando.*" *Theatre Topics* 24 (3): 167–174.

Bufkin, Jana, and Sarah Eschholz. 2000. "Images of Sex and Rape: A Content Analysis of Popular Film." *Violence Against Women* 6 (12): 1317–1344.

Butler, Judith. 1990. *Gender Trouble: Feminism and the Subversion of Identity.* New York: Routledge.

—. 1993. *Bodies That Matter: On the Discursive Limits of Sex.* 2nd ed. New York: Taylor & Francis.

—. 1999. *Gender Trouble: Feminism and the Subversion of Identity.* 2nd ed. New York: Routledge.

—. 2002. "Is Kinship Always Already Heterosexual?" *Differences: A Journal of Feminist Cultural Studies* 13 (1): 14–44. https://muse.jhu.edu/article/9630.

—. 2004. *Undoing Gender.* 1st ed. New York: Routledge.

Cameron, John H. 2014. "A New Kind of Hero: *A Song of Ice and Fire's* Brienne of Tarth." In *A Quest of Her Own: Essays on the Female Hero in Modern Fantasy,* edited by Lori M. Campbell, 188–205. Jefferson, N.C.: McFarland.

Carter, Cynthia, and C. Kay Weaver. 2003. *Violence and the Media.* Maidenhead: McGraw-Hill.

Cecil, Dawn K. 2007. "Dramatic Portrayals of Violent Women: Female Offenders on Prime Time Crime Dramas." *Journal of Criminal Justice and Popular Culture* 14 (3): 243–258. https://digitalcommons.usf.edu/fac_publications/2647/.

BIBLIOGRAPHY

Cogman, Bryan. 2012. *Inside HBO's* Game of Thrones. San Francisco: Chronicle Books.

Connell, R.W. 1990. "An Iron Man: The Body and Some Contradictions of Hegemonic Masculinity." In *Sociological Perspectives on Sport: The Games outside the Games*, edited by Robert E. Washington, 141–149. New York: Routledge.

—. 2000. *The Men and the Boys*. St Leonards, New South Wales: Allen & Unwin.

—. 2002. "On Hegemonic Masculinity and Violence: Response to Jefferson and Hall." *Theoretical Criminology* 6 (1): 89–99. https://doi.org/10.1177/136248060200600104.

—. 2005. *Masculinities*. 2nd ed. St Leonards, New South Wales: Allen & Unwin.

Connell, R.W., and James W. Messerschmidt. 2005. "Hegemonic Masculinity: Rethinking the Concept." *Gender and Society* 19 (6): 829–859. https://doi.org/10.1177/0891243205278639.

Conrich, Ian, and Laura Sedgwick. 2017. *Gothic Dissections in Film and Literature: The Body in Parts*. Basingstoke: Palgrave Macmillan.

Corker, Mairian. 1999. "Differences, Conflations and Foundations: The Limits to 'Accurate' Theoretical Representation of Disabled People's Experience?" *Disability & Society* 14(5): 627–642. https://doi.org/10.1080/09687599925984.

—. 2001. "Sensing Disability." *Hypatia* 16 (4): 34–52. https://doi.org/10.1111/j.1527-2001.2001.tb00752.x.

Creed, Barbara. 1993. *The Monstrous-Feminine: Film, Feminism, Psychoanalysis*. Abingdon: Routledge.

—. 2005. *Phallic Panic: Film, Horror and the Primal Uncanny*. Carlton, Victoria: Melbourne University Publishing.

Davies, Ann. 2007. "The Beautiful and the Monstrous Masculine: The Male Body and Horror in *El espinazo del diablo* (Guillermo del Toro 2001)." *Studies in Spanish & Latin American Cinemas* 3 (3): 135–147. https://doi.org/10.1386/shci.3.3.135_1.

Davis, Lennard J. 1995. *Enforcing Normalcy: Disability, Deafness, and the Body*. London: Verso.

DeCoste, D. Marcel. 2015. "Beyond the Pale? Craster and the Pathological Reproduction of Houses in Westeros." In *Mastering the* Game of Thrones: *Essays on George R.R. Martin's* A Song of Ice and Fire, edited by Jes Battis and Susan Johnston, 225–242. Jefferson, N.C.: McFarland.

DeKeseredy, W.S., and M.D. Schwartz. 2005. "Masculinities and Interpersonal Violence." *Handbook of Studies on Men and Masculinities*, edited by Raewyn Connell, Michael Kimmel, and Jeff Hearn, 353–366. Thousand Oaks, Calif.: Sage.

Doan, Laura L. 2006. "Topsy-turvydom: Gender Inversion, Sapphism, and the Great War." *GLQ: A Journal of Lesbian and Gay Studies* 12 (4): 517–542. https://muse.jhu.edu/article/202838.

Docherty, David. 1990. *Violence in Television Fiction*. London: Libbey.

212 REIMAGINING MASCULINITY AND VIOLENCE

Drabinski, E. 2013. "Queering the Catalog: Queer Theory and the Politics of Correction." *Library Quarterly: Information, Community, Policy* 83 (2): 94–111. https://doi.org/10.1086/669547.

Drummond, Murray. 2011. "Reflections on the Archetypal Heterosexual Male Body." *Australian Feminist Studies* 26 (67): 103–117. https://doi.org/10.1080/08164649.2011.546331.

Edelman, Lee. 2004. *No Future: Queer Theory and the Death Drive*. Durham, N.C.: Duke University Press.

Elliott, Karla. 2015. "Caring Masculinities: Theorizing an Emerging Concept." *Men and Masculinities* 12 (1): 1–20.

Ellis, Katie M. 2014. "Cripples, Bastards and Broken Things: Disability in *Game of Thrones.*" *M/C Journal: A Journal of Media and Culture* 17 (5). https://doi.org/10.5204/mcj.895.

Evans, T. 2018. "Vile, Scheming, Evil Bitches? The Monstrous Feminine Meets Hegemonic Masculinity in *A Song of Ice and Fire* and *Game of Thrones.*" *Aeternum: The Journal of Contemporary Gothic Studies* 5 (1): 14–27. www.aeternumjournal.com/_files/ugd/c8fb40_06ac011f45bc4d48af234da4e9b6dd7c.pdf?index=true.

Fernández-Villanueva, Concepción, Juan Carlos Revilla-Castro, Roberto Domínguez-Bilbao, Leonor Gimeno-Jiménez, and Andrés Almagro. 2009. "Gender Differences in the Representation of Violence on Spanish Television: Should Women Be More Violent?" *Sex Roles* 61 (1–2): 85–100. https://link.springer.com/article/10.1007/s11199-009-9613-9.

Ferreday, Debra. 2015. "*Game of Thrones*, Rape Culture and Feminist Fandom." *Australian Feminist Studies* 30 (83): 21–36. https://doi.org/10.1080/08164649.2014.998453.

Finn, Kavita Mudan. 2020. "Queen of Sad Mischance: Medievalism, 'Realism,' and the Case of Cersei Lannister." In *Queenship and the Women of Westeros: Female Agency and Advice in* Game of Thrones *and* A Song of Ice and Fire, edited by Zita Eva Rohr and Lisa Benz, 29–52. London: Palgrave Macmillan.

Flaherty, Kelly. 2016. "28 Fascinating Facts about the 'Game of Thrones' Costumes." *BuzzFeed*. www.buzzfeed.com/keelyflaherty/facts-about-the-game-of-thrones-costumes-you-probably-nev?utm_term=.jjjmy3A3W#.ftnA7rYrK.

Foucault, Michel. 1977. *Discipline and Punish: The Birth of the Prison*. 4th ed. London: Allen Lane.

—. 1979. *The History of Sexuality*. London: Allen Lane.

Frankel, Valerie Estelle. 2014. *Women in* Game of Thrones: *Power, Conformity and Resistance*. Jefferson, N.C.: McFarland.

Freedman, Tovia G. 1994. "Social and Cultural Dimensions of Hair Loss in Women Treated for Breast Cancer." *Cancer Nursing* 17(4): 334–341. http://journals.lww.com/cancernursingonline/Fulltext/1994/08000/Social_and_cultural_dimensions_of_hair_loss_in.6.aspx.

Freud, Sigmund. 1919. "The Uncanny." In *An Infantile Neurosis and Other Works*, 219–253. London: Hogarth Press.

BIBLIOGRAPHY

Garber, Marjorie B. 1993. *Vested Interests: Cross-Dressing and Cultural Anxiety.* London: Psychology Press.

Garland-Thomson, Rosemarie. 1997. *Extraordinary Bodies: Figuring Physical Disability in American Culture and Literature.* New York: Columbia University Press.

—. 2002. "Integrating Disability, Transforming Feminist Theory." *NWSA Journal* 14 (3): 1–32. www.jstor.org/stable/4316922?origin=JSTOR-pdf.

Genovese, Megan. 2019. "Audience Reception of Intersectional Genderbent and Racebent Casting in *Elementry.*" *Pop Culture Matters*, Proceedings of the 39th Conference of the Northeast Popular Culture Association, edited by Martin F. Norden and Robert E. Weir. Newcastle upon Tyne: Cambridge Scholars Publishing.

Genz, Stéphanie. 2016. "'I'm not going to fight them, I'm going to fuck them': Sexist Liberalism and Gender (A)politics in *Game of Thrones.*" In *Women of Ice and Fire: Gender, Game of Thrones and Multiple Media Engagements*, edited by Anne Gjelsvik and Rikke Schubart, 243–266. London: Bloomsbury.

Gerschick, Thomas J. 1998. "Sisyphus in a Wheelchair: Men with Physical Disabilities Confront Gender Domination." In *Everyday Inequalities: Critical Inquiries*, edited by Jodi O'Brien and Judith Howard, 189–211. www.wiley.com/en-us/Everyday+Inequalities%3A+Critical+Inquiries-p-9781577181217.

Gerschick, Thomas J., and Adam S. Miller. 1995. "Coming to Terms: Masculinity and Physical Disability." In *Men's Health and Illness: Gender, Power, and the Body*, edited by Donald Sabo and David F. Gordon, 183–204. Thousand Oaks, Calif.: Sage Publications. https://sk.sagepub.com/books/mens-health-and-illness/n9.xml.

Gjelsvik, Anne. 2016. "Unspeakable Acts of (Sexual) Terror as/in Quality Television." In *Women of Ice and Fire: Gender, Game of Thrones and Multiple Media Engagements*, edited by Anne Gjelsvik and Rikke Schubart, 57–78. London: Bloomsbury.

Gjelsvik, Anne, and Rikke Schubart, eds. 2016. *Women of Ice and Fire: Gender, Game of Thrones and Multiple Media Engagements.* London: Bloomsbury.

Goodnow, Katherine J. 2010. *Kristeva in Focus: From Theory to Film Analysis.* New York : Berghahn Books.

Gresham, Karin. 2015. "Cursed Womb, Bulging Thighs and Bald Scalp: George R.R. Martin's Grotesque Queen." In *Mastering the* Game of Thrones*: Essays on George R.R. Martin's* A Song of Ice and Fire, edited by Jes Battis and Susan Johnston, 151–169. Jefferson, N.C.: McFarland.

Hackney, Charles H. 2015. "'Silk ribbons tied around a sword': Knighthood and the Chivalric Virtues in Westeros." In *Mastering the* Game of Thrones*: Essays on George R.R. Martin's* A Song of Ice and Fire, edited by Jes Battis and Susan Johnston, 132–150. Jefferson, N.C.: McFarland.

Halberstam, Judith/Jack. 1993. "Imagined Violence/Queer Violence: Representation, Rage, and Resistance." *Social Text* (37): 187–201. https://programaddssrr.files.wordpress.com/2013/05/imagined-violence-queer-violence-representation-rage-and-resistance.pdf.

—. 1995. *Skin Shows: Gothic Horror and the Technology of Monsters*. Durham, N.C.: Duke University Press.

—. 1998. *Female Masculinity*. Durham, N.C.: Duke University Press.

—. 2005. *In a Queer Time and Place: Transgender Bodies, Subcultural Lives*. New York: NYU Press.

—. 2011. *The Queer Art of Failure*. Durham, N.C.: Duke University Press.

Hamming, Jeanne E. 2001. "Dildonics, Dykes and the Detachable Masculine." *European Journal of Women's Studies* 8(3): 329–341. https://doi.org/10.1177/135050680100800305.

Handyside, Fiona J. 2012. "Queer Filiations: Adaptation in the Films of Francois Ozon." *Sexualities* 15 (1): 53–67. https://doi.org/10.1177/1363460711432101.

Hanlon, Niall. 2012. *Masculinities, Care and Equality: Identity and Nurture in Men's Lives*. London: Palgrave Macmillan.

Hansen, Briana. 2016. "Twitter Hates Bran Stark from 'Game of Thrones' (and They Have a Point)." *HelloGiggles*, 5 June. https://hellogiggles.com/lifestyle/twitter-hates-bran-stark/.

Hansen, Helle Ploug. 2007. "Hair Loss Induced by Chemotherapy: An Anthropological Study of Women, Cancer and Rehabilitation." *Anthropology & Medicine* 14(1): 15–26. https://doi.org/10.1080/13648470601106335.

Harrison, Mia. 2019. "George R.R. Martin and the Two Dwarfs." *Routledge Companion to Disability and Media*, edited by Katie Ellis, Gerard Goggin, Beth Haller, and Rosemary Curtis. New York: Routledge.

Hart, Lynda. 2005. *Fatal Women: Lesbian Sexuality and the Mark of Aggression*. London: Routledge.

Harvey, Dan, and Drew Nelles. 2014. "Cripples, Bastards, and Broken Things: Disability in *Game of Thrones*." *Hazlitt*, 10 June. http://hazlitt.net/feature/cripples-bastards-and-broken-things-disability-game-thrones.

Heifetz, Danny. 2019. "Evil or Incompetent: The Bran Stark Edition." *Ringer*, 21 May. www.theringer.com/game-of-thrones/2019/5/21/18633468/bran-stark-king-iron-throne-evil-bad-ruler.

Helford, Elyce Rae. 2000. "Feminism, Queer Studies, and the Sexual Politics of Xena: Warrior Princess." In *Fantasy Girls: Gender in the New Universe of Science Fiction and Fantasy Television*, edited by Elyce Rae Helford, 135–162. Lanham, Md.: Rowman & Littlefield.

Helliwell, Christine. 2000. "'It's only a penis': Rape, Feminism and Difference." *Signs: Journal of Women in Culture and Society* 25 (3): 789–816. www.jstor.org/stable/3175417.

Hemmings, Clare. 2013. *Bisexual Spaces: A Geography of Sexuality and Gender*. Abingdon: Routledge.

Horstmann, Ulrike Maria. 2003. "'Boy!'—Male Adolescence in Contemporary Fantasy Novels." In *Images of Masculinity in Fantasy Fiction*, edited by Susanne Fendler and Ulrike Maria Horstmann, 81–102. New York: Edwin Mellen Press.

BIBLIOGRAPHY

Howe, Andrew. 2015. "The Hand of the Artist: Fan Art in the Martinverse." In *Mastering the* Game of Thrones: *Essays on George R.R. Martin's* A Song of Ice and Fire, edited by Jes Battis and Susan Johnston, 243–261. Jefferson, N.C.: McFarland.

Hughes, Sarah. 2015. "Has *Game of Thrones* Season Five Been Too Brutal to Enjoy?" *The Guardian.* 11 June. www.theguardian.com/tv-and-radio/tvandradioblog/2015/jun/10/has-game-of-thrones-season-five-been-too-brutal-to-enjoy.

Hutcheon, Linda. 2012. *A Theory of Adaptation.* Abingdon: Routledge.

Johnston, Susan. 2021. "Abjection, Masculinity, and Sacrifice: The Reek of Death in *Game of Thrones.*" *Men and Masculinities*: OnlineFirst Article. https://doi.org/10.1177/1097184X211044184.

Jones, R. 2012. "A Game of Genders: Comparing Depictions of Empowered Women between *A Game of Thrones* Novel and Television Series." *Journal of Student Research* 1 (3): 14–21. https://doi.org/10.47611/jsr.v1i3.100.

Kazyak, Emily. 2012. "Midwest or Lesbian? Gender, Rurality, and Sexuality." *Gender & Society* 26 (6): 825–848. https://doi.org/10.1177/0891243212458361.

Kilker, Robert. 2006. "All Roads Lead to the Abject: The Monstrous Feminine and Gender Boundaries in Stanley Kubrick's *The Shining.*" *Literature/Film Quarterly* 34 (1): 54–63. www.proquest.com/docview/226996499.

Kimmel, Michael S., Jeff Hearn, and Raewyn Connell. 2005. *Handbook of Studies on Men & Masculinities.* Thousand Oaks, Calif.: Sage.

Knox, S., 2018. "*Shameless*, the Push-Pull of Transatlantic Fiction Format Adaptation, and Star Casting." *New Review of Film and Television Studies* 16 (3): 295–323. https://doi.org/10.1080/17400309.2018.1487130.

Kristeva, Julia. 1982. *Powers of Horror.* New York: Columbia University Press.

—. 2012. *The Severed Head: Capital Visions.* New York: Columbia University Press.

Lacan, Jacques. 1977. "The Signification of the Phallus." In *Écrits*, 103–115. New York: W.W. Norton & Co.

Lambert, Charles. 2015. "A Tender Spot in My Heart: Disability in *A Song of Ice and Fire.*" *Critical Quarterly* 57 (1): 20–33. https://doi.org/10.1111/criq.12176.

Larrington, Carolyne. 2016. *Winter is Coming: The Medieval World of* Game of Thrones. London: I.B. Tauris.

—. 2017. "Gender/Queer Studies." In *Handbook of Arthurian Romance: King Arthur's Court in Medieval European Literature*, edited by Leah Tether and Johnny McFadyen, 259–272. Berlin: De Gruyter.

Larsson, Mariah. 2016. "Adapting Sex: Cultural Conceptions of Sexuality in Words and Images." In *Women of Ice and Fire: Gender*, Game of Thrones *and Multiple Media Engagements*, edited by Rikke Schubart and Anne Gjelsvik, 17–38. London: Bloomsbury.

Latham, J.R. 2017. "(Re)making Sex: A Praxiography of the Gender Clinic." *Feminist Theory* 18 (2): 177–204. https://journals.sagepub.com/doi/abs/10.1177/1464700117700051.

Lee, Esther. 2015. "Claire McCaskill Leads Charge to Boycott *Game of Thrones* after Brutal Rape Scene: 'I'm Done,' Missouri Senator Says." *US Weekly*. www.usmagazine.com/celebrity-news/news/claire-mccaskill-leads-charge-to-boycott-game-of-thrones-im-done-2015205.

Leederman, T.A. 2015. "A Thousand Westerosi Plateaus: Wargs, Wolves and Ways of Being." In *Mastering the* Game of Thrones*: Essays on George R.R. Martin's* A Song of Ice and Fire, edited by Jes Battis and Susan Johnston, 189–204. Jefferson, N.C.: McFarland.

McRuer, Robert. 2006. *Crip Theory: Cultural Signs of Queerness and Disability.* New York: NYU Press.

Manalansan, I.V., and F. Martin. 2014. "The 'Stuff' of Archives: Mess, Migration, and Queer Lives." *Radical History Review* 2014 (120): 94–107. https://doi.org/10.1215/01636545-2703742.

Mansbridge, J. 2017. "Adapting Queerness, Queering Adaptation: Fun Home on Broadway." In *Adaptation, Awards Culture and the Value of Prestige*, edited by C. Kennedy-Karpat and E. Sandberg, 75–94. New York: Palgrave Macmillan.

Mantoan, Lindsay. 2018. "Raven: Cersei Lannister, First of Her Name." In *Vying for the Iron Throne: Essays on Power, Gender, Death and Performance in HBO's* Game of Thrones, edited by Lindsay Mantoan and Sara Brady, 90–93. Jefferson, N.C.: McFarland.

Mares, Nicole M. 2017. "Writing the Rules of Their Own Game: Medieval Female Agency and *Game of Thrones*." In Game of Thrones *versus History: Written in Blood*, edited by Brian A. Pavlac, 147–160. Hoboken, N.J.: Wiley Blackwell.

Martin, George R.R. 2011a. *A Game of Thrones.* 4th ed. London: Harper Voyager.

—. 2011b. *A Clash of Kings.* 4th ed. London: Harper Voyager.

—. 2011c. *A Storm of Swords 1: Steel and Snow.* 4th ed. London: Harper Voyager.

—. 2011d. *A Storm of Swords 2: Blood and Gold.* 4th ed. London: Harper Voyager.

—. 2011e. *A Feast for Crows.* 3rd ed. London: Harper Voyager.

—. 2012. *A Dance with Dragons.* 2nd ed. London: Harper Voyager.

—. 2013. *The Wit & Wisdom of Tyrion Lannister.* New York: Bantam.

—. 2014. "I Broke the Internet." *Not a Blog*, 27 March. https://grrm.livejournal.com/362384.html.

—. 2015. *A Knight of the Seven Kingdoms.* New York: HarperCollins.

—. 2018. *Fire and Blood.* New York: Bantam.

—. 2019. "An Ending." *Not A Blog*, 20 May. https://georgerrmartin.com/notablog/2019/05/20/an-ending/.

Massie, Pascal, and Lauryn Mayer. 2014. "Bringing Elsewhere Home: *A Song of Ice and Fire's* Ethics of Disability." In *Ethics and Medievalism*, edited by Karl Fugelso, 45–60. Cambridge: D.S. Brewer.

Meyerson, Mark D., Daniel Thiery, and Oren Falk. 2015. *"A Great Effusion of Blood"? Interpreting Medieval Violence.* Toronto: University of Toronto Press.

BIBLIOGRAPHY

Miller, Julie. 2016. "*Game of Thrones* Finale: The Secret Symbolism in Cersei's Badass Gown." *Vanity Fair.* www.vanityfair.com/hollywood/2016/06/game-of-thrones-season-6-finale-cersei-dress.

Minowa, Yuko, Pauline Maclaran, and Lorna Stevens. 2014. "Visual Representations of Violent Women." *Visual Communication Quarterly* 21 (4): 210–222. https://doi.org/10.1080/15551393.2014.987281.

Misra, Sulagna. 2015. "Inside the Music of *Game of Thrones* Season 5." *Vanity Fair.* www.vanityfair.com/hollywood/2015/06/game-of-thrones-season-5-music.

Mitchell, David T., and Sharon L. Snyder. 2000. *Narrative Prosthesis: Disability and the Dependencies of Discourse.* Michigan: University of Michigan Press.

Moglia, Sarah. 2014. "Cripples, Bastards, and Broken Things: Disability in *Game of Thrones.*" *Skeptability,* 8 June. https://web.archive.org/web/20141021201923/http://skeptability.com/2014/06/06/cripples-bastards-and-broken-things-disability-in-game-of-thrones/.

Moyce, Audrey. 2018. "Brienne and Jaime's Queer Intimacy." In *Vying for the Iron Throne: Essays on Power, Gender, Death and Performance in HBO's* Game of Thrones, edited by Lindsey Mantoan and Sara Brady, 59–68. Jefferson, N.C.: McFarland.

Muso. 2017. "*Game of Thrones* Season 7 Opener Pirated 91.74 Million Times." *Muso Magazine.* www.muso.com/magazine/game-of-thrones-season-7-opener-pirated-91-74-million-times/.

Namaste, Ki. 1996. "Theory's Erasure of Transgender Subjectivity." In *Queer Studies: A Lesbian, Gay, Bisexual, and Transgender Anthology,* edited by Brett Beemyn and Michele Eliason, 183–203. New York: NYU Press.

Nel, David C. 2015. "Sex and the Citadel: Adapting Same Sex Desire from Martin's Westeros to HBO's Bedrooms." In *Mastering the* Game of Thrones*: Essays on George R.R. Martin's* A Song of Ice and Fire, edited by Jes Battis and Susan Johnston, 205–224. Jefferson, N.C.: McFarland.

Nickalls, Sammy. 2016. "*Game of Thrones* Has Officially Won More Emmys Than Any Other Drama." *Esquire,* 11 September. www.esquire.com/entertainment/tv/news/a48508/game-of-thrones-emmys/.

Orr, David. 2011. "Dragons Ascendant: George R.R. Martin and the Rise of Fantasy." *New York Times,* 12 August. www.nytimes.com/2011/08/14/books/review/george-r-r-martin-and-the-rise-of-fantasy.html.

Ostrander, R. Noam. 2008a. "Meditations on a Bullet: Violently Injured Young Men Discuss Masculinity, Disability and Blame." *Child and Adolescent Social Work Journal* 25 (1): 71–84. https://doi.org/10.1007/s10560-008-0113-5.

—. 2008b. "When Identities Collide: Masculinity, Disability and Race." *Disability & Society* 23 (6): 585–597. https://doi.org/10.1080/09687590802328451.

Oswin, Natalie. 2008. "Critical Geographies and the Uses of Sexuality: Deconstructing Queer Space." *Progress in Human Geography* 32 (1): 89–103. https://doi.org/10.1177/0309132507085213.

Patel, Charul. 2014. "Expelling a Monstrous Matriarchy: Casting Cersei Lannister as Abject in *A Song of Ice and Fire*." *Journal of European Popular Culture* 5 (2): 135–147. https://doi.org/10.1386/jepc.5.2.135_1.

Payne, Kelly. 2017. "Data of Thrones Part I: Screen Time, Episodes, and Death in *Game of Thrones*." *Looker*, 21 June. https://web.archive.org/web/20170624095836/https://looker.com/blog/data-of-thrones-part-i.

Petersen, Alan. 2003. "Research on Men and Masculinities: Some Implications of Recent Theory for Future Work." *Men and Masculinities* 6 (1): 54–69. https://doi.org/10.1177/1097184X02250843.

Phillips, Jennifer. 2016. "Confrontational Content, Gendered Gazes, and the Ethics of Adaptation in *Outlander* and *Game of Thrones*." In *Adoring Outlander: Essays on Fandom, Genre, and the Female Audience*, edited by Valerie Estelle Frankel, 162–181. Jefferson, N.C.: McFarland.

Prater, Lenise. 2014. "Monstrous Fantasies: Reinforcing Rape Culture in Fiona Mcintosh's Fantasy Novels." *Hecate* 39 (1/2): 148–167. https://search.informit.com.au/documentSummary;dn=86116984878043;res=IELLCC.

—. 2016. "Queering Magic." In *Gender and Sexuality in Contemporary Popular Fantasy: beyond Boy Wizards and Kick-Ass Chicks*, edited by Jude Roberts and Esther MacCallum-Stewart. Abingdon: Routledge.

Preciado, Paul B. 2018. *The Countersexual Manifesto*, translated by Bruce Benderson. New York: Columbia University Press.

Prosser, Jay. 1998. *Second Skins: The Body Narratives of Transsexuality*. New York: Columbia University Press.

Pugh, Catherine. 2018. "Harder and Stronger: Yara Greyjoy and the Ironborn." In *Vying for the Iron Throne: Essays on Power, Gender, Death and Performance in HBO's* Game of Thrones, edited by Lindsay Mantoan and Sara Brady, 79–89. Jefferson, N.C.: McFarland.

Pugh, Tison. 2008. "'There lived in the Land of Oz two queerly made men': Queer Utopianism and Antisocial Eroticism in L. Frank Baum's *Oz* Series." *Marvels & Tales* 22 (2): 217–239. www.jstor.org/stable/41388876.

Quintero Johnson, Jessie M., and Bonnie Miller. 2016. "When Women 'Snap': The Use of Mental Illness to Contextualize Women's Acts of Violence in Contemporary Popular Media." *Women's Studies in Communication* 39 (2): 211–227. https://doi.org/10.1080/07491409.2016.1172530.

Reed, J. Ann, and Elizabeth M. Blunk. 1990. "The Influence of Facial Hair on Impression Formation." *Social Behavior and Personality: An International Journal* 18 (1): 169–175. https://doi.org/10.2224/sbp.1990.18.1.169.

Roberts, Jude, and Esther MacCallum-Stewart, eds. 2016. *Gender and Sexuality in Contemporary Popular Fantasy: Beyond Boy Wizards and Kick-Ass Chicks*. Abingdon: Routledge.

Romano, Aja. 2019. "Why the Ending of *Game of Thrones* Elevated the Worst of Fan Culture." *Vox*, 20 July. www.vox.com/2019/7/20/18638718/game-of-thrones-ending-bran-stark-transformative-fandom.

Rosenberg, Alyssa. 2012. "Men and Monsters: Rape, Myth-Making, and the Rise and Fall of Nations in *A Song of Ice and Fire*." In *Beyond the Wall: Exploring George R.R. Martin's* A Song of Ice and Fire, edited by James Lowder, 15–27. Dallas, Texas: Smart Pop.

BIBLIOGRAPHY

Rubin, Henry. 2003. *Self-Made Men: Identity and Embodiment among Transsexual Men*. Nashville, Tenn.: Vanderbilt University Press.

Runstedler, Curtis. 2020. "Cersei Lannister, Regal Commissions, and the Alchemists in *Game of Thrones* and *A Song of Ice and Fire*." In *Queenship and the Women of Westeros: Female Agency and Advice in* Game of Thrones *and* A Song of Ice and Fire, edited by Zita Eva Rohr and Lisa Benz, 129–144. London: Palgrave Macmillan.

Schröter, Felix. 2016. "Sworn Swords and Noble Ladies: Female Characters in *Game of Thrones* Video Games." In *Women of Ice and Fire: Gender, Game of Thrones and Multiple Media Engagements*, edited by Anne Gjelsvik and Rikke Schubart, 79–104. New York: Bloomsbury.

Sedgwick, Eve Kosofsky. 1990. *Epistemology of the Closet*. Berkeley, Calif.: University of California Press.

—. 1993. *Tendencies*. Durham, N.C.: Duke University Press.

—. 2015. *Between Men: English Literature and Male Homosocial Desire*. New York: Columbia University Press.

Shaham, Inbar. 2015. "Brienne of Tarth and Jaime Lannister: A Romantic Comedy within HBO's *Game of Thrones*." *Mythlore: A Journal of J.R.R. Tolkien, C.S. Lewis, Charles Williams, and Mythopoeic Literature* 33 (2): 49–70. https://dc.swosu.edu/mythlore/vol33/iss2/7.

Shakespeare, Tom. 1999. "The Sexual Politics of Disabled Masculinity." *Sexuality and Disability* 17 (1): 53–64. https://doi.org/10.1023/A:1021403829826.

Shildrick, Margrit, and Janet Price. 1996. "Breaking the Boundaries of the Broken Body." *Body & Society* 2 (4): 93–113. https://doi.org/10.1177/1357034X96002004006.

Shuttleworth, Russell. 2004. "Disabled Masculinity: Expanding the Masculine Repertoire." In *Gendering Disability*, edited by Bonnie G. Smith and Beth Hutchison, 166–178. New Brunswick, N.J.: Rutgers University Press.

Shuttleworth, Russell, Nikki Wedgwood, and Nathan J. Wilson. 2012. "The Dilemma of Disabled Masculinity." *Men and Masculinities* 15 (2): 174–194. https://doi.org/10.1177/1097184X12439879.

Sjoberg, Laura, and Caron E. Gentry. 2008. "Reduced to Bad Sex: Narratives of Violent Women from the Bible to the War on Terror." *International Relations* 22 (1): 5–23. https://doi.org/10.1177/0047117807087240.

Smith, Brett. 2013. "Disability, Sport and Men's Narratives of Health: A Qualitative Study." *Health Psychology* 32 (1): 110. doi: 10.1037/a0029187.

Smith Rainey, Sarah. 2018. "The Pleasures of Care." *Sexualities* 21 (3): 271–286. https://doi.org/10.1177/1363460716688677.

Snowarkgaryan, Aejon. 2019. "[Spoilers]. *Game of Thrones* Characters Ranked by Screentime. Tyrion and Jon Are the Clear Winners Here. (Source-Type A Media Youtube)." *Reddit*, 23 May. www.reddit.com/r/gameofthrones/comments/bs1vea/spoilers_game_of_thrones_characters_ranked_by/.

Sontag, Susan. 1964. "Notes on Camp." *Partisan Review*.

Sparky. 2012. "The Disabled Can Play the *Game of Thrones*." *Fangs for the Fantasy*, 20 May. www.fangsforthefantasy.com/2012/03/disabled-can-play-game-of-thrones.html.

Spector, Caroline. 2012. "Power and Feminism in Westeros." In *Beyond the Wall: Exploring George R.R. Martin's* A Song of Ice and Fire, edited by James Lowder, 169–188. Dallas, Texas: Smart Pop.

Stanton, Rob. 2015. "Excessive and Appropriate Gifts: Hospitality and Violence in *A Song of Ice and Fire*." *Critical Quarterly* 57 (1): 49–60. https://doi.org/10.1111/criq.12173.

Stryker, Susan. 1994. "My Words to Victor Frankenstein above the Village of Chamounix: Performing Transgender Rage." *GLQ: A Journal of Lesbian and Gay Studies* 1 (3): 237–254. https://doi.org/10.1215/10642684-1-3-237.

—. 2004. "Transgender Studies: Queer Theory's Evil Twin." *GLQ: A Journal of Lesbian and Gay Studies* 10 (2): 212–215. https://doi.org/10.1215/10642684-10-2-212.

—. 2008. *Transgender History*. Boston: Seal Press.

Synnott, Anthony. 1987. "Shame and Glory: A Sociology of Hair." *British Journal of Sociology* 38 (3): 381–413. https://doi.org/10.2307/590695.

Tarnowski, A. 2019. "'Yet I'm Still a Man': Disability and Masculinity in George R.R. Martin's *A Song of Ice and Fire* Series." *Canadian Review of American Studies* 49 (1): 77–98. www.muse.jhu.edu/article/721886.

Tasker, Yvonne, and Lindsay Steenberg. 2016. "Women Warriors from Chivalry to Vengeance." In *Women of Ice and Fire: Gender,* Game of Thrones *and Multiple Media Engagements*, edited by Anne Gjelsvik and Rikke Schubart, 171–192. London: Bloomsbury.

Thistleton, John. 2015. "Retired General David Morrison Takes Aim at *Game of Thrones'* blatant violence." *Sydney Morning Herald*, 22 September. www.smh.com.au/national/act/retired-general-david-morrison-takes-aim-at-game-of-thrones-blatant-violence-20150922-gjrxhp.html.

Thomas, Calvin. 1996. *Male Matters: Masculinity, Anxiety, and the Male Body on the Line*. Champaign: University of Illinois Press.

—. 2008. *Masculinity, Psychoanalysis, Straight Queer Theory: Essays on Abjection in Literature, Mass Culture, and Film*. New York: Palgrave Macmillan.

Torrell, Margaret Rose. 2013. "Potentialities: Toward a Transformative Theory of Disabled Masculinities." In *Emerging Perspectives on Disability Studies*, edited by Matthew Wappett and Katrina Arndt, 209–225. New York: Palgrave Macmillan.

Trump, Donald. 2018. "Sanctions Are Coming." https://twitter.com/realDonaldTrump/status/1058388700617498625.

—. 2019. "The Wall Is Coming." https://twitter.com/realDonaldTrump/status/1081735898679701505.

VanArendonk, Kathryn. 2019. "King Bran? Really?" *Vulture*, 20 May. www.vulture.com/2019/05/game-of-thrones-king-bran-the-broken.html.

Ward, Dan. 2018. "'Kill the boy and let the man be born': Youth, Death and Manhood." In *Vying for the Iron Throne: Essays on Power, Gender, Death and Performance in HBO's* Game of Thrones, edited by Lindsay Mantoan and Sara Brady, 109–120. Jefferson, N.C.: McFarland.

Wassersug, Richard J., and Tucker Lieberman. 2010. "Contemporary Castration: Why the Modern Day Eunuch Remains Invisible." *BMJ* 341 (1). doi: 10.1136/bmj.c4509.

BIBLIOGRAPHY

Wedgwood, Nikki. 2009. "Connell's Theory of Masculinity: Its Origins and Influences on the Study of Gender." *Journal of Gender Studies* 18 (4): 329–339. https://doi.org/10.1080/09589230903260001.

Wilkins, Kim. 2016. "From Middle Earth to Westeros: Medievalism, Proliferation and Paratextuality." In *New Directions in Popular Fiction: Genre, Distribution, Reproduction*, edited by Ken Gelder, 201–221. Basingstoke: Palgrave Macmillan.

Winteriscoming. 2013. "*Game of Thrones* Wins Award Honoring Disability Awareness." *Winter is Coming*. http://winteriscoming.net/2013/10/22/game-of-thrones-wins-award-honoring-disability-awareness/.

Wittingslow, Ryan Mitchell. 2015. "'All men must serve': Religion and Free Will from the Seven to the Faceless Men." In *Mastering the* Game of Thrones*: Essays on George R.R. Martin's* A Song of Ice and Fire, edited by Jes Battis and Susan Johnston, 113–131. Jefferson, N.C.: McFarland.

Young, Helen. 2014. "Race in Online Fantasy Fandom: Whiteness on Westeros.org." *Continuum* 28 (5): 737–747. https://doi.org/10.1080/10304312.2014.941331.

—. 2015. *Race and Popular Fantasy Literature: Habits of Whiteness*. London: Routledge.

Young, Joseph. 2017. "'Enough about Whores': Sexual Characterization in *A Song of Ice and Fire*." *Mythlore* 35 (2): 45–61. https://dc.swosu.edu/mythlore/vol35/iss2/4/.

Index

adaptation 2–5, 8–9, 18, 25, 39, 59, 92–93, 108, 137, 140–141, 174, 180–186, 189–191
amputation 151, 155, 177

Baratheon, Joffrey 58–59
Baratheon, Stannis 79, 118–119
Benioff, David, and D.B. Weiss 3–4
Berlant, Lauren 83
Bolton, Ramsay 41–48, 66, 71–72, 119, 176–177
Brienne of Tarth 23, 88–89, 91, 106–125
  and Arya Stark 123, 190
  and chivalry 52, 91, 107, 114–117, 121–124
  and Jaime Lannister 107–109, 113–114, 116–117, 120–121, 123–124, 149–155, 158–161
Butler, Judith 14, 16–19, 29, 74–75, 91, 109–110, 129, 141, 171, 204

chivalry 52, 91, 107, 114–117, 121–124, 132, 154
Clegane, Gregor (the Mountain) 28, 32–40, 101–103
Connell, Raewyn 10–11, 13, 34, 50, 70, 76, 90
Creed, Barbara 20–21, 28, 30, 32, 35, 43–44, 48, 96–98, 103, 105, 138–139, 164–165

disability 127–129, 131, 139, 151, 155, 162
  see also amputation
Dothraki 1, 9, 196–199, 203
dragons 1–2, 103, 191–192, 200–201, 204–208
Drogo, Khal 1, 196–197, 203
Drogon (Daenerys's dragon) 199, 201, 203, 205–206
dwarf *see* Lannister, Tyrion

Elliot, Kara 11, 13, 73, 115

Faith Militant 98–99
fantasy genre 9, 15–16, 22, 29, 35, 53–54, 60–61, 78, 112, 114–115, 153, 165, 175
  and queerness 2, 13, 25, 89, 106, 109, 111–112, 142, 173
Frey, Walder 64, 185–189

Grey Wind (Robb's direwolf) 64–65
Greyjoy, Theon/Reek 41–43, 58, 66–74

Hodor 133–138
honour 23, 52, 79, 91, 114, 116, 118, 153, 159–160
  see also chivalry
Hutcheon, Linda 18

Ice (sword) 54–55, 58

The Imp *see* Lannister, Tyrion

justice 49–50, 53, 57, 67, 78, 82, 182, 193, 195
  see also chivalry

Kingsguard 106, 113, 131, 153–155
knight 29, 91, 106–107, 109–116, 121–124, 131–133, 139, 146, 151
  see also chivalry
Kristeva, Julia 13, 19–20, 30, 32, 55, 64, 100–101, 134

Lannister, Cersei 23, 29, 34, 37–39, 87, 89–106, 124–125, 146, 149, 155–161, 163, 183–184, 188, 197
Lannister, Jaime 97, 103–105, 107–109, 113–114, 117, 120–124, 127, 146–162
Lannister, Tyrion 82, 93–94, 108, 130, 144, 156, 162–171, 199–200

magic *see* supernatural and magic
Martin, George R.R. 3–4, 180–181
Melisandre 81
The Mountain *see* Clegane, Gregor

Needle (sword) 123, 179

Others *see* white walkers/Others

prosthesis 29, 45, 102, 108–109, 111, 113, 133

queer kinship 14, 23, 37–38, 46, 121–122, 125, 136, 141, 144–145, 153–155, 166, 169–170, 190
queer theory 13–16, 129

readers and reading 7–8, 21, 50
Red Wedding 64, 185–188
Reek *see* Greyjoy, Theon/Reek

Sixskins, Varamyr 174–179, 205
slavery and slaves 192–193, 195–198
Snow, Jon 41, 47, 52–53, 74–86, 144, 201–202
Stark, Arya 123–124, 174–175, 179–191, 205
Stark, Bran 49, 51–58, 73–74, 129–146, 171, 189–190
Stark, Eddard 49–62, 66–67, 69–70, 76, 78, 85, 124, 143, 199, 201
Stark, Robb 59–65, 75, 85, 131
Stark, Sansa 47–48, 119
Stormborn, Daenerys *see* Targaryen, Daenerys
supernatural and magic 1, 15–16, 22, 24, 37–38, 75, 98, 112, 124, 130–137, 139–142, 144–145, 173–177, 179, 182, 198, 205, 208

Targaryen, Daenerys (Dany) 1–2, 40, 82–84, 92, 162, 166–167, 169–170, 174, 191–208
Tarly, Samwell 82, 144, 170, 201
Tarth, Brienne of *see* Brienne of Tarth
Three-Eyed Crow/Raven 130, 132, 138–141, 143–145
transgender 88–89, 93, 96, 102–103, 108–111, 115

warging 133–138, 142–143, 175–178
Weiss, D.B. *see* Benioff, David and D.B. Weiss
white walkers/Others 56–58, 159, 178–179, 189